POWER!

HOW TO GET IT,
HOW TO USE IT

Michael Korda

BALLANTINE BOOKS • NEW YORK

The author and the publisher are grateful for permission
to quote from the following books:

The Glass Bead Game, by Hermann Hesse. Translated
by Richard and Clara Winston. Copyright © 1969 by
Holt, Rinehart and Winston, Inc. Reprinted by permission of Holt, Rinehart and Winston, Inc.

Journey to Ixtlan, by Carlos Castaneda. Copyright ©
1972 by Carlos Castaneda. Reprinted by permission of
Simon & Schuster, Inc., and by special authorization of
Ned Brown and Carlos Castaneda.

The Last Tycoon, by F. Scott Fitzgerald. Reprinted by
permission of Charles Scribner's Sons.

Library of Congress Catalog Card Number: 75-2263

ISBN 0-345-25195-4-195

This edition published by arrangement with
Random House, Inc.

Manufactured in the United States of America

First Ballantine Books Edition: October 1976

To the memory of
Brendan,
The Rt. Hon. The Viscount Bracken, P.C., M.P.

CONTENTS

Part One: POWER PEOPLE

Chapter One: THE POWER GAME   3

Chapter Two: STORIES OF POWER   18

    The Look of Power   19

    ". . .Go Tell Him About Dogs"   22

    "Joe Namath Was a Leader . . ."   33

    ". . . Maybe I'm a Weakling"   42

    "Power Means Love . . ."   50

Chapter Three: LIVING WITH POWER   56

Part Two: THE WORLD OF POWER

Chapter Four: THE POWER SPOT   73

    Power Lines   75

    Power Areas   81

    Power Groups   92

    The Power Dynamics of Office Parties   95

    Gossip Power   102

    TOO vs. TOP   107

    The Power Circle   115

Chapter Five: GAMES OF POWER   122

    Games of Weakness: "Avoid victories over one's superiors"   125

    "Nice Guys Finish First"   133

    Expand, Don't Climb!   139

    The Information Game   146

    "Nobody is Indispensable!"   153

    No-Power   157

    Games of Manners   161

Chapter Six: POWER EXERCISES   171

    "I'm Afraid I Have Bad News for You . . ."   173

The Mythology of Meetings   176
The Rituals of Power   181
"... None Will Sweat But for Promotion ..."   187
"Money and Sex Are Forces too Unruly for Reason ..."   194
"Stand Not Upon the Order of Your Going, But Go at Once"   198
"Men Must Endure Their Going Hence ..."   200
Chapter Seven: SYMBOLS OF POWER   207
Foot Power   208
"Phone Me in the Limo"   211
Status Marks—"A Gold-Plated Thermos Is a Man's Best Friend"   220
Furniture   230
Time Power   239
Standing-By   247
Chapter Eight: WOMEN AND POWER   251

Part Three: LOVE OF POWER

Chapter Nine: POWER RULES   295
ACKNOWLEDGMENTS   306
NOTES   307

"Sometimes, to those around him, he seemed so idealistic as to be innocent. He never talked about power and he did not seem to covet it. Yet the truth was quite different. He loved power and he sought it intensely, and he could be a ferocious infighter where the question of power was concerned . . . Part of his strength appeared to be his capacity to seem indifferent, to seem almost naïve about questions of power."

—David Halberstam, on
Robert McNamara,
THE BEST AND THE BRIGHTEST

"Liking power, he despised those who preferred glory."

—Douglas Hurd
TRUTH GAME

PART ONE

Power People

CHAPTER ONE

The Power Game

The only way to learn the rules of this Game
of games is to take the usual prescribed
courses, which require many years; and none
of the initiates could ever possibly have any
interest in making these rules easier to learn.

—Hermann Hesse
THE GLASS BEAD GAME

The only limits of power are the bounds of
belief.

—H. Wilson
ON CRAFTS

The purpose of this book is to show you how to use, recognize and live with power, and to convince you that the world you live in is a challenge and a game, and that a sense of power—*your* power—is at the core of it.

All life is a game of power. The object of the game is simple enough: to know what you want and get it. The moves of the game, by contrast, are infinite and complex, although they usually involve the manipulation of people and situations to your advantage. As for the rules, these are only discovered by playing the game to the end.

Some people play the power game for money, some for security or fame, others for sex, most for some combination of these objectives. The master players (some of whose games we shall study) seek power itself, knowing that power can be used to *obtain* money, sex, security or fame. None of these alone constitutes power; but power can produce them all.

No matter who you are, the basic truth is that your interests are nobody else's concern, your gain is inevitably someone else's loss, your failure someone else's victory. In the words of Heinrich von Treitschke, the German philosopher of might, "Your neighbor, even though he may look upon you as his natural ally against another power which is feared by you both, is always ready, at the first opportunity, as soon as it can be done with safety, to better himself at your expense . . . Whoever fails to increase his power, must decrease it, if others increase theirs." [1]

It would be difficult to sum up the position of the average person more succinctly than this. Von Treitscheke's analysis of the human condition, despite what might at first reading seem to be a familiar streak of German paranoia and depression, in fact applies to a good many jobs, marriages and love af-

fairs, and represents, for a lot of people, a way of life.
Since the people who live their lives along these lines
have a marked tendency to find their way into positions of power that threaten or block the rest of us,
learning to play the power game is a means of self-
defense.

Why do people wake up to discover the promotion
they expected has been given to someone else, the
raise they counted on has not materialized, that they
have been retired before they wanted to go, are no
longer invited to meetings, or worse yet asked to
attend so many that it's obvious the real action is
going on somewhere else? The answer may, of course,
be simple incompetence—it is unfortunate that stupidity, drunkenness, and laziness often intervene in
the game, obscuring its otherwise perfect logic—but
above a certain level of play it is safe to assume the
losers have been defeated by superior players, have
failed to pay sufficient attention to their own moves
and those of others, and are now obliged to pay the
price.

For that matter, the same ebb and flow of power
can be observed in every kind of human intercourse;
the same rules apply to love affairs as to office warfare. Who does not know the dangerous moment in
any relationship when one person's need for the other
becomes strong enough to shift the balance of power?
The power game is played in bed as fiercely as elsewhere, if not more so, and marriage is perhaps the
best school for the player who wants to study and
master the use of power in its most subtle form, over
a long period of time.

To play the power game, it is first necessary to discover for yourself what power *is*. The student of

power ought to begin by learning to recognize its manifestations in every aspect of life—for all life is a training ground, and every human exchange is an opportunity for testing the player's ability. The masters play the game twenty-four hours a day, with parking lot attendants, spouses, lovers, headwaiters, agents of the IRS, traffic policemen, their fellow workers, their superiors and their subordinates, instinctively trying to control every situation in which they find themselves and to place as much of an obligation as possible on the other person. To the master player, even the most ordinary human encounter is completely fascinating, offering incalculable opportunities for practice. Some of the best players I know developed their basic techniques in such places as fruit markets, where the choice of the individual pieces of fruit one wants as contrasted to those being palmed off on one, can be used to study such concepts as resistance under pressure, feigned hesitation, whining and compromise. Childhood itself teaches us many useful techniques—playing one parent off against the other, withholding affection, throwing up when all else fails—but most people forget these valuable techniques in the process of becoming adults. School, on the other hand, provides lessons in the power game which are seldom forgotten by anyone, particularly the ability to look busy and industrious when one is in fact doing nothing, and the essential knowledge of how to deal with bullies, or become one.

The trick is to develop a style of power based on one's character and desires. With that foundation, it is possible to hone the moves of one's own game to a fine, cutting edge. Those who were bullies at school often develop a very sophisticated repertoire of bullying techniques in adult life, though they may eventually find themselves at a disadvantage if they meet a more powerful bully; those who learned as children to deal with bullies by means of flattery, cunning and a display of weakness, usually go on using these defenses against adult bullies with the same success. The most successful players of the power game can do both, and don't mind looking foolish or weak when it's useful—a certain amount of ego destruction is not a bad thing.

The instinct for power is basic to men and women —as Nietzsche observed, "Wherever I found the living, there I found the will to power" [2]—but it is usually thought of as one of mankind's less attractive characteristics, along with violence and aggression, with which it is often confused. Most people do not like to admit that they want power, which is why they never get it, and those who do have power go to endless lengths to mask the fact. Some politicians, like the late Lyndon B. Johnson, openly relish the trappings of power, but the contemporary American style of power is to pretend that one has none. To confess that one *has* power is to make oneself responsible for using it, and safety lies in an artfully contrived pose of impotence, behind which one can do exactly as one pleases. In an age of clamorous victims it is easier to join in the clamor, to follow the inspired lead of the Mafiosi who demanded our sympathy because they were discriminated against as Italo-Americans, just another minority group, no connection to the guys who make their living from loan-sharking, narcotics, illegal gambling and prostitution. The "man of respect" gave way to the complaining victim as the power style of organized crime at just about the same time that the urban middle-class was making the same discovery.

The old ideal of "walking tall," of exuding an aura of power in all its physical and psychological terms was a potent weapon in the traditional arsenal of urban man. The city-dweller's motto toward his fellow-man has always been "Don't tread on me!" until recently. Cringing was thought to be wrong, the ideal cringe-figure being of course Uncle Tom, that lovable old darky who represented so perfectly what whites hoped (but inwardly doubted) the blacks felt toward them. With the onset of urban disintegration, power moved into the streets in the alarming form of the blacks themselves, who learned to ritualize their demands for power in a series of attitudes designed to suggest that they *welcomed* confrontation: the swaggering walk, the coldly contemptuous stare, the eye-dazzling display of high-pimp clothing styles, all conspired to make the black *street-visible*, to suggest that ordinary, wage-earning blacks were connected to the threats of armed violence of the radical left and the frightening reality of urban crime. In response to this, the white urban middle-class—those who did not flee to the suburbs—retreated, learned to walk *small*, to avoid confrontation. Showing that one had power was asking for trouble, and admitting, what is more, that one might possibly be held responsible for second-rate education in the ghetto, crumbling housing, insufficient medical services, rapacious landlords, corrupt police . . .

It was easier and more sensible to pretend that we were all victims of the system, whether we lived in the ghetto or a twelve-room duplex apartment with a view of the park. The fact that it had been *our* system, that we lived well in part because other people lived badly, was something we found it convenient to ignore, now that it was under attack—which explains the unusual phenomenon of people within the system, the beneficiaries and architects of it, so to speak, joining with those outside to denounce it. Hence it was possible for Leonard Bernstein to claim that he "understood" the Black Panthers at his much-publicized party in their honor, for it was evident that there was no percentage in defending the system that had made it possible for him to acquire a cooperative apartment in the first place and which was designed to ensure that his neighborhood was safe, the education in his district first-class, the garbage on his street picked up every day, if that system was going to be destroyed. None of the crew had any desire to go down with the ship, as it were, and even the first-class passengers were eager to prove that they had been press-ganged on board or had never sailed on her at all. And why not? Half the people in Washington who had worked to get us into the Vietnam war later joined the antiwar campaign as if they had never had anything to do with what happened. What people had always done instinctively in their private and business lives was suddenly elevated to a living philosophy.

Now that sex is a subject that can be openly discussed, power seems to be the one dirty little human secret we have left to hide. The most familiar comment on power is that of Lord Acton: "Power tends to corrupt and absolute power corrupts absolutely." [3]

Yet in our age, the consequences of *not* playing the power game are generally considered worse. Acton's view of power has been superseded by the general belief that power is *good*, that "all weakness tends to corrupt, and impotence corrupts absolutely." [4] If we believe in anything in the last quarter of the twentieth century, it is in the extension of power, the drive to dominance. Not to reach for power, in the contemporary view, is to limit one's potential, to set a limit to one's consciousness. Two world wars, Darwin and Freud, have finally brought most Western men to the realization that existence is finite, that death is real. There are no longer any plausible substitutes for success and fulfillment in this life, nor any comforting belief that failure here below will be rewarded in some way above. We have no alternative to present apotheosis; stripped of our uniqueness as human beings by Darwin, exposed to our own inadequacies by Freud, compelled to live with the knowledge of our immense potential for violence and irrationality by history itself, we are left to fabricate our own substitute for immortality. Power—"the ability to bring about our desires" [5]—is all we have left.

In former times, power was a game of the elite, a violent activity like jousting or fox-hunting that occupied the time of those who already had enough to eat. The majority of people were hard put to survive, and any doubts that they might have about their position in society were answered by the religious leaders of whatever faith had been imposed upon them. Cecil Alexander's familiar and moving Victorian hymn, which began optimistically enough with "All things bright and beautiful, All creatures great and small . . ." went on to express the more brutal realities of the traditional social contract:

> The rich man in his castle,
> The poor man at his gate,
> God made them, high or lowly
> And order'd their estate.

Work and prayer were the lot of the unleisured classes, and given the nature of preindustrial society, work tended to absorb most people's energies fully.

In our age, work is a less absorbing experience, especially for people with office or "managerial" jobs. Few modern offices bear even a superficial resemblance to those Dickensian counting houses in which clerks worked long, exhausting hours under fierce direct supervision and discipline. In fact time lies heavy on most people's hands today, and there is ample energy left to use in improving one's position. What is more, we now have a democratic attitude toward work: formerly it was believed to be a harsh *necessity*, part of God's judgment on mankind for that fatal gastronomic error in the Garden of Eden, an inevitable misery that would be redeemed, if at all, in Heaven; today we believe that work is an *opportunity*. Learn a trade, get a job, make something of yourself, *be* someone! Work is no longer an end in itself but a means of changing ourselves, of rising. We no longer view the places where we work as treadmills but as ladders. And how much more interesting is the climb than the work itself!

Psychoanalysts, who differ on most things, agree that "the will to power" is an essential expression of our humanity, though they seem unable to recommend just how this instinct should best be used. "Achieve! Arise! Conquer!" exhorted Alfred Adler, "Whatever name we give it, we shall always find in human beings this great line of activity—this struggle to rise from an inferior to a superior position, from defeat to victory, from below to above." [6] True enough: rising "from below to above" is so universal an ambition that it is almost pointless to discuss the morality, or even the common sense, of such a desire. We believe in ambition as we once believed in salvation; indeed, some power games exist largely to supply the *illusion* of a hard-fought contest in lives and careers that are in fact unconditional surrenders.

As a species, we want to believe that we're fighting for the leadership of the herd even when we're merely grazing peacefully on the edges.

Thus it is easy enough to understand why we need power—without it we are merely cogs in a meaningless machine. The more difficult question is why we need work. Very few people, after all, can be said to *enjoy* working, and as society becomes more complex and technological, and jobs are broken down into ever smaller specialities offering a constantly decreasing opportunity to be involved in the whole process, the number of people who enjoy their work is likely to decline still further.

In an age when the Puritan work-ethic seems irrelevant, there are primarily four reasons for working: 1) Habit; 2) Pleasure; 3) Money; 4) Power.

Habit is a significant factor. Most people are inclined to fall into a steady routine of work, simply because anything else would require imagination, invention and a spirit of adventure. Accepting the routine of work gives meaning and order to lives that would otherwise be chaotic and unbearable. It's not so much that people like work as that they fear having nothing to do and no place to go for eight or more hours a day. How else to explain the depression that comes over men facing retirement, even in cases when they are leaving with a generous pension and a fat bundle of stock? Work is a habit-forming drug, and the habit is hard to break.

With the exception of skilled craftsmen—a vanishing breed—few people work for pleasure. Most people don't *mind* working, but feel that it's both indecent and wasteful to *enjoy* it openly. Half the reason for working at all is the hold it gives us over other people. In domestic situations, work can be used to justify almost anything: impotence, impatience, refusing to wash the dishes, falling asleep on the sofa after dinner, a whole variety of excuses, demands and special pleadings. Few men are inclined to come home from a day's work and say how much they enjoyed it; there is more to be gained by affecting fatigue, despair and tension, as if the working day were a terrible sacrifice on behalf of one's loved ones. Women at home have their own ways of exacting a tribute from others for work performed: nobody has anything to gain from admitting that they like their jobs. Then too, there is always the suspicion that a person who enjoys working may simply not be working hard enough. It is safer to complain along with one's colleagues, and to hope that the complaints will suggest that one's salary is being earned, and should perhaps even be increased.

By contrast, people who are interested in power know how to work, and usually work hard. They have a purpose beyond merely making money or filling up time, because they want their work to lead somewhere, to reward them in terms of autonomy, independence and self-satisfaction. Only the person who understands power can extract the maximum benefit from his work, however skillfully it is performed.

As a reason for working, the desire for money obviously remains a powerful one, but in our society it is increasingly irrelevant—not that Americans are any less strongly motivated to accumulate wealth than in the past, but as a dream wealth has faded in the era of the bureaucrat, the "junior executive," inflation, credit cards and high taxes. Few people can hope to acquire great wealth—fewer still even suppose it possible—and almost everyone who works is involved in an organization of one kind or another, within which the limits of their monetary ambitions must be contained.

It is the desire for *power* that keeps most people working. What we are offered is no longer the opportunity for unlimited wealth, but the chance to acquire limited power, with the advantage that its satisfactions cannot be taxed and are not subject to depreciation or the depredations of international speculators. In modern corporations money is no longer the goal —or the goad for that matter. The most successful corporate executive can hardly hope for more than an increasing sufficiency in terms of income, and the real goal of most employees is to build up enough benefits to tide them over the usually impecunious period from retirement to death, assuming always that they survive to undergo this dreary foretaste of death itself. Like Christianity, the corporation offers comfort in the problematic future in exchange for sacrifices and good deeds in the present. A Golden Age on Social Security is the modern equivalent of Hell.

Still, you cannot motivate people solely by threatening them with penurious old age—you must offer them some motivation for the present. The opportunity to acquire and wield power provides just such a motivation; thus most corporations find it in their interest to encourage power games. Hence, in every organization there exists a *built-in* or "house" power game, the rules and rewards of which are established by the management. The astute player must play the company game as well as his own, while being aware that winning someone else's game is not necessarily winning his own—indeed, victory in a game that has been established by the management of a company, or has developed as part of the company's traditions, may ultimately involve *losing* his own game. The player should therefore automatically distrust most promotions, titles, symbols of office and raises when they are offered to him—which is not to say that he should turn them down or denigrate them openly. It would be wise to remember the following warning: "Power cannot, strictly speaking, be given to another, for then the recipient still owes it to the giver. It must in some sense be assumed, taken, asserted. For unless it can be held *against* opposition, it is not power and will never be experienced as real on the part of the recipient." [7] What is *given* to us, however attractive it may seem, is almost always a trap.

Corporations are perfectly happy to give power and prestige to the people who work for them. Power is cheaper than raises; anyway at the top, senior executives can hardly hope to keep more than half of what they're paid. Nor is it in the corporation's interest to give anyone a guarantee of substantial retirement benefits, even if inflation made that possible—uncertainty pays dividends in performance. What keeps people working is the *promise* of security—if they actually *had* it, they might stop. Hence the organization has an interest in encouraging the natural propensity of men and women toward self-aggrandizement, if only by means of symbolic rewards. Furniture is cheaper than bonuses; it is depreciable, and can be used in any case for the next incumbent.

Since what people want most is power over others —"managing people," as the euphemistic business phrase goes—the average corporation functions as a kind of broker, providing those who want power with a certain number of people over whom they can exert it. This costs nothing; every organization always has plenty of people so unimportant or easily replaceable (assuming they were ever necessary in the first place) that it is simple enough to satisfy the power cravings of even the most incompetent executives by giving them someone to tyrannize. For years this has been the real function of secretaries in the minds of many men.

But the kind of power the corporation can give us has its disadvantages—take the person who has the power to decide on salaries. This is a coveted power position, since it allows the holder the maximum possibility of increasing his ego at other people's expense, together with the assurance that he will be courted, flattered and feared. On the other hand, the ordinary person who holds such a job is often condemned to be underpaid himself, since his position is usually dependent on the ability to hold salary increases to a predetermined amount. He cannot exercise his power and at the same time give himself the substantial raise he deserves, or at any rate expects.* In people is a sham. However much he may be feared, his case, as in so many others, the power over other he has lost the power game in being given power; his control over others is a substitute for real gains for himself.

The power game player, on the contrary, will never allow himself to be placed in this position. He does not regard the company's interests as identical with his own. If asked to enforce economies he will do it,

* My feelings about power are not in any way sexist. Women should have their share of it, and experience tells me they will use it in much the same ways men do. However I have thought it better not to burden the reader with such cumbersome devices as "he/she" or the constant use of the word "person." Most of the actions I describe can be attributed just as easily to a woman, and where there are differences, or when I'm referring to a woman, I will make this clear.

but never at his own expense. His aim will be to cut salaries by ten percent and use his success at doing this in order to get a twenty-percent increase for himself.

Power, as we shall see, pays off.

It is not enough to want power, or even to *have* it. It must be used creatively. And it must be enjoyed.

The use of power as a weapon of aggression makes monsters of us. The feeling that power is a wearisome burden ("If only you understood how hard it is to be the one who has to make decisions . . .") is self-destructive. Power must be the servant, not the master.

In *The Act of Will*, Robert Assigioli describes very precisely the value of play as a means of dealing with life in a passage that might serve as an eloquent description of the power game: "One of the best incentives is the instinct to play . . . Thus the danger is avoided of making life too rigid and mechanical, rendering instead interesting and colorful what would otherwise be tiresome duties. All with whom we are associated can become our cooperators (without knowing it!). For instance, a domineering superior or an exacting partner becomes, as it were, the mental parallel bars on which our will . . . can develop its force and proficiency . . . Talkative friends or time-wasters give us the chance to control speech; they teach us the art of courteous but firm refusal to engage in unnecessary conversation. To be able to say 'no' is a difficult but useful discipline. So the Buddhist saying goes: 'An enemy is as useful as a Buddha.' "[8]

CHAPTER TWO

Stories of Power

He could leave the Archives to the archivists, the beginners' courses to the present set of teachers, the mail to his secretaries, and would not be neglecting any serious matters. But he did not dare leave the elite to themselves for a moment. He had to keep after them, impose himself on them and make himself indispensable to them. He had to convince them of the merit of his abilities and the purity of his will; he had to conquer them, court them, win them, match wits with every candidate among them who showed a disposition to challenge him—and there was no lack of such candidates.

—Hermann Hesse
THE GLASS BEAD GAME

Only power can get people into a position where they may be noble.

—Alfred Kazin

The Look of Power

Some people seem to have been born knowing how to use power, sometimes even formed by nature in its image.

It isn't necessary to be six feet tall and built like a football tackle, but there are some physical signs that hint at power—a certain immobility, steady eyes, quiet hands, broad fingers, above all a solid presence which suggests that one belongs where one is, even if it's somebody else's office or bed.

It is possible to cultivate some of these signs of power, and even to adopt certain idiosyncrasies that will make one the center of attention in any group, but nothing can substitute for that combination of self-control and personal magnetism that naturally powerful people have.

It helps to have a large face, with at least one overpowering feature—General de Gaulle's nose or President Johnson's ears are examples—but failing this gift from the gods or the laws of genetics, the apprentice power-seeker would do well to take a good look at himself (or herself) in the mirror, thus putting to good use the time that would otherwise be wasted in merely shaving or making-up. After all, when people look at you, your face is the first thing they see, and very possibly the only thing they'll remember.

You might think there is little you can do about your face, short of plastic surgery, but this is not altogether true. We live behind our faces, while they front for us. We may easily ignore how badly they are serving us. Try looking in the mirror, and saying, in a firm, reasonable and believable voice, "I think my work entitles me to more money than I'm making now, and I know I can get more, as a matter of fact, but I'd prefer to stay here." If your eyes look shifty and blink a lot, and your lower jaw is pushed forward pugnaciously, your face is giving you away, and in a real encounter your superior will probably conclude that you don't have any job offers and probably don't even believe that your work is worth what you're already making. By practicing in front of a mirror, it is possible to develop a firm, trustworthy gaze, and a confident, relaxed mouth.* We may not be able to make ourselves beautiful, but we can learn to control our facial reactions, to eliminate the more obvious signs of nervousness.

Despite the recent popularity of beards and mustaches, these are seldom useful in playing the power game, since they are still often assumed to hide a weak upper lip or a lack of chin, and are, of course, unavailable to women players. Men with beards almost always look as if they had something to hide, and very often do, and the majority of mustaches look like half-hearted compromises between shaving

---

* Facial "power problems" include licking the lips and biting them, any twitch of the mouth, particularly at the corners, blinking and excessive eye movement. EEM is the easiest defect to correct—one merely has to practice looking at a fixed object without showing boredom. It is possible to prevent involuntary twitching at the corners of the mouth by applying Xylocaine anesthetic ointment before an important meeting, but the effect is temporary, and if too much ointment is used the lips become numb and speech is slurred. A friend of mine went to Japan to have his eyes widened, in order to acquire a more frank and open gaze, but the operation is not cheap once you have added the cost of air fare, and only worthwhile for an aspiring politician, which he is.

20

and growing a full beard, thus giving an impression of uncertainty.

It is useful to learn to sit still while others are fidgeting—many a businessman has benefited from his rocklike immobility in times of crisis, which is bound to give the impression that he alone is in control of himself—while in fact he may simply have nothing useful to suggest or have failed to understand just how bad things are. Gradually, people who sit still and keep quiet acquire a reputation for common sense and reliability, and even toughness, particularly since they seldom offer an opinion before hearing what other, more impetuous souls have to say. This is a talent which can be learned in time—a few weeks of Yoga instruction may help, or reciting large parts of *The Oxford Book of English Verse* or baseball scores to oneself during business meetings. The main thing is to be silent, impassive, alert in appearance and yet at the same time, *visible*.

Clothes can sometimes help to make one visible, but nothing annoys other people more than eccentricity in clothing. In corporations where a "shirt-sleeve" atmosphere reigns, it is possible to acquire high visibility by always wearing a jacket, which makes one look more solid, conservative and reliable than anyone else.

Feet have their uses. Most people cross their legs when seated, so a certain aura of solid power can be projected by planting the feet firmly on the floor. Feet can be used much more subtly, as we shall later see.

Executives who sweat heavily may find it worthwhile to invest in a powerful air-conditioner, even at the risk of making other people shiver, since perspiration is usually considered a sign of tension or lying. None of these tricks, however, can substitute for the advantages of a good, strong, well-controlled face.

". . . Go Tell *Him* About Dogs"

Those who have such a face are thrice-blessed. Take my friend Jack: imagine a tall, lean man, radiating strength and power, endowed by nature with a thrusting, powerful nose (even the nostrils are large, which is a good sign of power in both people and horses), hooded, bright-blue eyes, fierce eyebrows and prominent cheekbones. Jack knows by instinct how to assume "the power position." Without even thinking about it, he faces the entrance in any restaurant or bar, with his back to the wall, knowing that a man with his back to the door is apt to be nervous and ill-at-ease, unable to prevent himself from looking over one shoulder. In conferences, Jack sits with his back to the window so that others have to look into the glare of the sun to see him.

He speaks in hushed whispers, so you have to lean forward to catch what he's saying, thus putting you at an uncomfortable angle and creating an illusion of "bowing." Like all good power players he never sweats and has absolute control over his bladder; no matter how long the meeting or luncheon, he will not be the first to leave the table for the bathroom, since the first person to go is apt to be considered weak by the rest, even if they all go a few minutes later. (Players doubtful of their ability on this score might well emulate the British royal family, for whom it is customary to prepare for public appearances by drinking as little as possible for several days beforehand, and eating a low-bulk, high-protein diet —one may be thirsty, but one is not likely to have to ask to be excused just when a destroyer is to be launched or the Lord Mayor of Sheffield knighted.)

Jack is a business advisor of world-wide fame, with a genius for the unconventional deal that throws everyone off-balance. He went from a Brooklyn high school in the Depression to an enormous office of his own in the Seagram building on Park Avenue. The conference room looks like a bank vault, all stainless steel and polished brass, with a glass table big enough for a meeting of NATO. Yet his personal office looks like something a street-corner notary public might have in Bensonhurst—battered old furniture, dusty file folders all over the floor, a grandfather clock that doesn't work—an office which emphasizes that its occupant doesn't need all the gleaming show of power outside. In fact, these two styles of decoration correspond to Jack's two basic styles of power. When he meets you in the outer office, surrounded by telephone consoles with gleaming buttons, chrome-plated lighting fixtures from George Kovacs, rugs that look like modern tapestries and wall hangings that look like antique rugs, Jack projects tireless strength, resolution and efficiency. He is crisp, impersonal, forever flashing quick, concise orders to people over the intercom system. The carefully contrived lighting gives his face a glow of good health. In the presence of such indefatigable energy and purpose, it seems pointless to resist.

When he's in his private office, he slips naturally into another style, his shoulders slump, he complains that he's exhausted, that he's too old to take the red-eye flight back from L.A. and drive straight from Kennedy to the office, his hooded eyes no longer project power, but rather infinite fatigue. Lost amidst huge piles of paper, he draws on your sympathy, inquires after your ailments and describes his own, recommends a doctor for your bad back, offers you a tranquilizer while cautioning you not to take it. When necessary, he can shift quickly from one style to the other, until his opponent is thrown completely off-guard, never quite sure whether it's the efficient financial wizard or the doting uncle he has to deal with. Jack has no trouble in switching from one role to the other: both are real, and it is instinct, rather than cunning, that guides him.

Jack understands power, all right, it's his stock in trade. He appears in people's offices without being announced by the receptionist so that they look up from their desks to find him standing there. He knows how much it's worth not to give them time to tell the receptionist to keep him waiting for a few minutes; he catches them with their jackets off, their ties loosened, busy making calls to their girl friends on their private telephones or joking with a secretary, and already he's a step ahead, like a man who has walked into a woman's bedroom and found her naked.* No receptionist stops him anyway: he looks as if he owns the whole company and is about to evict the entire staff, possessions and all, leaving

---

* Or, to be fair, a woman walking into a man's bedroom and finding him naked! In either case, the naked party is more embarrassed than the clothed party and has nothing left to hide. The person who has been surprised nearly always feels guilty about the encounter, and thus loses power to the intruder. Full exposure is a kind of surrender.

them standing on the street with their coffee mugs, ecology posters and the ashtrays their children made in crafts class, wondering what happened.

From the very beginning of his career, he has known better than to ask for favors—he grants them willingly enough, but makes sure that there's no way of returning them. The balance is always on *his* side. He acts with impassive, but instinctive, generosity. At the end of one long and unsuccessful negotiation, an executive, sensing that they had reached a dead end, paused to admire Jack's watch, a slim, gold Patek Phillipe with a mesh-gold bracelet. "That's a terrific watch," he said, "is it expensive?" Jack shrugged. "Four hundred dollars," he replied. "I'd like one," the executive said, "is that list or net?" Jack allowed himself a smile, and taking off the watch, he placed it on the desk and rose. "Net," he said, "but the watch is yours. If we can't make a deal on the contract, we can always make a deal on the watch." Before the astonished executive could reply, Jack was gone, leaving his opponent to struggle with the dilemma. Did he owe Jack four hundred dollars? Or the list price? Or four hundred dollars minus reasonable depreciation? Or, God forbid, *nothing*? Could he give the watch back? Despite repeated telephone calls, Jack refused to discuss the watch, or even acknowledge its existence, and by the time the two men met to renew their negotiations on more substantive matters, the executive had very little on his mind but the question of the watch, and easily gave way on most of the points Jack had wanted him to concede in the first place.

If he had been smart, he would have sent the watch back by registered mail, but as Jack later pointed out, "He really *wanted* the watch. So I made it the most expensive watch he'd ever buy."

Jack moves automatically to establish his territorial imperative. At the luncheon table, sitting opposite you, he gradually moves his pack of cigarettes, his gold Dupont gas lighter, his reading glasses, his butter plate and water glass, if necessary, closer and closer to the center of the table, finally crossing the invisible boundary until they encroach on your table space. By the time the meal is served, he has you surrounded, while you're leaning forward across his belongings to hear what he's saying. The table has become a chessboard, and you suddenly find *his* pieces on your side of the board, threatening your king. He has checkmated you before you even knew the game had started.

He always brings his hat and overcoat into your office, so he can drop them on your couch or chair, thus establishing a territorial right, rather than hanging them up outside. He often asks to use your telephone, a reasonable enough request that nobody would refuse. Since you are likely to leave while he's on the telephone—which is only polite—you return to find him sitting at your desk, your telephone (an obvious Freudian symbol of power in form and function) in his grip. This sight is enough to unbalance a great many otherwise shrewd men.

If Jack has any weakness, it is sentimentality, an affection for certain people so strong and passionate that it even seems to surprise Jack. He has learned to manipulate people, but not to be indifferent to them, which makes his task just that much harder, since he basically wants to make everybody happy, even when he's won. Even when his opponents have been defeated, when every clause has been altered to his satisfaction, he leaves them with the impression that they have made a successful compromise. He never claims or celebrates a victory. If there is any way to defeat him, it lies in his sense of justice, as spontaneous as it is genuine. Many of his clients are "waifs and strays," people Jack has met who need him, and who somehow touch his inner depths of paternal kindness, Jack's desire to right the world's wrongs. Perhaps it's simply that a life spent dealing with the vast intangible problems of oil leases, conglomerate real estate deals and Latin American resort hotels fails to satisfy his own needs. However that may be, Jack can often be found playing the power game for small stakes, or no stakes at all, like a successful doctor who puts in two afternoons a week at a free clinic, or secretly treats a patient too poor to pay.

One of these doctors, as it happens, is his brother. He is one of those saintly, old-fashioned doctors one imagines no longer exist, a stooped, powerfully built man, with an innocent face and the clear eyes of a natural diagnostician. His love is medicine, and he may well be one of the last people in the country to believe in the Hippocratic oath and the Declaration of Independence without reserve. So you have to imagine, if you can, one of those Gerald Greene-type doctors of the old school, living out in Canarsie, with an old frame house and garden near Avenue U and 69th Street at the back of beyond in deepest Brooklyn, somewhere behind the Floyd Bennett Naval Air Station and lost between the parking lot of the new Macy's and endless stretches of pastel-colored asphalt-shingled houses, filling stations decorated with bedraggled plastic flags fluttering from limp wires, sinister-looking taverns with windows just large enough to comply with New York State Liquor Law requirements, and public high schools optimistically designed to resemble Mt. Vernon and now surrounded by cyclone fences and covered in graffiti—Checkpoint

27

Charlies on the Berlin Wall of sporadic racial violence, appearing in the Manhattan newspapers only as backgrounds to photographs of plastic-visored tactical patrolmen and screaming mobs of housewives and anti-bussers . . . In other words, it's a neighborhood "in transition," physically a kind of peninsula, sloping down toward Sheepshead Bay, its grimy beaches littered with worn-out tires and junkyards and ramshackle horse stables and odd little industrial pockets that process malodorous plastics or specialize in the repainting of stolen cars; sociologically, it's changed from Jewish to Italian to black, not quite fast enough to satisfy the blacks, but fast enough to drive out the Jews, who have long since fled to Larchmont and Great Neck, and to anger the Italians, who have moved in after the Jewish exodus. This process means—you have to picture it, if you're not a New Yorker—that whole areas look like Dresden in 1945, vast reaches of rubble punctuated by weather-worn signs promising vast urban reconstruction projects under the guidance of some long-departed mayor, synagogues that are now Muslim temples, storefronts that have been covered in plywood to serve as the local offices, or armed strongpoints, of the Italian-American Anti-Defamation League, pseudo-Irish bars whose names are changing from "The Shamrock Grill" to "Mecca," a furniture store which has taken on a new lease on life as the center for a brotherhood of "martial monks" in green robes with black cords, who teach the disciplines of Kung Fu, Karate and Judo and are generally suspected of supplying young blacks with drugs, automatic weapons, or both. It is not a happy place to live.

At one time, the neighborhood supported a good many doctors—GP's who knew their patients, made house calls, and carried barley sugar for children in

their pockets. As the neighborhood changed, they
fled, into retirement or the suburbs, and for most of
the residents, medical care is now something connected to interminable forms and performed in the
huge, scary hospital that looms on the horizon next
to the few high-rise housing developments and the
Con Ed gasometers. Except for Jack's brother, who
stayed, learned a little Italian, took to *schmoozing*
with the parish priest instead of the rabbi, but found
himself, in the end, isolated in the ebb tide of social
disintegration. Drug addicts journey out from Bed-
ford-Stuyvesant to break into his office, he cannot
make house calls at night for fear of being mugged,
the picket fence around his house is torn down while
he's sleeping, delinquents remove the hub caps and
the MD plates from his car, graffiti appear on his
door. Where once he received respect, he is now
harassed.

All of this has happened without Jack's being
aware of it—he loves his brother, but their paths
seldom cross, and each thinks the other an innocent.
Los Angeles is closer to Jack than Brooklyn by now,
and not surprisingly when he told me the story of
his brother's distress, it was in the dim light of the
Polo Lounge of the Beverly Hills Hotel, where I
had just rescued him from an argument with a
drunken businessman, whose parting shot to us was
"I don't care what you say, I'd rather control technology than be President any day, and that's what
I'm doing. All my life I've worked for 'fuck-you'
money, so I can say 'fuck you' to *anyone*, and I'm
saying 'fuck you' to *you!*"

"A yokel," said Jack with contempt as he guided
me to a table. "He has some system for a back-pack
dispenser that keeps beer ice cold. You strap it on
vendors and they hawk ice-cold beer around the

stands at sports arenas. That's technology? That's *power*? Tom Swift and his back-pack beer-keg? I'll tell you how to use power, if you want to know.

"You know my brother, right? Maybe you don't know that one of my clients is a Mafia don—except that we refer to him as a man accused of underworld activities, right? We'll call him Mr. Pietro, okay? He's a very important man in certain circles, and has a lot of power in Brooklyn, where he runs a number of business establishments. Personally, I like him—he's a warm, generous guy who looks after his relatives, which I admire. I think he's set them up with Carvel stands from one end of Long Island to the other. He once told me, 'They can't do no harm selling ice cream, but the only guy I'd trust a hundred percent to run an ice cream stand would be a diabetic. At least he wouldn't steal the stock.' Anyway, Pietro is in federal prison right now, and I see him every once in a while on his personal investment business. His professional business, I don't want to know about.

"Pietro was the last guy on my mind when I went out to see my brother for his birthday, something I hadn't done in a long time. When I got out to Brooklyn in the limo—I figure I left there on the subway, when I go back it's going to be by limo—I could see my brother looked worried and unhappy. I prodded him a little, and he told me what was happening around there. Ten years ago he could have gone to the rabbi or the cops, but now, who knows? Well, I figured I'd do something about it on my own, without telling him, so after lunch—one of those big lunches like the whole menu of the Stage Delicatessen, only with lace tablecloths—I went out for a walk in the old neighborhood, and after a couple of blocks I see this corner candy store, the kind that sells papers, and magazines, and about a million other things, and it's the center of the neighborhood, right? Well, there's this old guy at the counter, a ghinny, big white mustache, apron, set up so he can see the whole street. So I go in, and I square off my shoulders, and when I'm standing right in front of him so he can't see out the door—I make it clear I'm deliberately blocking his vision—I look him right in the eyes. 'Can I get you something?' he asks. 'No,' I said, 'I have come to bring you a message from Mr. Pietro. The message is this: *Don't mess with my* consigliere's *brother!* I am Don Pietro's *consigliere.* The doctor is my brother. That's the message.'

"So this guy looks at me and opens his eyes wide. 'Why tell me?' he asks. 'What can I do? Kids, who can control them these days? They do all sorts of things, their parents don't care, the neighborhood isn't safe. You got blacks moving in, our own kids don't show no respect, even the priest don't feel safe. Tell your brother he should buy a dog.' I just looked at him without blinking. 'Don't give me that,' I said. 'I'm not authorized to have a discussion, I don't want to hear about dogs, I'm empowered—right? *empowered*—only to give you a message, that's all, and you heard it. You got the message from Don Pietro. What you do is your business, friend. You want to talk about dogs, you go tell *him* about dogs.'

"Well, since then my brother tells me things have changed. His fence has been fixed, nobody touches his car, there's even a carful of neighborhood guys watching his front door at night to make sure he doesn't get mugged, all of them carrying tire irons and plumber's wrenches. He's a happy man. He thinks the neighborhood has become a very nice place. I haven't told him what I did, and I haven't told Pietro I used his name either, not that he'd mind

—he has a sense of humor and he's against crime in the streets himself. I used power. And nobody even knows I did.

"I don't want my name on the screen because credit is something that should be given to others. If you are in a position to give credit to yourself, then you do not need it."[1] This statement (it is Monroe Stahr, the Hollywood producer, speaking in F. Scott Fitzgerald's *The Last Tycoon*) represents the most subtle view of power—and the rarest. Few people who have power, or want it, can forgo self-advertisement (for this reason, powerful people are seldom good at keeping secrets). People like Jack who like to use power *invisibly* are rare. In Malcolm X's phrase, "Power is best used quietly, without attracting attention"—[2] a judgment that was dramatically confirmed when he went public with his power and was cut down by a submachine gun.

The most talented power players prefer to operate behind the scenes, getting what they want with the minimum of publicity and fuss. They have learned that it is better to set things up quietly and patiently so that what they want is *offered* to them. Confrontation produces friction, and friction slows progress.

For most people in organizations, however, the main attraction of power lies precisely in its visibility. The role of *éminence grise* does not appeal to them. Nor does modern life favor secret power: we don't mind being led, but we want to see our leaders in action, to share their struggles vicariously. We like open diplomacy, "up-front" power confrontations in our politics and plenty of interesting power games at work. Every business organization thrives on power games, perhaps because the satisfactions of most people's work are limited and they will generally put up with a good deal in return for the pleasure of watching others struggle for power. It's at once a spectator sport and a participatory one, since everyone, however unimportant, can play a role, take sides, make judgments, feel involved in something more dramatic and interesting than their own limited task. Thus a flamboyant seeker after power is likely to attract far more supporters and sympathizers than a quiet plotter.

People who enjoy the public appearance of power can rise very fast. They become stars, celebrities in their own small worlds, they build their own legends by wielding power openly; they are born leaders.

"Joe Namath Was a Leader . . ."

David Mahoney, the fifty-two-year-old chairman, president and chief executive officer of Norton Simon Inc, is "accustomed to the fast track."[3] The track has always carried him toward power and success, and indeed he moved so fast and looked like such a winner that "the way has always been cleared for him by older men."[4] The son of a Bronx construction worker thrown out of work by the Depression, Mahoney runs a conglomerate whose sales exceeded one and a half billion dollars in the fiscal year ending June 30, 1973, and whose activities include soft drinks, packaged foods, cosmetics, liquor, fashions and magazines.

The executive offices of Norton Simon Inc. on

Park Avenue seem to have been designed to reflect the presence of power and money, in a quiet, self-assured style that is peculiarly late twentieth-century American. The "reception area" (it is far too big to be called a waiting room) is dimly lit, decorated in shades of brown, as silent and overpowering as a Pharaoh's tomb, and probably not much less expensive to build. The walls are hung with enormous abstract paintings, the kind of bland but costly art that is at once inoffensive and soothing, the carpet is a dark brown and beige basket-weave design, the furniture is stainless steel and leather—not so very different in spirit from a first-class passenger lounge at any airport—one almost expects to see a miniskirted waitress appear to take one's order and to hear the subdued moan of Muzak. What makes the difference is *money*. Everything here is solid and expensive, and despite the size of the rooms, one doubts that these chairs and couches are often occupied—they are here to fill up space.

The corridors are equally dark and hermetic, though an open door reveals a glimpse of a surprisingly cheerful ladies' room, brilliantly lit and decorated in brightly modern flowered chintz and white plastic. Mahoney's own outer office is a big, quiet room with a spectacular view of New York, a conference table covered in painted blue linen, womb-like armchairs in tan suede leather, ornate cigarette boxes filled with Tareytons (Mahoney's brand), a table in fake alligator hide on which sits a copy of David Mahoney's interim report to the shareholders for the three months ending September 30, 1973, tastefully bound in blue-gray parchment paper. The white curtains sway gracefully in the breeze from the ventilating system, the windows are sealed, and from the other side of the door that leads to Mahoney's

private office come the sounds of a spirited argument
in which the phrase "operating capital" recurs frequently. It is like being in the control room of a
spaceship starbound for profit.

When the door opens, the captain himself appears,
a lean, tall, handsome man in his early fifties, wearing a checked suit, a blue linen shirt, black patent
leather Gucci loafers and a thin Florentine gold wrist
watch which he never looks at. Mahoney has the
rugged, expressive and self-deprecating good looks
of the young John Huston or Jason Robards, Jr.—
one can imagine him easily as Hickey in *The Iceman
Cometh*. The first thing that strikes one about him
are his eyes, large, intelligent, shrewd and of a daz-
zling blue intensity that is instantly persuasive and
disarming. Mahoney seems to know how to use his
eyes—he looks straight at you, doesn't ever seem to
blink, leans forward across the table to bring them
closer to you, twists himself in his chair to keep
them at the level of yours. He has the quality of a
hypnotist or an actor—there's something unlikely
about him as a businessman, except that the eyes
can go awfully cold when he's asking you questions.
Unlike Jack, Mahoney is in constant motion, chain-
smoking, pouring himself Sanka from a stainless steel
coffeepot, gesturing, tilting his chair back, but his
feet stay firmly planted on the floor, and he has Jack's
habit of pushing his belongings across the table very
gradually, a gold lighter, his ashtray and his silver-
plated mug making their way inexorably toward you
as he talks.

It is difficult to imagine Mahoney radiating anything but vitality. His physical presence is striking—
he is lean, tanned in mid-winter, one of those people
who would attract attention anywhere. He has a
charm like that of John F. Kennedy (another Irish-

35

American success story), although the only photographs in the room are two autographed color spreads of President and Mrs. Nixon from a *McCall's* story.

"Power is a lever . . ." Mahoney says. We are chatting about his responsibilities, his meteoric career, and Mahoney is trying to define just how he got where he is. "Is power persuasion or force?" he asks, shrugging, "or manipulation?" He pauses to ask if I have read Alan Watts, gracefully works Newton's Third Law into his conversation, quoting it exactly, dismisses people who have disagreed with him with a genial "God bless 'em," picks up a phone and says, "Tell them it's for six o'clock and we're going to have to move them back," then he goes on to discuss how he runs his business. For Mahoney sees power as a means of getting things done, is uncomfortable with the idea of power as an abstraction, a quality he *has* rather than a working tool. He is interested, as he says, in "how, not why."

"There's no autonomy in the *world*," he says. "There are damn few things I could just *do*. Do I feel that I want to run things, and make the decisions? Yes. But I've always been a line operator." He pauses. "Basically, for all the companies I've worked for, I've had to be a moneymaker. There has to be a leader to make things work, somebody who has whatever that intangible quality is." Mahoney searches for an example, obviously reluctant to use himself. "Joe Namath!" he says. "He had the power; he was a leader." Mahoney smiles broadly, and I understand why Namath comes to his mind, for Mahoney excelled at baseball and basketball at Cathedral High School in Manhattan, and realized that skill and the will to win in athletics was the only way he would ever get a college education. Playing basketball to win took him to the University of Pennsyl-

vania's Wharton School and, in a sense, finally to
this office. He is still playing to win, and has a fellow feeling for athletic stars, whose problems on the
field he likes to compare to his own. So far as his
own success is concerned, he is content to say that
"Ever since Moses came down from the mountain
with the tablets, the world has been moved by salesmen. I'm a salesman."

As to running a company, Mahoney sees his role
as getting the best out of people, a form of salesman-
ship itself. He likes "to ratify good decisions, not
make them, to orchestrate people," but one can
imagine that he has no trouble in orchestrating them
toward the decision he wants made, and he does not
deny a capacity to manipulate people and enforce
discipline. "I much prefer a consensus," he says, "but
I don't trust total agreement. If two people agree all
the time, one of them is unnecessary."

On the question of using his power toughly, Mahoney is ever so slightly evasive, in part because of
the story of a power game he is said to have played
on the executive who had been running Norton
Simon Inc.'s Canada Dry division for two weeks.
When the latter pointed out that the division couldn't
possibly meet its figures for the year, Mahoney told
him to "be on budget by the six-month mark." When
he asked what would happen if he couldn't make it,
Mahoney is said to have replied, "Then clean out
your desk and go home."[5]

This story worries Mahoney a lot, and he is at
pains to point out that the Canada Dry executive did
in fact "make his figures," and is still with the company. "These things aren't personal. What I want to
know is not why you are down, it's When are you
going to be up? Give me the how, not the why. I'm
prepared to listen to the reasons, and I can under-

stand good reasons, like a strike in a bottling plant, but I want to know how you're going to climb out of something like that. If you can't make it you'd better have a damn good reason and a plan." For the first time, a hint of Mahoney's toughness shows through as he dismisses the subject abruptly: "Anyway, he *agreed* to those figures, they were *his* figures!"

Figures play a large part in Mahoney's conversation, and in fact he explains his own position by saying, "All I am is the sum total of everybody else's figures." How does he ensure that everybody meets their figures? Mahoney talks about "the process of getting things done," about persuasion, incentives ("You fill people's needs for money, security, whatever it is, everybody wants something, after all, even if it's only a good table at the Pump Room"), then reluctantly considers the possibility that his power relies on an element of fear. "People fear things, sure, they sometimes fear me. You fear anyone or anything that can cause you a problem. People's fear of me is really their fear of *themselves*. If they're performing, they don't have anything to fear. There's probably fear in every organization, and it's natural. The first time you disagree with the boss the fear starts. It can't be helped."

Mahoney quickly points out that the constructive use of power is not easy for him. He dislikes firing people—"It's the most difficult decision, hard enough when it's people you know and like—you know their wives, homes, children—but it's even harder when it's people you don't know, when you close down a whole plant because you have to." For a moment he looks grim, perhaps it's a decision he's in the process of making, then he smiles suddenly and adds, "You have to take the job seriously, but not take *yourself* seriously. Otherwise work is a drudge."

How does Mahoney feel about money? Did he always want power, wealth, success? "I just always knew I never wanted to be poor," he says, and recalls seeing a limousine waiting outside a theater when he was a child and thinking it meant "power and security." He rises to his feet without having looked at his watch, apparently aware that it is nearly six o'clock. "But limousines and things like that wear off," he adds. "You get a lot of perquisites, and they're important to your ego. To me, it goes back to the money end of it. I don't want it to be unrewarded. I've earned it." He apologizes for leaving, but has an exercise class at Alex and Walter's Gym at six-thirty, and the limousine is waiting downstairs. At the door he pauses and turns back. "With power comes responsibility," he says intently. "When you have a string on the company—*it has a string on you.*" And he's gone, moving with the graceful speed of an old athlete.

Clearly Mahoney doesn't mind the string. Part of his charm is that he *doesn't* take himself altogether seriously: power is a game, he plays it well, he wins a lot, loses sometimes, but obviously gets a lot of excitement out of it. He is not, as another major corporate executive has been accused of being, "a total-control freak whose need for power can never be satisfied."[6]

Of course it's easier to play the power game so disarmingly from a position like Mahoney's, and with his natural grace (the *New York Times* recently compared him to Robert Redford, which gives you some idea of his star quality). As for his subordinates, he controls them by means of whatever *they* want—as someone once remarked of Harold S. Geneen's hold over ITT's executives, "He's got them by their limos."[7] Still, Mahoney is a smoothie, which makes him very rare in his world, where it is more common to rely on inducing "a tension [that] goes through the company, inducing ambition, perhaps exhilaration, but always with some sense of fear."[8]

Inducing fear is the kind of power that most people understand best, and in many offices one can see scenes that remind one of carnage in the jungle—the stifled shrieks of the victim, the triumphant cry of the successful predator, the hushed and subdued twittering of those who have been spared and tell themselves after each kill, "Thank God it wasn't me this time." Lots of people *like* to be feared, and don't feel they have power unless they are. Aggression is their strategy; anger is their favorite weapon.

To a limited extent it is possible to control people through fear, if only because most people will do anything to avoid a scene. In the words of Erich Fromm, "the animal reacts to threats to his existence whether with rage and attack, or with fear and flight [and] flight seems to be the more frequent reaction."[9] Some people become adept at the art of intimidation, a tactic which is often useful at meetings, where it is possible to single out a scapegoat and attack him suddenly and outrageously. If the attack is unexpected, the shock and surprise will prevent other people from coming to the scapegoat's defense, which is a valuable way of concealing the attacker's own deficiencies. Most people are happy to follow a strong lead, even if it's in the wrong direction. As power moves go, however, this method is primitive and dangerous. Open confrontations easily get out of control, especially when they take place in public, and successful power players soon learn to avoid them.

A fierce display of temper is sometimes a useful device, but usually falls into the realm of *defensive* games. Most executives, however senior, are inclined to avoid head-on collisions with colleagues who are "thin-skinned" or notoriously short-tempered. It's simply too much aggravation.

All the same, while people who lose their temper easily are frequently given enormous privileges and freedom simply to keep them quiet, they seldom rise to any real position of power. The most they can do is to frighten intruders away from their nests by a ritual display of anger, like the male fiddler crab, which waves its left claw "as a warning to other males . . . and to delimit territory".[10] In the average human executive, the equivalent signs are predominantly facial—the cheeks become flushed and pouchy, the eyes fixed and sometimes bulbous, the lips stiffened in the center, but trembling at the extremities. Following the territorial patterns of human beings, explosions of temper are always most severe when they take place *outside* the individual's office, since his rage is intensified by the insecurity of standing on space that doesn't "belong" to him. Wise executives therefore prefer to have such confrontations in the office of the person likely to lose his temper—on his own ground he is more capable of giving way.

Such manifestations of anger generally derive from insecurity, and as people rise in the hierarchy, they usually learn to control themselves and to calm others, aware that power lies in "the production of intended effects,"[11] rather than in violent self-display. While a lot of powerful people start out as "tough guys" because it's an easy, fast game for a certain kind of gutsy player, most of them soon learn to rule by reason. The trick is to make people do what you want them to and *like* it, to persuade them that they want what *you* want.

". . . Maybe I'm a Weakling"

W. Michael Blumenthal is a case in point. The president and chairman of the Bendix Corporation, which had revenues of nearly two billion dollars in the fiscal year ending September 30, 1972 (and earnings of $56,400,000), Blumenthal acquired an almost legendary reputation for being "a tough guy," who was, in the words of a former employer, "arrogant and overly aggressive." A *Fortune* story on Blumenthal began with a warning paragraph: "Visitors to the Bendix Corp. headquarters in Southfield, Michigan, should be advised not to stand near any closed doors. There is too much danger that they will be knocked flat by W. Michael Blumenthal . . . Blumenthal doesn't just enter a room—he explodes into it, and a bruising bump awaits anyone who happens to be in his way."[12]

This dramatic picture irritates Blumenthal, as one quickly discovers in talking to him, but it is also possible to guess that there was a time when it would have pleased him immensely. For Blumenthal is a very special kind of industrialist, perhaps the first and most successful of a new breed—men who have succeeded in the academic world and in government, then gone on to cash in their IQ's in industry for astronomical salaries and stock options. Blumenthal taught economics at Princeton University and turned down an offer of tenure to go to work for Crown Cork International, a producer of bottletops, served for two years in the State Department, and spent four years as chairman of the U. S. delegation to the "Kennedy Round" of international trade negotiations, the youngest person ever to hold the title of

Ambassador. Looking at him, it is difficult to imagine
him knocking anyone flat—he is thin and gray, a
youngish man whose hairline has receded and whose
most noticeable facial characteristic is a firm, pugnacious jaw. Blumenthal has none of the obvious signs
of physical vitality that would make David Mahoney
stand out in any group; on the contrary, he looks
stooped and tired, and the combination of his extreme pallor and a gray suit makes him seem almost
invisible. Sitting quietly on a commuter train, Blumenthal would look like an accountant going home
to New Jersey, a middle-aged man with other people's worries on his mind who knows he ought to get
some exercise and fresh air, and also knows he won't.
But Blumenthal almost never sits quietly; he is a flu-
ent, impatient, nonstop talker. He manages to hold
his irritation under control most of the time, but it is
clearly a Herculean effort, and the least interruption
produces a state of complete tension in him, resolved
only when he can plunge back into the conversation
and get it under his control again. Clearly, he has
been forcing himself to listen to people instead of
lecturing them, but he hasn't altogether succeeded
in this transition so far, and has acquired from somewhere the odd habit of sticking his tongue out as far
as it will go, almost stretching it downward, when
hearing someone out. It doesn't seem rude; perhaps
unconsciously it's the only way he can hold himself
back from cutting off the speaker and regaining the
conversational initiative.

Rudeness is very much on his mind, as we sit in
his suite at New York's Regency Hotel, surrounded
by the modern appurtenances of power and wealth—
for Blumenthal is accompanied by his personal assistant and by Bendix's vice president of public relations, his limousine is waiting downstairs to carry

him to an appointment, and he has offered to fly me up to Boston with him later on in the afternoon on Bendix's JetStar in case we need to continue our conversation. And indeed, he *isn't* rude; he's even gracious, but his impatience is a warning of the violent temper concealed beneath the polite exterior.

"I wasn't rude," he says, "but I may have been a little—*abrasive*. My press was: Able guy, getting the job done, but abrasive." For a moment, Blumenthal is silent, leaving the word "abrasive" hanging in the air, and I can't help remembering a phrase of David Mahoney's: "I'd accept abrasiveness as the price of competence any time, if I have to." Blumenthal looks up at the ceiling for a moment, then goes on: "Experience has taught me to relax, to let nature take its course. You learn how to get your way differently . . . To be successful in using power you have to have a *sense* of power. I would define that as a gut-feel of being able to predict with some degree of certainty how people will react in certain situations, so you can predict when there is going to be trouble over something. You also need an understanding of what motivates people in a positive sense, and in a pejorative sense, you need manipulative skill. *Manipulative.* I hate that word. It's using people almost in the negative sense, to your advantage . . . Still, so far as my previous press is concerned, all those stories about my being abrasive, *pushy*, I do have an image of myself now as being sufficiently skilled in manipulating people so that I don't need to operate that way any more . . ."

There is still something of the professor about Blumenthal, but what strikes one most is that his habits of speech, his precision, his "can-do" enthusiasm, his commitment to energy ("Energy," he says, "is the basic requirement of power") are all reflections of the Kennedy Years, hangovers from that period when it was thought possible to link the academic and the political worlds and produce a new style. Today, only Kissinger remains as the greatest triumph of this unlikely marriage, and in many ways, Blumenthal, another German-Jewish refugee who made good in the academic world, then left it to seek greater power, resembles him. His voice is less accented, but he too uses the language in a precise, professorial way, is addicted to such neo-Kennedyisms as "gut-feel," "getting the other fellow on board" and "excellence" in a way that is slightly nostalgic, and shares Kissinger's impatient contempt for those less intelligent than himself and for the professors who went into government and failed to learn that "there was no way to get your thing down the road unless you could get the right fellows on board with you." Under the circumstances, it is hardly surprising that Blumenthal's PR man uses phrases like "the criteria of relatedness," and says of his boss, "He's above all things an efficacious man. Efficacity for him is the equivalent of *memento mori* for the existentialists." One imagines that the purchase of sets of the *Encyclopaedia Britannica* and dictionaries of quotations must have soared in Southfield, Mich., when Blumenthal took over Bendix.

Like most people who have acquired money and power, Blumenthal denies an interest in money, and despite the suite at the Regency, one senses that he means it. "I don't have a primary interest in money at all," he says. "I was making five thousand dollars a year as a professor, in 1958, and I was thrilled when I got thirteen thousand as the assistant to the president of Crown Cork, but that wasn't the reason I left

45

Princeton, and it isn't the reason I left the government for Bendix. I left Princeton because I'm bored by the requirements of being a first-class scholar—for that you have to have a lot of *Sitzfleisch*, the ability to sit on your rear, researching." What motivates Blumenthal is "the exercise of power," the desire to go beyond any imposed limitations. When he first came to Washington, he was impressed by the people around him, but as he points out, "the higher up you went and the closer you got to these very powerful people, you found they were no different from anybody else, and you were just as smart . . . You look at a guy who could be President of the United States, and you say to yourself—I could do it as well as he could. Maybe power is the gall to think that about yourself. As the Germans say about important people, 'They also cook with water' . . . What interests me is the opportunity to excel in the use of my talents without any restrictions on them."

In common with most modern executives, Blumenthal isn't even slightly interested in ownership. Asked if he would like to own Bendix, he reacts with great emphasis, speaking abruptly for the first time. "It's not ownership that counts—it's control. And as chief executive that's what I've got! We have a shareholders' meeting next week, and I've got ninety-seven percent of the vote. I only *own* eight thousand shares. Control is what's important to me . . . To have the control over this large animal and to use it in a constructive way, that's what I want, rather than doing silly things that others want me to do."

As for the means of control, Blumenthal sees it as the ability to select and motivate people, a process which he admits he has had to learn by experience since those days when he acquired a reputation as a man who knocked people over in his haste to get his own way. "When you have a two-and-a-half-billion-dollar business, it's quite clear you will fail unless you can be very selective. The ability to decide where to put your time becomes critical. If you're really good at picking people, you use your power *through* them without stifling them. I work very hard at not recruiting yes-men, and that's hard to do in a big company, because if you knock them over the head two or three times, they will *become* yes-men." Blumenthal scowls momentarily, then says, "I tell them all the time, 'I don't want you to *be* yes-men!'" His expression as he says this, raising his voice for the first time, is a little like that of the Blue Meanie in *Yellow Submarine*, who would never take yes for an answer.

It is a familiar problem of power: how to control people without making them subservient. Blumenthal, a man of quick intelligence, has managed to learn the importance of listening to other people, however impatient he may seem, largely because he has moved into a business where it's necessary to deal in areas of technology and science that his education hasn't prepared him for. "I'm an operator," he says, "a synthesizer, not an intellectual. One of the elements of success is the ability to do a quick study. When I went into government, I got into the kind of work where I had to learn enough to be able to operate in a wide variety of fields in which the language was technical and the facts mysterious. Commodity trade. What the hell did I know about commodity trade? What does *anybody* know? You have to come down to basic issues, policy questions. Take computers. Most business executives are scared of those devils. Our company spends something like twenty million dollars a year on them, so they're important.

47

You learn to ask, 'Can you tell me what that means?' "

Blumenthal rises and goes to the phone, dials quickly and asks, "Did Lisa make an appointment for me?" There is a pause. He sticks his tongue out—perhaps it's only a nervous reaction of boredom. He nods and puts down the receiver, then smiles broadly. "Power! I was just trying to get an appointment at the barbershop! You learn quickly to accept the fact that I can say I'd like to have a car waiting downstairs at one-twenty—I see we're already four minutes late—because I want to be at a certain place by one-thirty . . . Or I want a plane to fly me to Boston at six-thirty tonight, things of that kind, you learn to expect. They look like power to other people, but they're just a convenience." He struggles into his coat and picks up a heavy briefcase, waiting in the hall, ready for him. At the door, he turns for a moment to say goodbye, and adds: "When you have a strong ego, and the strength to use your power, you learn by experience that it is best in life to listen to people who can help you make a decision, and to *defer* to people, sometimes against your better judgment, because you've learned by experience that it's wise to defer to them for any number of reasons. Then you go home in the evening with this gnawing feeling in your insides, asking yourself, 'Am I abdicating my responsibilities, am I reduced to the role of an arbiter? Why am I not that strong chief executive? Maybe I'm just a weakling.' "

*   *   *

To men like Mahoney or Blumenthal, power is a technique. They are high priests of a system, who seek control over *things,* justifying their own ambition in terms of efficiency. The more things you can control (and "things" includes people, of course), the more power you have. But their power is to a very large extent impersonal. As one person said of Blumenthal, "An organization of 87,000 people tends to surround its chief executive with a certain amount of awe," which is certainly true, but ultimately one can influence the work of 87,000 people only by indirect means. A chief executive often plays small power games with his immediate staff just like a minor executive in a small company, for the very good reason that it is only over his immediate entourage that he can exert power directly and visibly; in power terms, the human touch counts for a great deal, and power over people one knows is always more satisfactory than power over large numbers of strangers.

At the same time, size diffuses power. Blumenthal, God knows, is no "weakling," despite his own fears, but the sheer size of his company forces him into the role of a conciliator, however aggressive he is by instinct.

Even a man like Henry Ford II, though he conveys "an unmistakable aura of power that inspires respect, awe and sometimes downright fear," [13] is obliged to operate within the confines of what amounts to a large, private bureaucracy. Though it is true enough that "Ford *is* the boss, he always was the boss . . . and he always will be the boss," [14] his role is still that of a high-level manager, not an autocrat. When asked why he had allowed the company to embark on an advertising campaign that he disliked, he replied, "They wanted it, so there it is." [15]

Those who desire *personal* power are very different. Instead of controlling a portion of the existing world, they set out to create their own. A well-known motion-picture director once told me, in all serious-

49

ness, that when he made a movie he was God. "I have the world in my hands," he said, "I can make it come out any way I want, decide who lives and who dies, who gets punished, who gets to live happily forever after. In between pictures is my seventh day. I rest." This is, of course, a somewhat romantic and self-indulgent view of power. After all, even the most despotic movie director usually starts with somebody else's story, and has to deal with actors, art directors, writers, technical problems, the studio money-men and many other obstacles to independent creativity. Still, it's a common enough point of view—those who aren't satisfied with power over *things* want to create complete worlds that are reflections of their own power. Nothing will satisfy them but omnipotence.

The omnipotent look powerful in their own worlds, but their position has its weaknesses. People like Mahoney or Blumenthal could seek power elsewhere, and probably will someday, people like Jack get their power by playing a game against the rest of the world; people who create worlds in their own image in order to feel powerful end up needing their employees more than their employees need *them*. In the quest for absolute power, they become servants and victims.

"Power Means Love . . ."

On the outside it's a perfectly ordinary town house in the mid-Sixties of Manhattan, just off Fifth Avenue, a quiet side street from which it is possible to hear

the noises made by the animals in the Central Park
Zoo. There is nothing flashy about the exterior, no
indication that this is the residence and private office of Robert Guccione, owner and creator of *Penthouse,* who has built a girlie magazine into a vast
international empire by keeping one step ahead of
Playboy in nudity. Inside, however, it is a vision of
opulence, somewhere between Mae West's bedroom
and a night club in style. What is not covered in
antiqued, smoked mirrors is covered in gilt, marble
or velvet. William Randolph Hearst would have felt
at home among the gilded cherubim, the heavy
drapes and the ormolu furniture, if only the ceilings
were higher.

Guccione's secretary, a statuesque young woman
with long blond hair, dressed in a very short white
minidress, leads one up the stairs to his office, a room
of indescribable chaos, which must once have been
a library and is now filled with books, records, telephones, photographs, layouts, posters and clothes.
Guccione himself seems at ease here, within reach of
the telephones that allow him to exercise a personal
control over his transatlantic empire. He is a tall,
heavyset man, possibly in his early fifties, though it
is hard to tell, dressed in a skintight sueded buckskin
shirt-suit, open to the navel to reveal a hairy chest
crisscrossed by heavy gold chains and ornaments,
among them a gold Penthouse Club key. He has a
strong face, rather like that of a Roman emperor of
the Late Empire, dominating but self-indulgent and
easily bored. There's an uneasy feeling of discrepancy
between the Guccione who talks about *Penthouse* as
a cultural influence on the future of American life
("The things we are embarking on are going to be
very important in the life of this country") and the

tough, ambitious boy from New York who made his way from a job in a London dry-cleaning firm to take on Hugh Hefner, via cartooning and art direction. Guccione is certainly persuasive enough, but one feels that he's trying too hard for sincerity when he talks about social goals and freedom of speech and changing life-styles, that he's rehearsing himself in the role of a "communicator" and entrepreneur for some imaginary stockholders' meeting in the not-too-distant future. He is more relaxed, and on the whole more convincing, when he talks about the way he runs *Penthouse*, and the reasons for his success ("Even as a kid, I was a leader").

To Guccione, his business is, in his words, "a family." "To some people," he says, "power means respect, power means love. They must be needed." There is little doubt that Guccione is one of these people—his is a personal view of power, very unlike the cool drive for excellence and control that characterizes Michael Blumenthal or the orderly sense of priorities that enables David Mahoney to function. All are powerful men, but Guccione sees himself as *Penthouse*, it's not that his ego is involved in it—it *is* his ego.

"In my little world," he says, giving a deprecating nod to the row of telephones, "I have absolute power . . . As power corrupts, it also mellows. I'm very patriarchal to begin with. I take an extraordinary interest in people's problems . . . But there's only one boss—that's me! It's a benevolent dictatorship."

This is a point of view that is comparatively rare among powerful people, most of whom prefer to seem more than they are until they've succeeded, then go to a great deal of trouble to seem *less* than they are, often denying that they have any power at all. For

Guccione, each day is an opportunity to prove his power, and he clearly relishes every moment. Obviously he is in the process of transforming himself from a tough entrepreneur into a culture-figure of sexual liberation and a business success story. It seems to be very much on his mind, obliging him to take on a tone of sweet reason which doesn't appear to suit him and with which he isn't altogether comfortable. Just as he's telling me that he doesn't want to dominate anybody ("I always give the other guy the benefit of the doubt"), his secretary brings him a cup of coffee, and he spills a drop on his new buckskin trousers. "I *told* you I want a saucer!" he shouts, suddenly coming alive, and it is apparent that indeed there is only one boss here. He smiles again, as if to reassure me that this flash of temper isn't really him, then quietly begins to talk about his power, but now that his temper has appeared, he can't quite conceal it. "Power is something you have—just another tool at your disposal. Big companies *had me under their fucking knuckles!* Power gives you a new *weapon!*" As Guccione talks about "big companies," his face changes—it swells with passion, the smile lines vanish and he seems to me, to be honest, a little frightening.

Slightly startled myself, I get up and walk around, while Guccione dabs at his trousers and reaches for a telephone, for here, perhaps not entirely to my surprise, is an authentic tyrant, a man who values power as a personal prerogative, who doesn't have doubts about it . . . But Guccione, who has just completed the telephone call, has turned suddenly gloomy. "When a man really makes a success of his life," he says, "ninety-nine percent of his friends vanish. I have never changed, but I feel rejected by the people

I used to know and love." This is a common complaint of people who have acquired power, and perhaps a justifiable one—it changes relationships. Somehow the path of power is seldom the path of love. Guccione still wistfully wants both, hopes to bridge the gap. *"Penthouse,"* he says, "is like a family. You think of everyone as a brother, son, cousin, sister. You treat them with respect . . . You're giving love and attention to people who sometimes think it's just another job." He stares into space, a man with money and power, who wants the impossible from the people who work for him. "I've even had plans," he adds thoughtfully, "for buying an estate and moving my key people into it. It's feudal. But it would be nice. It could happen . . ."

There's no doubt about it, whatever the inner satisfactions are, it's hard to play God. It's easier to rule by committee, to *influence* things rather than running them to the last detail, but the temptations at the top of the power tree are heady—the higher up you go, the easier it is to assume that you know what is best for people, to feel *responsible* for them. Power over people! What an intoxicant: it's better than drugs, better than alcohol, not only better than sex but part *of* it. Still, we have to ask ourselves if that's the kind of power we want. We can learn a great deal by studying the very powerful, whatever their power style, but for most of us the purpose of power is not to make ourselves responsible for others, but to protect ourselves. The wise man soon learns that omnipotence is servitude. Too much power over other people can be almost as bad as falling into the clutches of people who think they have the right to run your life.

CHAPTER THREE

Living with Power

He suffered the fate of all who exercise a natural and initially unconscious power over other men; this power is not exercised without a certain cost to its possessor.

—Hermann Hesse
THE GLASS BEAD GAME

It is strange desire to seek power and lose liberty.

—Francis Bacon
ESSAYS, II, Of Great Place

Without power, we might as well be trees, rocks, oysters, whatever you like, estimable objects in the sight of God, useful even, obeying the complex laws of Nature, but without the capacity to alter the world, *to control our own lives*. The abyss opens before us, the bottomless gulf of living a life controlled by others, the humiliation of *submission*.

I remember a day, long ago, from another world, when the movie business was still a game of autocrats, before television humbled the great tyrants of the West Coast, leaving them rich but impotent, when I went to the pool at the Beverly Hills Hotel for my swimming lesson. One of the great studio heads was floating on a rubber raft, smoking a cigar. For weeks he had been "making himself unavailable" to an elderly screenwriter, refusing to answer telephone calls, breaking appointments, keeping the old man in tortured suspense, until finally he had let it be known that he would consent to hear him out at 3 P.M. at the pool. When the writer arrived, he could see the producer floating like an obese and hairy water lily in the middle of the pool, available to anyone who could swim out to him. What the producer knew was that the writer couldn't swim. Like a condemned man, the writer retired to don a borrowed pair of swimming trunks, and while the producer's aides smirked and giggled at the cabana, he ungracefully waded across the shallow end of the pool, with the timid courage of the damned, until the water reached his chin. But the producer, using his hands as flippers, moved his raft out into deeper waters, foot by foot, until the writer found himself floundering in the pale, chlorinated water—a nightmare scene of sadism taking place under the creaking palm trees of Southern

California, to the noise of small children happily paddling and beautiful young women slapping suntan lotion on their expensive bodies, bodies like those which had no doubt once been available to the writer when he had been "hot" and owned his own house on South Rodeo Drive, with a tiled pool and a guava tree. Bravely he splashed his way toward the ever-receding raft, attempting to explain why his contract should be renewed as he gulped in distasteful mouthfuls of water. Sometimes he vanished beneath the surface altogether, only to reappear, still talking. At last, when he began to look dangerously exhausted, the pool guard dived in after him. As he was hauled back to the poolside, one of the great man's aides leaned over, lighting a cigarette with a gold Dunhill lighter, and said firmly, slowly, loudly, as one might talk to the senile or the hard of hearing, "Okay, he saw you and he heard you. Now you can get dressed and go."

Hobbes notwithstanding, nothing is quite as "brutish" as life among civilized man; the sudden violence and uncertainty of primitive life can hardly compare to the degradations of our society. A moment's weakness, and we are at the mercy of monsters, real ones too, not the supernatural figures of the savage's imagination. Power is a means of protecting ourselves against the cruelty, indifference and ruthlessness of other men.

This does not mean that we have to become monsters ourselves. Whether or not power is, as Henry Kissinger says, "the ultimate aphrodisiac" [1] (and one hopes it's not), in itself it is neither good nor evil. We can learn to use it in order to be more free, to make life happier and more productive for ourselves and others, or we can use it as "a vehicle of an ego which takes no consideration of guilt and innocence, but merely of what it can get." [2] The object of power is to survive in a difficult world.

Nor is it wise to think of power as a compensatory mechanism. Those who seek power to make up for some real or imagined physical defect are in for an embittered and angry life. Napoleon was not necessarily driven to succeed because he was short, as many seem to believe; he succeeded because he was Napoleon. Height is an obsession with people who hunger after power in the wrong ways. Perhaps men still believe that height has something to do with the size of the penis, despite the assurances of the Masters and Johnson report on this score. Perhaps it's just that for a certain kind of man the thought that anyone can literally look down on him is unsufferable. On the rare occasions when Harry Cohn dined out, he was said to place a telephone book surreptitiously on his chair. "Elevator shoes," which promise an additional two inches in height, appeal to the same insecurity.

There is no doubt that short men are inclined to seek out some means of making up for their lack of height—Winston Churchill's long cigars and funny hats perhaps served this purpose; L. B. Mayer used to receive visitors from behind his enormous, wall-like, curved desk, and whenever he was photographed signing a contract with a star like Clark Gable, who would have towered over him, the star was seated next to Mayer on a lower chair, so that their heads were level.

In some circumstances, nations can fall over the question of a man's height. Paul Reynaud, the Premier of France in 1940, was under the domination of his mistress, Hélène de Portes, an unattractive woman of a certain age, who loathed the British and was in every way defeatist. Her influence on Reynaud was considerable, even absolute, and was said to be based largely on the fact that he was small and she alone could make him feel tall and powerful. As one observer said, "Had Reynaud been three inches taller, the history of the world might have been changed." [3]

Height means something to people, and it's wise not to forget it. The chairman of one great conglomerate is said to have a pedestal behind his desk so that he appears to be about a foot taller than he really is when he stands up to greet somebody, and it is rumored that a stockholders' meeting had to be delayed because an underling had forgotten to place the pedestal behind the podium. It is certainly true that he likes to have short men around him; one's chances of success at this particular corporation are vastly increased if one is under five foot eight inches in height. Indeed, being tall is dangerous there. The chairman loves to humiliate people who are taller than he is, and sometimes promotes them just so that he can make them suffer. "Big is dumb, short is smart," he once told an executive who had displeased him. Another executive, when asked why he continued to work at a company which paid him less than he could have gotten elsewhere, replied, "Well, it's the only place I know where everyone in the top management above me is shorter than I am. I feel comfortable around here. Where else can a guy five foot nine feel *tall*?"

* * *

If shortness supposedly spurs us on to power, health is usually taken as a sure sign of *having* it. Years ago, I remember seeing Robert F. Kennedy walk into a roomful of people in Dark Harbor, Maine, all of them rich and healthy, and noticing that he positively *radiated* good health and energy, not unlike David Mahoney, but on a higher plane of intensity. "God!" breathed the woman beside me, "look what power does to you. I wish I had it!"

It is a curious sign of our admiration for power that we associate power and health; in former times, power was popularly supposed to lead to worry, illness, premature aging and baldness, rather like masturbation. Today, we expect the powerful to glow with health, and they mostly do. The successful exercise of power, like a satisfactory sex life, tends to make people feel good about themselves, whatever the real state of their health, and constant excitement tones up the system wonderfully.

Of course power takes its toll too. Erik Erikson has pointed out that Martin Luther, a man with an enormous need and drive for power, suffered all his life from constipation, a misfortune which obsessed the great reformer to the point that his spiritual breakthrough took place while he was sitting on the toilet. Erikson points out that Luther was "compulsively retentive," [4] that he stored up his energies and his knowledge as if aware that they would someday be released in a single, explosive moment, a purgative flash that would at once cleanse Luther himself and the Church. Odd as it may seem, constipation is often the price of power, even among less titanic figures than Luther, perhaps because powerful people are not only anxious to control everything, but determined not to let *go* of anything. Be this as it may, the use of laxatives seems to increase as power increases, and a good many of the powerful people I know not only suffer from constipation, but discuss it quite openly, as if it were proof of their success, a form of self-imposed suffering. I have seen a motion picture halted every morning at nine-thirty so that the director—a man of great fame in the movie business—could go off and fight the daily battle with his recalcitrant bowels. As he left, the cast and the crew wished him success, and on his return he would describe exactly what had happened, or not happened, in graphic detail. Gradually I came to realize that knowledge of the daily state of his bowels was a kind of status symbol. Think of it: actually being able to force people to discuss his shit as if it were a subject of fascination. What greater proof of power than to force a hundred people, maybe more, to pretend that they cared about what he did on the toilet. Not for nothing did Joseph Mankiewicz once remark in another context that "the whole world is wired to Harry Cohn's ass."

As if that weren't enough, a group of researchers has found that power (and "achievement orientation") correlates very highly with serum uric acid, the substance in the blood that is responsible for gout, and which is considered "a possible risk factor in coronary heart disease." [5] Serum uric acid is high among powerful, successful men, and at its lowest among the unemployed, a depressing piece of information for the ambitious to consider. Blood pressure and serum cholesterol both increase among those who have "responsibility for others" in a working situation, which makes it hardly surprising that nearly thirty percent of the businessmen who responded to one nationwide survey felt that their jobs "had adversely affected their health." [6]

The kind of jobs that lead to power naturally involve stress and responsibility, but I strongly suspect that the businessmen who felt their health was affected were simply responding to the "suffering quotient." This is an extension of the Puritan pleasure/pain principle, in which pleasure must be expiated by an equivalent or greater amount of pain, and implies that all power, insofar as it is enjoyed, must be justified by suffering. The basic proposition is simple —I am not supposed to like power, though it's what I most want, therefore I must pretend that it has been thrust upon me by others against my will; and I must convince everyone around me that it is a painful burden, that I'm suffering on *their* behalf. Often, no sooner is a person promoted than he begins complaining about the demands made on him and the sacrifices he has had to make. On one level, this is an attempt to placate one's rivals, to suggest that they wouldn't have liked the job if they had got it, but on a deeper level, it comes from the feeling that while it may be all right to *have* power, it is wrong to *enjoy* it.

Not surprisingly, many powerful people are hypochondriacs. On the one hand, they want to command and control; on the other, they want to be comforted and appreciated. One way of bridging these conflicting demands is to suffer openly, publicly, constantly —to show by coughing, sneezing, groaning, limping and wheezing that they are stretched beyond endurance by the demands of power. A recent survey of vacation habits concluded that powerful executives "have been turning away from extended, uninterrupted rest periods. Many of them are not even taking their full allotment of vacation . . . Mentally, they are never away from the office . . . Like any natural warrior, the executive is more comfortable at the front, however exhausted or exposed to danger he may be, than he would be if safe behind the lines. He would rather fight than rest." [7]

Note the romanticism of this comment: "the natural warrior"—the notion that work is like fighting in the front lines, the suggestion that the executive is actually exposing himself to danger by staying at his desk . . . In fact, many senior executives who stay at their desks do so because they are bored by their families, or because they are afraid to let anyone discover the office can be run without them. For some, it is worth staying in the office all summer simply in order to be able to say, "I never take vacations." It is part of the suffering quotient.

The complaints of powerful people about stress, tension and overwork are mostly bogus, and when they're real, they're self-imposed. It's a form of guilt, the fear that Thackeray may have been right when he wrote that "Every man who manages another is a hypocrite," [8] that it's wrong to love power.

Yet love it we do. In the words of novelist Patrick Anderson, "It's like a woman you want to stay in bed with forever. But that's not all, not for the best people. There's all you can do with power, if you're smart and tough and lucky. You get kicked in the teeth every day, but sometimes there'll be those moments when you've done everything right, when everything breaks your way, and then you're soaring, you've won your game, whether or not anyone else knows it or understands it or even gives a damn." [9]

Perhaps herein lies a key to the difficulty we have in coping with power—it is perhaps the most personal desire we have, since even the intimacy of sex is usually shared with someone else. Power, by contrast, is a *private* passion, the winning and the losing are internal, only we can know whether or not we've won our game.

"Power!" says The Rev. John J. McLaughlin, the controversial Jesuit who was a deputy special Presidential assistant, and seemed to function as chief exorcist to the defunct Nixon White House. "What do we know about it? We don't know anything about it. We have sex education—why don't we have power education? You can train yourself to handle power." [10] True enough, though one wonders, judging from Father McLaughlin's support for such temporal matters as the Christmas bombing of Hanoi, the mining of Haiphong and the President's stand on Watergate, whether he himself is able to perceive the difference between what he describes as "two views of power . . . an opportunity for an ego-trip, and an opportunity for service." We don't in fact know much about power, and given the way history is taught in this country, when it's taught at all, it's surprising we know anything. In every century, men have used power well, or destructively and self-servingly, and a careful study of history could show us what kinds of power corrupt and why. If we don't know it's because we don't *want* to know.

No sooner had the scandal of Watergate been revealed than sermons began to appear on the evils of power, as if the White House under Richard M. Nixon had been the palace of Nebuchadnezzar. Yet what was Watergate but an example of the price of impotence? The rationale for the burglary—and all that followed from it—was insecurity and envy, the baffled fear on the part of the President and his assistants that even *in* the White House they were somehow powerless, the inner sense of worthlessness that made them fear they had no right to be there, and might at any moment be found out, revealed as weak and ordinary men.

George Allen of the Washington Redskins, Mr. Nixon's favorite football coach, was perhaps unconsciously speaking for the President when he remarked, "The winner is the only individual who is truly alive. I've said this to our ball club. Every time you win, you're reborn; when you lose, you die a little." [11] But power is not based on winning all the time. A man who has to win every battle is asking the impossible of himself and the world, and is likely to collapse the first time he encounters defeat. A powerful man, by definition, is able to survive failure and humiliation, to draw some deeper wisdom from them, to practice what John F. Kennedy called "grace under pressure."

The essence of power is the ability to cope with the demands of life, not to react like a paranoid at every real or imagined threat, or waste one's life and energy trying to submit everything to one's own control. The world is a disorderly and dangerous place, and always has been, and the man of power must learn to live in it comfortably. It is one thing to have a sense of order, but quite another to impose that sense of order on the rest of the world—no amount of power is sufficient for that, and one can only fail in the attempt. We can only control others to a limited degree, and the world is full of men who *seem* powerful in their little world, but are in fact chained to their desks like galley-slaves to the oar. On and on they labor, far into the night, because they fear one moment of inattention or hesitation will undermine their power. One could see these traits in former President Nixon—the joylessness, "the endless struggle for control," [12] the compulsive need to be "on top," the tortured attempts to disguise even small defeats and failures as victories of some kind, the endless pleas for sympathy and understanding, the feeling that life is nothing but a tough challenge, in which hard work and the will to win count for everything. It is not power—perhaps not even the abuse of power—that is at the root of the "White House horrors," as John Mitchell called them. "The thing that is completely misunderstood about Watergate," said former White House special counsel Charles Colson, "is that everybody thinks the people surrounding the President were drunk with power . . . But it wasn't arrogance at all. It was insecurity. That insecurity began to breed a form of paranoia. We overreacted to the attacks against us and to a lot of things." [13] There is no doubt that "a high level of self-pity influenced the style of the Nixon White House," [14] and self-pity is not an emotion one connects with a sense of power. What is more, it led inevitably to blunders, inefficiency and bad management. A truly powerful group of men might well have succeeded in burglarizing the office of Daniel Ellsberg's psychiatrist or tapping Larry O'Brien's telephone—neither feat would seem insuperably difficult. But these were frightened amateurs who felt themselves ill-equipped to play in the big leagues, and constantly needed to reassure themselves that their fears about "the enemy" were justified.

Nor was the Nixon Administration unique in this respect. Many of the people we *think* are powerful turn out on closer examination to be merely frightened and anxious. It is a mistake to assume that the position and the person are the same thing. A man may have a resounding title, a great position of authority, money, influence, but if we notice that his hands are constantly fidgeting on his desk, that he can't look us in the eye, that he crosses and uncrosses his legs as if suffering from a bad itch in the crotch and that when the telephone rings, he can't make up his mind whether to pick it up or ignore it, we can then, I think, safely conclude that he is not a man of power. However humble our own position, we have a chance of getting whatever it is we want. How often we fail to recognize this, how long it takes us to learn the difference between real and simulated power, what opportunities we waste, not to speak of time!

Often we look for power where there is only fear, greed and self-interest. We have to learn to recognize the signs of power and to fight subtly, ruthlessly, constantly for our own. As nations carry on diplomacy and war to maintain their own independence, so we too must play the games of power in order to be ourselves, to avoid "being lived by [events], rather than living them." [15] What is at stake is our ability to be the person we want to be, rather than being the person others want us to be. What we all want is what Rollo May describes as "sense of significance . . . a person's conviction that he counts for something, that he has an effect on others, and that he can get recognition from his fellows." [16]

Thus, trivial as power games may sometimes seem, they are a means of defining who we are, of preserving both our freedom of action and our ability to effect change. We learn, early on in the schoolyard, that things often go badly for bystanders, that engaging ourselves in events may lead to their turning out in our favor, rather than against us. When you pick up the telephone, write a letter, join in a conversation, you are—like it or not—initiating a game, at the end of which you will either feel pleased with yourself or have the nagging sense that you have somehow been diminished, reduced in significance. Nothing is static; every action makes us more or less than we were before. Even the most mundane office is a place in which to test our power. Every moment in the day offers us the opportunity to try our skills, to enjoy our triumphs, to learn something from defeats—for we cannot always be victorious. Most of us think power lies elsewhere, in the next office, on the floor above, in the White House, beyond our reach. But it is all around us; we have only to seize it. It does not lie beyond the everyday activities of our lives, but *in* them.

Power is a myth, but we do not have to journey to the deserts or undergo any long initiation to learn its meaning and master its mysteries. When Carlos Castaneda, the anthropologist and student of power, complained to his mentor Don Juan that he was not really qualified to follow his guide on the path to power and knowledge in the frightening loneliness of the deserts and the mountains, that if he could perhaps "disentangle" himself from his commitments as a twentieth-century urban man and go and live in the wilderness, he might fare better, the old man pointed to the busy streets of a modern town, and said: "This is your world . . . You are a man of that world. And out there, in that world, is your hunting ground. There is no way to escape the *doing* of our world, so what a warrior does is to turn his world into his hunting ground. As a hunter, a warrior knows that the world is made to be *used*. So he uses every bit of it. A warrior is like a pirate that has no qualms in taking and using anything he wants, except that the warrior doesn't mind or doesn't feel insulted when he is used and taken himself." [17]

PART TWO

The World
of Power

CHAPTER FOUR

The Power Spot

... the Game was virtually equivalent to worship, although it deliberately eschewed developing any theology of its own.

—Hermann Hesse
THE GLASS BEAD GAME

You are hunting power and this is your place, the place where you will store your resources.

—Carlos Castaneda
JOURNEY TO IXTLAN

To the person who works merely because work is an unfortunate necessity, the place in which it is done is convenient or inconvenient, pleasant or unpleasant, but not of any basic significance in itself. To the person who plays the power game, on the other hand, it is the board on which the game is played, a fascinating world of infinite possibilities. An office, for example, can be seen as a chessboard or a battlefield, depending on the nature of one's game and psyche. It is also a world which we inhabit for at least eight hours a day, and which provides all the risks, opportunities, dangers, triumphs, defeats and demands of the larger world outside. It has its own landscape and natural features, which must be approached as the hunter approaches his environment, its own trails and paths and watering places, where the inhabitants can move and congregate in comparative freedom from the attention of predators, places where the natural cover is good and other places where danger can be scented, where the power of the predator is in the air.

In every corner of even the most banal office there are ritual objects with which people mark their own place of safety or power—the poster taped to the wall, the photographs of children or lovers or vacation spots, framed diplomas, stuffed animals, carefully calligraphed phrases or poems—the list is endless, but the instinct to mark one's place is the same. Everyone feels the need to make their spot theirs by right, even if it's only a desk in the typist's pool, and all attempts to impose a clean and uncluttered scheme of impersonal design ultimately fail for this reason. Even in modern banks, where the desks are exposed to the full view of the public by plate-glass windows and where the rules are fairly rigid about the display of personal objects, one can see the evidence of this need. At night one can walk down Park Avenue and see the long rows of gleaming desks, identical, clean of scattered papers, but on every one there is an object that is meaningful to somebody, a homemade ceramic ashtray, a miniature plastic football helmet, a pink plastic rose, a Charlie Brown desk calendar . . . In offices which are hidden from the public's sight, personality markers flourish, usually growing more expensive and permanent in nature as the salary and size of the person's office increases, but leveling off at the $40,000-a-year mark, at which point a professional decorator is usually responsible for the office's appearance.

Power Lines

It is important to develop an eye for the "geography" of power in the office. Generally speaking, offices are based upon a corner power system, rather than a central one, because the corner offices tend to be larger and more desirable. The closer one is to the center, the less powerful one is, just as the offices in the middle of a row are less powerful than the ones at either end of it. Power therefore tends to communicate itself from corner to corner in an X-shaped pattern, leaving certain areas as dead-space in power terms, even though they may contain large and comfortable offices with outside windows.

A glance at the diagram will reveal that an "outside" office, however desirable it may be because of

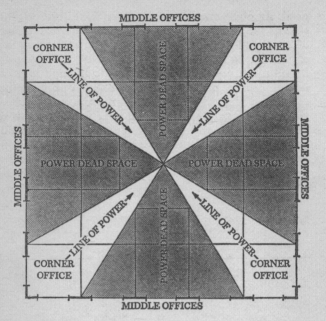

its window, is in fact a less powerful place to be than an inside office within the area of power, and it may well be better to stay inside the power area, forgoing a window, until such time as one can acquire a corner office. People who move to "outside" offices in the middle of the row, in the power deadspace, tend to stay there forever, decorating their offices with bizarre collections of junk and meaningless magnetic wall charts, and earning less than $30,000 a year until they're retired.

The conference room, if there is one, should be at the center of the office, where the power lines bisect. Any attempt to place it elsewhere usually ends in its being abandoned and turned into something else, or used only for meaningless and time-wasting staff conferences. Any attempt to exert power from a middle office is likely to fail, unless the people in the corners are singularly inept, senile or in the habit of drinking three double martinis at lunch. Even then, their power position may protect them. I know of one man who managed, by a series of adroit moves, to obtain a corner office by the age of fifty. Once in it, he put up photographs of his children, took up golf with an obsessive energy, and spent his day on the telephone or at his club arranging for golf partners and auditioning for outside directorships. Eventually, his younger colleagues managed to strip him of his functions, and his authority within the corporation declined. He was no longer invited to meetings, cash-flow reports no longer appeared on his desk, he was taken off the office distribution list for information reports, an enraged executive even had his name removed from the interoffice telephone directory. Nobody, however, was willing to commit the ultimate indignity of depriving him of his office. As a result, instead of being fired or forcibly retired, he stayed on to the age of sixty-five. So long as he stayed in that corner office, he was at one of the four poles of power, however he spent his day, and was therefore protected.

In another, similar, case, the man in the corner office posed more severe problems. He took to heavy drinking, even going so far as to train his secretary to mix Manhattans. The problem was that he remained active and ambitious, interfering in the management of the corporation, refusing to accept any diminution of his authority and generally holding back progress. It seemed impossible to dislodge him, and the other members of the management group more or less resigned themselves to living with him until mandatory retirement or death solved the problem. A solution, however, was eventually found: expedient reasons were invented for moving to a new building, and the obstructive executive was given a large and luxurious suite of offices in the middle of an outside row in the corporation's new headquarters. Here, out of the power area, he was no longer in a position to interfere, and quickly slipped into obscure semiretirement. As one of the participants recalls, "It was a stroke of genius, I mean, we couldn't move him out, and he wouldn't go, and as long as he was there in that office, we couldn't do anything with the company. So we moved the company. Still, when you come to think of it, it's weird. Because we couldn't move one man, we moved three hundred fifty people to two floors in a new building, at a cost of hundreds of thousands of dollars and God knows what inconvenience—and it was worth it!"

Anyone who has ever tried to reallocate office space can testify to the existence of certain fixed patterns which are almost impossible to disrupt—offices which people don't want to abandon even for the lure of larger, lighter ones, secretaries who have acquired territorial rights so strong that they cannot be moved, pieces of furniture that have acquired totemic significance. Certain power spots are obvious—for example, executives always prefer to have their offices protected from easy access, while most secretaries, because acting as a lookout against unwanted intrusions is part of their function, prefer to have an open view. Thus, an executive office that is out of the traffic mainstream is desirable, while a secretary is likely to prize a position that gives her a view in as many directions as possible. It is interesting that most executives, valuing privacy for themselves, as-

sume that their secretaries would be grateful to have
their desk space walled off with a partition, not
realizing that a secretary may prefer to forgo privacy
for the advantages of good sight-lines. (Even among
the highest and most securely protected of the executive elite, it is usual for the desk to be positioned so
that its occupant can look up and see the door, not
so much out of politeness as because nobody likes to
be caught unawares.)

If your function is precisely to *protect* another person, you need to see approaching danger in time to
take precautionary measures and give a warning.
Thus the more a secretary is exposed to other people's
view, the more powerful her own position is likely to
be. While the office of the President of the United
States is closed off by a solid door, and guarded by
armed secret-service men, his secretary's desk is in a
kind of open corridor, with a view down a passage-
way and out toward the White House Rose Garden.
Doubtless the secretary to the President could have
a more private office if she wanted one, but her
power is dependent on her ability to see who is approaching. The fact is that access to the President's
office is guarded by the secret-service men, but the
fiction is preserved that the President's secretary
checks the approaching visitor, greets him or her and
goes through the motions of arranging access to the
President. The secretary's desk retains its significance as a power spot even though the appointments
are actually made by the President's assistant, and
the armed guards at the door check any visitor
against their list and authorize entry into the office.
To give the secretary a "better" office in the President's terms, that is to say one which is more secluded and private, would be to deprive her of power.

If the view is important, so is proximity. In most

cases, power diminishes with distance. Put someone's assistant next to his superior's office, and he benefits from being close to the source of power. Promote the assistant to a larger office that is further away, and his power is likely to decrease. Only if he is given a title and a job that allows him to create his own power base can he benefit from moving. I have known at least one assistant to an aging senior executive resist every temptation to move to a better office, well-meant as these suggestions were. Seated in a kind of cubbyhole beside the great man's office, a dark, hot closet full of filing cabinets and coatracks, he fought to protect his position until he had a title of his own. No secretary would have worked in that airless little cubicle, but Sidney stayed in it, and for many good reasons. It had a door that led into the executive's office, thus giving Sidney a right of access without going past the executive's secretary, and another door opening out onto the corridor, so that he could see everybody coming and going. Well-wishers told him that he was crazy: it was too noisy, he had no privacy, it was too close to the men's room, how could he work there?

"So long as I sat there," he recalled, as we talked in his luxurious new office, "I had it made. I got to know everyone who came in, if they had to wait, they came in and leaned on my desk, or used my phone to confirm lunch dates, and everybody assumed that I must know everything that was going on. When I first moved into that god-awful hole, the only thing I insisted on was a telephone with several lines and an intercom line to my boss. I don't think I ever used it, but when he made a call, one of the buttons would light up on my phone, and anyone in my office would have a sense of my being *connected* to him. It's the proximity to power that counts, not space, a carpet, or a window. Anyway, sitting where I was, I didn't have to *do* anything, whereas if I'd moved to a real office, people would have passed by and asked themselves who the hell I was and what I was supposed to be doing. I'd have had to justify my existence, which is hard to do when you're just beginning. Being next to a man with power justified it for me. What's more I got good marks in everybody's eyes for not being pushy or ambitious. I turned down the offer of a more comfortable office, and people thought that was a nice gesture of loyalty, or humility, or just generally being a harmless person. If I'd moved to a big new office, people would have hated my guts in a week."

Power Areas

One should study the arrangement of an office and try to see it as a coherent landscape. In many offices, the center of power is on a lower floor than the rest of the organization. I know of one large investment bank which has two floors at the top of a Wall Street skyscraper; the reception room and the working staff are on the higher of the two floors, while a narrow staircase takes the visitor downstairs to the offices of the senior executives. This arrangement is by no means uncommon, and may be the result of an atavistic memory of World War II—if the building is going to be bombed, the more floors between you and the bombs, the better, and the more dispensable members of the organization therefore go on the upper stories of the building, the ultimate center of power being, of course, the cellar. In ordinary terms of power, however, a business in which the senior executives have retreated to a floor below the working staff is usually one in which they have also abdicated any direct responsibility for day-to-day operations, allowing a separate and more active hierarchy to flourish above them unsupervised. When the senior executives are on the floor above, they usually exercise a tighter control over the organization. This may simply be because it's easier to walk downstairs than to climb upstairs—beyond a certain age, the difficulty of climbing a flight of stairs discourages interference, but the fact remains that anyone seeking power would do well to choose a company in which the President and his closest associates are on the floor below, rather than on the floor above.

Obviously to be avoided are offices built on the open plan, with few, if any, walls and partitions. It may well be that "an open office encourages openness in people," [1] but openness is not necessarily desirable, and the justifications for removing executives from their offices and placing them out in the open together are seldom convincing. After all, they're not supposed to be communicating with each other on a free and open basis, even if that were possible, which is unlikely; they're supposed to be developing ideas, competing, running things and making decisions. The rationale for an open office is democracy and sociability, but the fact is that chief executives who insist on them basically don't trust their senior employees and want to keep their eyes on each and every one of them. This paranoid view is frequently masked by talk about "productive intercommunication" or the "business sociability factor," but the fact remains that the executives are out in the open at their desks like typists in the Army, and their boss is in a position to see all of them, like a master sergeant. One of the first steps toward giving people autonomy was

to give them privacy, and deprived of it they are reduced to the role of clerks in a Victorian counting
house. Even in the most open offices, a closed space
usually exists for such delicate operations as firing
somebody. The real problem is that people in open
spaces are not working for themselves, or on their
specific task, but for an audience of fellow workers
and superiors. It isn't so much "sociability" that's en-
couraged, as the art of looking busy, and when the
chief executive of a corporation wants to get out of
his office and sit among his vice presidents, it is more
likely to be because he doesn't *trust* them than because he wants to engage in open dialogue with them.

It is precisely where power is valued and symbolized
that power can best be sought. Places in which the
management has tried to eliminate the signs and
symbols of power, to encourage "openness," are places
in which the leadership is determined to retain all the
power in its own hands and to prevent the growth of
any alternative centers of power below them.

Extreme architectural innovations should be seen
as warning signs by the wary player of the power
game, whatever their form. For someone who wants
to rise swiftly, it is not encouraging to learn that the
four partners of one investment managing concern
share a big circular desk in a corner office (which
they refer to rather threateningly as "the war room");
executives who spend their working hours as close
together as this are unlikely to take much notice of
the people who work for them—the whole game is
being run, as it were, for their own amusement. Extremes of office decoration are usually a reliable sign
that it is difficult for the newcomer to obtain power.
One company I know of has its senior executives
segregated on the top floor of the building, in a kind
of garden-penthouse overlooking New York's harbor,

reached by a small private elevator which is simply, but expensively, decorated with a Renoir landscape. The floors below look like any other office, the usual mixture of shabby and modern; the penthouse is full of English wood paneling, French eighteenth-century furniture, enormous hunt tables, breakfront libraries, *chinoiserie* commodes, paintings and furniture gathered from every antique shop in Paris and London. Adams fireplaces have been hacked out of ancestral walls to be recessed into offices without chimneys, Regency wine coolers which once held bottles of champagne now serve as telephone tables, at one corner of the office stands a carved and gilded horse from an old fairground carrousel, the rest of which, together with its steam-driven machinery, is packed away in crates somewhere below.

An office like this as good as warns you that you aren't going to get any power until you have the key to that private elevator, and the people up there in the penthouse are not likely to want to see you have one. Indeed, a setup with sharp divisions like this is partly *intended* to keep the lower echelons in their places. Like a medieval castle, it serves to remind the peasantry of their humble station and to discourage the ambitious and the troublesome. Some offices carry the stronghold theory to extremes—one has executive quarters built like bank vaults in stainless steel (including the floors!), giving the impression that the management feels it necessary to defend itself from an armed uprising. With its steel walls, doors, floors and Venetian blinds, the power center of the office looks like the guardroom of a modern prison—one almost expects to see an emergency button that will seal the doors and pour Mace into the outer offices at the first sign of unrest. Another company has executive offices in dark slate, with narrow slits for windows and rough-hewn granite blocks as partitions. Once again, it seems to have been built with an eye to potential hand-to-hand combat, an effect strengthened by the remark of one vice president, who proudly described his office as "the fighting bridge." [2] When executives talk about their offices in terms of combat, it is seldom the outside world they have in mind. It is mutiny they are thinking of, not the competition.

A careful look at an office can reveal whether power is centralized or distributed in some pattern. If it shows signs of being firmly centralized, it may be as well to go somewhere else; if it doesn't, then it's necessary to study the pattern. For instance, one should try to discover the extent to which the occupant of a corner office has been able to extend his or her territorial rights, and in which direction. Most executives try to build up a buffer zone of subordinates, intruding into the middle outer offices on both sides as far as they can, and also reaching out toward the center of the office. Architectural features sometimes get in the way, but the impulse to reach out is very strong, and department heads are often anxious to secure some small beachhead a long way from their own domain in the hope of gradually taking over the space between their own power center and this isolated outpost. No matter how complicated the construction problems involved are, they will then attempt to create a single corridor of access running the length of their territory, and to seal off its end in a kind of Berlin Wall, obliging the visitor to go back out into the hall to get to the next office in line. Failing this, they will attempt to take over portions of the hall itself, using bulletin boards, posters and wall decorations to lay claim to the portion of the common hallway that runs through or past their territory, so that a stranger walking down the hall immediately realizes that he has crossed an invisible frontier into another department.

Part of the territorial power game consists of making surreptitious inroads on your neighbor's space or seizing neutral ground with a token force. Large filing complexes are particularly valuable in this game, since they require space and are not as a rule needed at the very center of the power area. An excellent example of this can be found in the offices of a large recording company, where the contract files were placed under the nominal supervision of a new and junior vice president, though in fact they were tended by the legal department, which, inconveniently enough, was on a different floor. The vice president took the files under his wing because he could see that they were a valuable property. It wasn't necessary at first to do anything with them—they were just there, lending prestige to his corner of the office, their contents obviously central to the company's business, if only in a symbolic sense, since most of the information they contained had long since been transferred to IBM tape and stored in some computer center. Still, in the unlikely event that anybody should want to consult these bulky files, he had control over access to them, and even set up a complicated security check over them. The more carefully the files were looked after, the more important they could be made to seem, and thus the more important he would be. It was a very nice little move in his own personal "Monopoly" game, more than justifying the amount of space the filing cabinets took up in his area and not imposing any real burden on him.

From a business point of view, however, they represented an asset without any potential for growth, and growth is a central factor in power. Their new owner therefore undertook "a sweeping reorganization of

the contract files," which involved the purchase of a
large number of expensive horizontal filing units,
hiring a filing clerk to put every contract into a neat
new color-coded folder and a central file-keeping index
system. The result was a swift growth in the size of
the files, if only because the new cabinets were far
more bulky than their shabby predecessors. Since
they had now outgrown the corner in which they had
been placed, it was necessary to find a new home for
them, and the vice president shrewdly lobbied for an
office some distance away from his own area, rather
than simply trying to add one more office adjacent
to his territory. The alternative being to stack the
cabinets in the hall (or admit that they were useless),
they were moved to the new office, and he was able
then, over the period of a year, to gradually seize the
offices in between, thus gaining about two hundred
feet of space and turning the files into a potent power
symbol. So far, nobody has pointed out that their
contents are recorded on the company computer, or
that both the legal and the accounting departments
maintain up-to-date Xerox copies of each contract.
The point is that these are the *originals,* and therefore have totemic significance. There they sit, occupying space formerly belonging to the merchandising
department, guarded by a young woman who has
nothing else to do but prevent open access to them
and log them in and out in the unlikely event that
anybody should want to consult them. It won't be
long before the man with the filing cabinets takes
over merchandising. Why not? He's got them out-
flanked.

"Hell, filing cabinets are chickenshit," said Mark
Haendel, a man I know who works for a major television network. "When I first came here, we had a
guy who was making merchandising tie-ups with the

network's shows, you know, toys, games, cocktail napkins, stuff like that. He was doing it out of one small office, and he saw what everyone else was doing, and decided to grow. I was working for him then, and what he did was to fill up his office with so much junk that he needed a display area. At that time, we were in an old building on Lexington Avenue, and space was tight, but the network had leased part of an old hotel off Third Avenue, and since everybody was embarrassed at making money off floating rubber ducks and Indian chief make-up kits for kids, they moved us over there. It was a weird place. There was a health club on the roof, two floors full of hookers and most of the rest were network offices in hotel rooms. Some guys who were divorced or separated actually moved in there, I mean why not —with the hookers and the health club and the coffee shop downstairs, it was a perfect life. Everybody had to go over to the corporate headquarters once a week to sign for their pay check, and the secretaries had to go over to get pencils and typewriter ribbons, but apart from that, we were pretty much on our own. My boss knew just what he was doing. He took over room after room, suite after suite, until he had a whole floor. We had merchandising racks, display rooms, strange guys developing new toys and games, we built up files, an international licensing department, we got ourselves our own screening room. I thought he was crazy—he was expanding so fast that we didn't even know what we were doing half the time, but he told me not to worry. 'Listen, Mark,' he said to me, 'right now this corporation is building a big new building over on Sixth Avenue. When we left the old one, we had a couple of rooms, right? When we move back in, they're going to have to give us half a floor. Just remember that every senior executive with kids gets one of everything we do, compliments of this department.' Of course, he was right. When the new building was ready, we had a whole department to move in, with display rooms, conference rooms, big offices, everything you could want. It was beautiful. The only trouble was that they'd installed a central computer system, and when they got it working, they discovered we'd been losing money for two years. Even then, we were okay. Nobody was going to wind up a department that had half a floor of office space, and people had gotten used to receiving the toys and things, I mean, they weren't about to start going out and paying money for birthday presents and Christmas gifts after two years of getting them by the gross on the cuff. All they did was give my boss a title and put a financial guy in under him, with authority to straighten things out. After all, you don't fire a guy for expanding too fast—that's optimism. Today, he's got the audio-visual cassette department as well, and he's making a hundred thousand dollars a year, and the only thing he really knows is how to grab for space, and to have everything under his control painted the same color, so people can see just how big his area is. It's always primrose yellow—even the men's rooms. I think he has his own painters in the closet, ready to go out at a moment's notice and paint up another office yellow so people will know it belongs to him. By now, I think he could just have the painters in at night to paint an office yellow, and people would assume it was his and whoever was in it was working for him. If he ever gets to be the chief executive officer, I guess he'll have the building painted yellow."

The use of color is not all that unusual in marking off the space under one's control. Color is one of the most effective ways to establish the visual image of an area. There are now even "executive color consultants," who analyze the worried businessman's character and appearance to find the colors most conducive to his personal power. Once the "basic power color" has been found, they advise their clients on matters ranging from office decoration to shirts, ties, socks, cars and the formica in their kitchens at home. One man threw away his clothes and spent $1,800 to refurbish his wardrobe in his power color, while another not only had his office repainted, but insisted on having his new car resprayed.[3] The president of one corporation not only had his own "color palette" drawn up, but sent his major executives out to have *their* individual colors selected, then had their offices redecorated accordingly. "I feel ten years younger," he was reported as saying, "and their performance is up ten, fifteen percent." Not every corporation is likely to seek the help of the consultant whose claim to fame is that he selected the clothes for one of the "ten best-dressed men in Sacramento" (Liberace presented the award), but many discover the value of marking their territory by means of color, whether they pick it themselves or pay $175 to be told what it should be.

One executive of my acquaintance has what might be called a "thing" for blue. She began by having a blue carpet installed in her office, then had the furniture re-covered in blue corduroy, then had the walls and even the Venetian blinds painted blue. Soon her secretary's chair was replaced with a blue one, and a blue IBM Selectric II typewriter with a blue ribbon appeared on her desk. Gradually, blue began to spread outward from her office, as her power increased, a tide of blue that touched filing cabinets, desks, floors, coffee mugs and water coolers. Since the other executives had no comparable obsession with color, the growth of this one highly visible color theme was all the more striking, and soon came to acquire almost a threatening force as a symbol. The people who worked for her tended to wear blue, simply because it matched their surroundings, but what had begun as a joke or a habit before long became a badge of loyalty, and the heads of other departments trembled when their secretaries turned up for work in blue dresses, as if they had unmasked themselves as the Fifth Column of an enemy army. Until one of them discovers a rival color power, the office will just go on getting bluer every day.*

Color is not the only way to establish control over space, though it is perhaps the simplest and the most obvious. More subtle forms of decoration can be used. In one Wall Street financial office, two rival executives have been competing for years with ship prints and Audubon prints. You can tell just whose area of power you're in by looking at the walls, and when one is ahead of the other, corridors take on a nautical or nature-loving aspect, depending on whose fortunes are on the rise. In other, more conservative offices, where decoration is in the hands of higher authority, the limits of a power area are established by such things as identical pen and pencil desk sets, cork wall boards or magnetic wall charts. The main

* Most people seem to regard blue as the most powerful color, provided it's reasonably dark. Yellow is sometimes thought to be frivolous and weak, beige and tan are too neutral to convey a sense of power, red is frightening to many people and dark browns depressing. White gives people a sense of space and freedom, so one can conclude that the most powerful combination of colors for an office would probably be white and dark blue, with perhaps a small hint of red to inspire fear.

thing is to find something nobody else has, appropriate it as a symbol and use it to establish territorial rights. If there is no other way, certain ways of placing furniture can sometimes be used to establish such rights. In many offices all the desks in one department or power area can be seen to face the same way, usually toward the head of the department, as Mohammedans face Mecca when praying.

Power Groups

Generally speaking, people tend to stay away from power areas, as if dangerous radiation emanated from them, but power-seekers should learn to identify them and learn to live there. Areas in which a great many people congregate are seldom power areas, since people generally collect together for safety. In a lot of offices, you can see where these safety zones have been established by the wear and tear on the linoleum and the rub-marks against the walls. By mutual consent, certain places are set aside where people can talk, drink coffee and relax, without interference from management. A similar grouping inside a power area would almost certainly attract unfavorable attention.

Thus, secretaries will leave the power area to drink a cup of coffee and chat, whereas people outside the power area can and do stay where they are. Some meeting areas are departmental, purely local areas of safety closed to people from other departments, others are integrated, in the sense that people from every department can meet within their limits at ease. The most important safety areas are those *near* a power area, since they tend to attract senior power game players as well, who emerge from time to time to join the rank and file, largely to seek assurance that they still have power.

A careful analysis of any office will show that there are certain places in which even the most powerful people are able to mingle with their inferiors on a relatively equal basis. Sometimes it's the reception area, where, for a moment, everyone is equal as they struggle into their coats. A secretary may hesitate to speak to the chairman of the board in the hall, even though they're both walking down it at the same pace, and may even drop behind deliberately so as to allow the chairman to go first and avoid initiating a conversation. Then, as they enter the reception area, she may well speak to him. In power terms, it's a neutral area, not quite *in* the office, but still a part of it, so an exchange between them becomes not only possible, but mandatory. After they have negotiated the door and entered the elevator, conversation once more becomes impossible. They have now *left* the office, and have no connection with each other—in all likelihood, a cheery exchange in front of the receptionist's desk will be followed by their standing in separate corners of the elevator, eyes fixed on the flashing numbers above the door so as to avoid further visual contact.

If the reception room is an area in which free communication between people at different power levels is—briefly—possible, other areas in the office exist for the purpose of power displays. Certain corners, meeting rooms and hallways are likely to be used as arenas for the more powerful executives, who will either stand there looking busy in order to make their presence visible, or create informal hallway meetings in the open to make a display of power. Such meetings are best avoided, since decisions and comments made as a public display of authority are almost always ill-advised. Groups in power areas are always searching for a victim to prove they belong there. It's difficult to display power in public without humiliating someone. If you want to catch the ear of someone powerful, it's usually better to do it as he passes the receptionist than when he's standing near his office holding court.

Still, an astute observer of power will notice that no powerful person likes to be sealed up in his office forever, however luxurious it is. The rituals of power must be completed in public, and the powerful are obliged to reaffirm their membership in the power structure at regular intervals and following an established pattern. Where people take their coffee breaks together power players will usually emerge from their own offices and join the group, but will seldom become part of it, preferring to stand slightly to one side, and as far away from other power players as possible. If these encounters take place in a hallway, as is frequently the case, the power player will usually try to get his back against the wall and position himself near a doorway that leads to some open area. He is thus protected from the approach of people who might come up behind him, and able to move rapidly away from the group. The important thing is to place himself so that he can never be surprised or trapped, preserving a quick escape route. Few power players are at ease in other people's offices (unless they're playing the kind of aggressive territorial game that involves taking over an opponent's power space by coming in and putting their feet on the desk), and for this reason they prefer to draw people out into the corridors and hallways (neutral ground) as much as possible.

Certain corners of hallways and corridors thus acquire the social functions of a Middle Eastern bazaar or the main street of a frontier town, until meeting there eventually becomes like membership in an informal club, and a newcomer may find himself excluded or ignored until one of the power players has recognized his existence and his right to participate.

Within their own sphere, people with power are subject to extreme pressures of rivalry and competition, in conflict with others who are either determined to strip them of power or refuse to admit that they have any in the first place. Thus those who have power are in a sense dependent upon those who *don't* —as a sort of testing ground. This phenomenon explains why office parties are necessary, and why they are invariably held outside the power area itself, however inconvenient this may be in terms of space or access.

The Power Dynamics of Office Parties

An office party is primarily an opportunity for those with power to meet their constituency, either by standing in a corner to see how many people move their way, or by mixing in to test their power over certain individuals. If you watch any office party, you will see that those who have power usually arrive late and seize a corner for themselves if they can. Those who are unsure of themselves tend to stand near the door or by the bar, whether it's a formal one or one improvised from a desk, since this way they are in the flow of traffic and are almost bound to be greeted and engaged in conversation. Astute players avoid these positions, however, since the object is to make the flow of traffic eddy toward *you*, gradually building up a circle of supporters and adherents so that there will tend to be a fixed knot of people at each corner of the room, and a restless mass in the center, trying to decide to which corner they should move. In large organizations, where parties require several rooms, either in the office or in a hotel, the same phenomenon will repeat itself in each room—the powerful people will move to the corners, as far as they can from their competitors, and will stay there, gathering supporters around them. Those who fail push their way back out to the door, in the hope of attracting passers-by, but this is a sign of defeat, and people who are reduced to this position normally leave the party early, pleading work or a headache.

At a certain point, the people who have power will usually abandon their corner positions and move together toward neutral territory, where they form a circle, with their backs to the people who don't have power. Their first act is to display themselves and seek confirmation of power from the rank and file. Once this has been accomplished, they move naturally toward one another and close ranks, the powerful separating themselves instinctively from the non-powerful. To a power game player the timing of this movement is interesting to observe, and sometimes useful. In the first phase, a powerful executive will hew his way into a corner and make himself easily available to anyone, from secretaries to middle-management personnel, joking, belittling his colleagues, passing his glass out for someone to take back to the bar and refill. This is the moment when an ambitious person can move in on a powerful person without seeming pushy or giving offense. In the second phase, any approach or attempt at familiarity will be taken as an intrusion, and possibly even rebuffed. When people who have power need others, they make themselves available; when they have had enough, they make themselves unapproachable. The moment when the senior executives, having collected enough people in their corners to assure themselves of their power, begin their movement into the center of the room, is the moment to break away from them. It is a sign that the period of familiarity is over—what could have been said to them with ease two minutes earlier, would now give offense.

This power nucleus will always form by instinct fairly close to the bar. From the corner, surrounded by underlings, they can easily get another drink without leaving their power position, but standing together in a closed circle, they can't, nor will the inner rivalries between them allow any of their number to perform this kind of service. They must therefore position themselves within easy reach of the bar, taking over one corner of it as their own. On rare occasions, the design of a room prevents this. I have seen one party given in a large hotel suite which had a carpet with a large embroidered medallion in the center, immediately below a crystal chandelier. At the point when the power players abandoned their corners, they automatically formed a circle below the chandelier, standing on the medallion which offered them a perfectly visible and distinct power spot. Unfortunately, it was at some distance from the bar. Nobody could approach the spot, and those on it were unwilling to leave, so for some time the senior executives stood together with empty glasses, irritated but rooted to the spot, until an understanding secretary sent a bartender over to take their orders.

In these circumstances, powerful people rarely sit down. Sitting at this type of social function is a kind of defeat, not only because it projects fatigue and a general lack of energy, but also because it prevents movement and puts the sitter at a disadvantage in terms of height. Participants in the power game will remain standing even when they have one leg in a cast and are obliged to lean on a cane, as I myself have frequently witnessed!

One can easily assess the relative importance of senior executives by watching their behavior at parties. Those who are most sure of themselves find a corner; those less sure of themselves place themselves in the middle of the traffic stream; the least secure players circulate around the room, avoiding the corners, which are already occupied, but attempting to form a circle of followers large enough to give them a visible constituency of their own. In almost every case, such people will move in a counter-clockwise circle, starting from the point of entry, in order to keep their right hand (the normal power side) toward the exterior of the room and the corners. They may be talking to the people on their inside (i.e., to the left as they make their circle), but the true focus of their attention and concern is the outside, where the power corners are. At the point when the people in the corners make their way toward the center, the people circling the room can then spiral inward to meet them, as unobtrusively as possible, as if they had never been trapped among the powerless in the first place.

Thus a general scheme of an office party, much simplified, will look like this in the first phase:

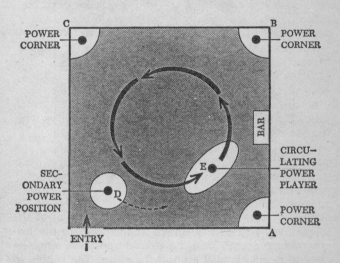

The power player who is circulating around the room usually hopes to seize one of the corners in case its occupant has to abandon his position to go to the bathroom or take a telephone call, and the power player in the "secondary power position" (by the door), will often move to the right and start a circle of his own, slightly larger than the existing circular power pattern.

In the second phase, everyone moves inward, as we have seen:

It is obvious that the player following a circular pattern is in an advantageous position at the moment when the inward movement begins, since he

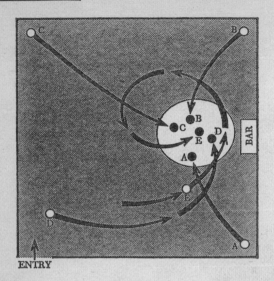

ENTRY

can circle in and establish the actual position of the power spot, while the person at the door, in the layout shown above, is in the weakest position, since he has to make his way around the room. The people in the corner must move very fast indeed if it's not to seem that they are merely joining those who are circling the room, and it is usually the one nearest the bar who makes the first move, his object being to arrive at the power spot before any of his competitors have reached it, and to make it seem as if he had chosen it, and they had followed his move. The player at point A is in the best position, since he is nearest the bar and in a corner, and he is likely to move out of his corner at just the point when circular player E is at the far side of the room, opposite the bar, thus effectively making E the last player to arrive, or the next to last, after the player in the

100

door. Generally speaking, this move will take place by mutual consent about a half-hour to an hour after the beginning of the party (the beginning being computed from the moment that a major power player has arrived). In many cases, it is the moment when any fun that is going to be had begins, since the period when the power players are displaying themselves and recharging their power at the expense of the rest of the people present is basically a formality. It isn't that they would necessarily frown on dancing, drunkenness, or the seduction of young women; it's merely that they have a purpose to be accomplished before there is time for any of these things. Indeed, the movements of this ritual will take place even when they have arrived late and the party is already out of control. I have been present at one party where the power players were delayed by a last-minute meeting, and arrived in a hotel room to find the ice already melting in its cardboard tubs, the male guests with their coats off, some of them dancing and others sitting on the floor, and one young lady dancing on a tabletop with a lampshade on her head and the front of her minidress unbuttoned to the navel. Embarrassed and fretful, they nevertheless took up positions of power exactly as described here, and went through the obligatory motions. The most they could do was to curtail the time span and form their power circle as quickly as possible, like settlers taking refuge from hostile Indians in the circle of their covered wagons.

The power circle, once formed, can only be broken up by mutual consent, but the period of time can be quite short. It need only be long enough for the members to assure each other of their status, and display it to the others in the room. At a dull party, the members may stay together for an hour or more, turning the power group into a kind of meeting; at a lively one, five minutes may be enough. Once the circle has been broken, each member is free either to leave or join in the fun. No power player is likely to walk into a party and enjoy himself until he has completed this two-part display of power—to do so would be to separate himself from the other players, and would automatically cost him status. On the other hand, once the power display has been accomplished, a member of the power group may get drunk, dance, take off his jacket, flirt or wear a lampshade on his head— the breaking of the circle renders him "invisible" to his peers and he has established his membership for the evening.

Gossip Power

Gossip has always come in for a bad press, and the person who is interested in power should certainly avoid gossiping to anyone. That does not mean it's a bad idea to *listen* to gossip. Quite the contrary: all gossip is worth hearing if you are strong enough to resist commenting on it, embellishing it, or passing it along. It pays to be a good listener, and to cultivate the habit of nodding wisely, as if you already knew about whatever you've been told. By carefully cultivating silence and reticence it is possible to build a valuable reputation as a person who knows a great deal and has probably been pledged to secrecy by some higher authority. Thus, if someone says to you, "Isn't it fantastic, did you know that X is having an affair with Y and that Z is about to be fired?" the proper response is not, "No kidding!" or "Tell me more." It is to sit impassively and say "Mmmm." If these are useful pieces of information, you can file them in your mind for later use, if they are not, you have taken no position on them. In either case, you have given the impression that you already knew all about it. This is all the more important when the gossip concerns your own affairs. If someone comes up to you with a sad and commiserating expression and tells you how sorry they are to hear that the promotion you hoped for is going to be given to your rival, the proper thing to do is to nod sagely and praise the other person's abilities and human qualities, even though it may be the first hint you've heard that you have been passed over. Later on, you can rage, or attempt to rectify the situation, but one of the first rules of playing the power game is that all bad news must be accepted calmly, as if one already knew and didn't much care.

I know of one case where two rival vice presidents were seeking a senior managerial position. One of them wrote a long and persuasive memorandum to the chief executive officer, explaining why the other person was temperamentally unsuited for the post. When this unwelcome news was told to the first person, he reacted by calmly praising the wisdom, talents and company loyalty of his rival, allowing it to be thought that he already knew about the memo, indeed that it had been *shown* to him. News of his reaction swiftly spread throughout the office, and the memorandum was defused. Some days later, he met the chief executive officer in the elevator (by design) and referred to the now-famous memo jokingly. The great man laughed, and dismissed it with a wave of his hand. The job, he indicated, was his. In cases like this, anger, immediate action and a public display of emotion are invariably fatal. The best thing to do is to strike a noble and calm posture, and repeat it in front of as many people as possible. The news will quickly make its way back to the senior management people without your having to call them. In this sense, gossip is useful—it represents both an informal (if unreliable) information system and feedback to higher levels of management.

There are various ways in which news, or rumor, travels. It works something like a river system: there is invariably a headwater of mysterious origin, then a mainstream from which tributaries branch off to every department. Once you have traced the main river to its source, it is perfectly possible to pick up whatever news you want from the tributaries—the water is the same. The gossip of people who have no power and no real knowledge of events is important only if you already know the stages by which the news traveled to them, since you then know where it came from and can guess with fair accuracy just how it may have been distorted and changed in its passage along the channel. If you don't know the geography of the system, then all gossip is meaningless.

By observing who talks to whom, in coffee breaks and at lunch, which people commute together, or ride in the same car pool, you can fairly easily map the system. If you know that the vice president in charge of public relations commutes with the treasurer's assistant, and that she in turn often eats lunch with your department head's secretary, and that *she* drinks coffee with *your* secretary, you can trace a piece of news that sounds as if it might be true or interesting back to its original source by the simple expedient of finding out with which member of the executive committee the vice president lunched on the day before you heard the news. Once you know the source, you may well be in possession of a valuable piece of information that will allow you to anticipate certain actions on the part of the management, or predict major changes in personnel. If your secretary, for example, points out that the whole office is worrying about the health of an executive in his late fifties, and if you know the channels through which gossip flows, you may be able to trace the story back to a member of the executive committee, in which case you can be sure that the executive's retirement has been discussed at a very high level, and that ill health is going to be the reasons given for his dismissal. It's also worth bearing in mind that gossip is often used to test people's reaction to a decision, as a kind of informal polling system that allows higher management to gauge the feasibility of a plan or a personnel move. If the entire office is indignant about the forced retirement of this executive, the idea may well be dropped without anyone's having to admit that it was a real possibility. If the gossip creates no waves, then those in positions of authority can move to implement the decision with confidence. It's not so much that they need popular support, unlike politicians, though they may from time to time solicit it; it's that they aren't always sure of what to do, but are generally in no position to ask for advice, since that would diminish their authority. If a thing seems doubtful, it is always useful to have an informal means of testing its effects. Thus gossip plays a real role in management technique, providing the powerful with a channel of communication to the powerless which can be used without loss of face.

It can also be used to spread bad news before it's officially announced, in order to make the actual announcement less painful and surprising. Thus a decline in profit sharing or a drastic ceiling on salary increases will almost always be rumored for several days before they are made official, and the actual announcement comes as an anticlimax. Bad news of this kind, when it makes its way along the gossip system, is nearly always a deliberate leak. Good news, on the other hand, is usually kept secret until the last moment, since all senior corporate officers naturally enjoy announcing it.

Immediately before the end of the year, there is always a wealth of rumors about people who aren't going to get the raises they expected, who will, indeed, be lucky to stay on. This kind of leak is designed to soften the blow and make life easier for the person who will eventually have to make the announcements on a personal basis. Usually, these rumors are exaggerated; if someone hopes to get $5,000, the best thing is to allow him to think he will get nothing and let him sweat it out for a few days or weeks, so that he'll accept the $2,000 you intend to give him without arguments, and will even be grateful. In much the same way, the gossip system can be used to warn someone that he's going to be fired in order to facilitate the task of the executive who has to do the firing, and also serves as a means of warning people whose performance is unsatisfactory.

It must always be remembered that gossip, unlike river water, flows both ways. The people who pass on gossip downward also feed it back, and anyone who receives information is supposed to return the favor. Few companies have any real espionage system, but almost all organizations have an informal one which works very effectively. However big or small an organization, the people at the top will eventually hear about what is happening at the bottom, but seldom along the lines of the conventional hierarchy. At every level executives are reluctant to pass along bad news about the people under them, if only because their failures can easily be held against those above them. The internal gossip system acts as a counterweight to this phenomenon, providing top management with a sense of what people are *actually* doing and saying, as opposed to what their superiors think they *should* be doing. Few department heads are likely to inform their superiors that a certain executive is drinking too much and frequently comes back from lunch at 3:00 P.M. with his tie askew and his buttons in the wrong buttonholes, but by means of the gossip system, the news is sure to travel to the top management almost instantly, bypassing the department head and reaching the president of the company long before the department head has even decided to inform him.

TOO vs. TOP

Nobody interested in power can afford to ignore the existence of this system of alternative management, without which no business could survive for long. All tables of organization, and most titles, are meaningless, and the more carefully worked out they are, the less they are likely to have to do with any recognizable reality. Just as information-flow in an office is geared to gossip rather than to any formal information system, so almost every other function in places of work is duplicated by an informal, alternative system. The person who is able to see the place where he or she works as it *is*, in terms of power, instead of as it's presented, is better equipped than a more conventionally minded player. Most committees meet to ratify decisions that have already been made long before, most memoranda simply convey ideas and plans that have already been discussed and decided upon by other people; surveys and reports, however elaborate, are usually designed to justify plans that have already been made or to serve as expensive rationalizations for decisions that were taken before the "facts" were ever put on paper. In most offices, the majority of the staff is employed in preparing explanations for actions that have already been taken, and in building up a case for projects that are already under way.

Take a large conglomerate which is in the bottling business and plans to get rid of its breweries to concentrate on soft drinks. The chairman of the board and the president of the company will discuss it first, perhaps taking the day off to drive up the coast for a round of golf and go over the problem in the open air, "away from the phones," as they say. By the time they have packed their clubs in the car, the whole office will know what they are considering, since each of them will have spent the previous week asking for financial reports on the beer business. By the time they come back, determined to inform the executive committee of their decision, the people in the beer business will already be telephoning their friends for jobs, the brewers' union will already be organizing committees to save their jobs and the financial reporters will be on the telephone to ask if the rumor is true. The alternative information system is simply stronger and more effective than management in most businesses, and the only effective way to outwit it is to leak a rumor, then do the opposite. An interesting exercise for anybody who wants to play the power game effectively is to draw up the "table of organization" (TOO) of his or her company as carefully as possible, in terms of its formal structure, putting everybody's name, title and function in neat, identical little boxes, with lines indicating the chain of command. A handsome chart like this will fill up an hour or so of time in a pleasant and constructive way, and in some companies may even exist in printed form, saving you the trouble of drawing up your own.

Once you have completed it, take a sheet of tracing paper and add to the chart the names of people who are *not* on the TOO, but who play significant roles in determining what happens in the company, or simply influence the way decisions are made. You may have a nice little box for X, but if his secretary is a strong-minded, interfering and gossipy lady with whom you suspect he has been sleeping for years, then her name should clearly be placed beside his. Perhaps Y is a genial drunk who has held onto his job for years by getting things for his superiors, from free theater tickets to first-class air seats at tourist prices, while his assistant is bright, and in fact runs the department. The assistant's name must be placed beside his. Now redraw the little boxes so that everyone gets a rough circle equivalent to his or her relative power. If Y's assistant is beginning to eat lunch quite frequently with Z, you may feel that the assistant should have a larger power circle than Y's. Now connect all these circles with lines of power, that is, lines of varying thickness indicating friendship, obligation, dependency, private alliances, rivalries, etc.

You will now have two quite different charts, one marked TOO, the formal table of organization of the company, the other marked TOP, the "table of power," which shows how things actually work.

Let us take a simplified example of higher management in an imaginary company. At the top is the board of directors and the president. Below them is the chief executive officer; below *him* is the vice president of operations, to whom the various department heads report. The TOO might look like this:

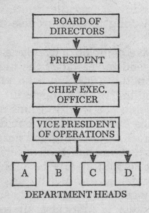

Now let us assume that the chief executive officer is approaching retirement and that his secretary is a dominating and powerful figure in his life, that the president and the vice president of operations play golf together, that department head A went to school with the vice president of operations and that department head D used to sleep with the executive officer's secretary. We can begin, in a very simplified way, to draw up a TOP as opposed to a TOO, bearing in mind that other factors have to be considered, and that the lines of power are so complex that they form a spider's web of contacts and obligations that overlap the established chain of command, and frequently obliterate it.

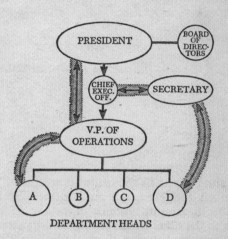

DEPARTMENT HEADS

The personnel listed are the same, but we now have quite a different picture of the power structure. Note that the thick, shaded lines indicate channels of power outside the formal structure and superseding it, and that the size of the circles indicates real power and influence, irrespective of formal position in the hierarchy. The reason I chose circles instead of larger or smaller rectangles is that circles seem less "rigid," more suggestive of the fact that people's power is subject to almost daily variations, and is never fixed. The circles should be shaded to show the person's maximum power potential and minimum power limit like this:

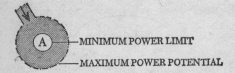

The small circle in the center represents A's actual position on the TOO, the outer dotted circle represents the maximum amount of power A can exert relative to the other members of the organization, the shaded area in between them represents the extent to which A's power fluctuates according to such variables as health, willingness to seek the vice president's support, the profitability of his department, etc. If his area of power on your chart were to balloon beyond the outer circle it would begin to approach the vice president's in size, in which case the chart would indicate that he may be about to replace his old schoolmate or that his old schoolmate is going to have to find a way of firing him to secure his own power area. If his circle of power diminishes to the same size as that of the other department heads we can assume that his alternative power channel has been cut off (in which case the other department heads, who will have been jealous of his position, may combine to destroy him), or that the vice president's own power is on the wane (in which case we can look for department head D's circle to grow). The main thing to realize is that your TOP is concerned with movement, not with a static explanation of who reports to whom. The amount of information to be taken into consideration may seem enormous (Does the president's wife play a major role in making decisions, in which case she too should be included?), but therein lies its value.

The time spent in thinking about the real power of the people you work with, and the means by which they communicate and exert their power, will give you a sense of the real structure of relationships, which is always far more complicated and subtle than it appears to be. If the chief executive officer always wears blue shirts and you suddenly notice that department head A has taken to wearing the same kind of shirt and frequently lunches with the chief executive officer, you can sensibly assume that something is happening, and looking at your TOP, you may conclude that the chief executive officer is attempting to deprive the vice president of operations of his ally and dependent and is beginning to succeed, in which case you can also expect to see department head D having many earnest conversations with the chief executive officer's secretary, his protector, since he will be afraid of losing *his* special position.

Every change, however small, in one relationship leads to a shift in the others, in which event new channels between people are opened up overnight in order to safeguard everybody's position in the TOP. Almost everybody maintains a fallback position, or several, in case a sudden change should occur. Department heads B, C and D will almost certainly maintain some sort of relationship with A, just in case his connection to the vice president should become a significant factor, or his protector's circle of power should suddenly envelop the chief executive officer's. By the same token, A is likely to maintain cordial relationships with D because of the latter's special position, just in case A's protector begins to decline in power. By these means, people attempt to ensure their power, relying on small social contacts— lunches, after-hours drinks, a shared cup of coffee, an occasional friendly office chat—to indicate their willingness to accept a new system of alliances if the old one collapses. Those who are interested in power are not likely to write anyone off until they're actually fired and out of the game. After all, life is full of surprises: a system of power is a delicate structure, which can collapse and be reconstructed in a quite different form overnight, unlike the TOO, in which it is merely necessary to insert a new name in the rectangle. The TOO represents a fixed system into which people are placed to fill specific functions; the TOP represents the results of these people's ambitions and their interaction with each other: a change in personnel changes the whole relationship, rather than simply replacing one player with another.

It is valuable to understand and exploit this system of alternative management, and to school yourself to read the signs that identify its presence. Very often, distribution lists of information sheets, reports and magazines will give you a clue. In most cases, the company reports, or any document of an official nature, will be circulated from person to person in the order established by the TOO—that is, the official structure of authority. On the other hand, informal items like trade magazines usually follow distribution lists made out by a secretary, and are likely to be sent in the order of the TOP. The secretary doesn't bother following the official structure of authority; he or she puts the names down in the order of their *real* importance. The difference is likely to be very instructive.

By the same token, it is worth looking at the order in which groups of people enter elevators, since they tend to board the elevator in turns established by the TOO, following the official order of precedence by title, and to leave the elevator according to their TOP positions, the time of ascent or descent giving them an opportunity to reposition themselves in the order of their real power. Allowances must be made for men who sometimes defer to a woman, but in general people enter the elevator by seniority and leave it in the order of their relative positions in the power structure.

The Power Circle

As a general rule, meetings are somewhat unreliable as indicators of real power. Needless to say, those who have substantive power will always try to arrange matters so that meetings are held in their own power spot, rather than in somebody else's or on neutral ground. The accomplished power player would far rather crowd a dozen people into his or her office, however uncomfortable it is for everybody, than hold a meeting in comfort somewhere else. Unless the meeting is so formal that there are predetermined places, as in an old-fashioned dinner party, the person whose meeting it is (all meetings are the property of somebody) will try to arrange matters so that he or she sits facing away from the window, so that the others get the sun in their eyes, while those attending the meeting will attempt to take up positions as close as possible to the leader's desk or chair. The object is to appear to be associated with the power that has called the meeting, rather than being part of the larger group that has been called in. This is particularly true of meetings in which people are going to be told they have to make a greater profit, or spend less, or stop coming in at ten in the morning. By placing himself close to the meeting leader and facing in the same direction, even if it means forgoing a chair and balancing on the window sill, the student of power can make it seem that he already knows what is going to be said, approves of it, *and that it doesn't apply to him*. For this reason, many people make a practice of arriving early for meetings and hovering near the desk of the power figure, dithering around long enough so that there are no seats left, and nothing for them to do but stand or lean behind the power figure, facing out toward the seated audience. This, however, is not a position of power—it's a form of self-camouflage.

In meetings where people are seated around a table, whatever its shape, the order of power is almost always clockwise, beginning with what would be the number "12" on a clock face, and with power diminishing as it moves around past positions at three o'clock, six o'clock, nine o'clock, etc. People will go to a great deal of trouble to get themselves in the position that corresponds to their place on the TOP, arriving long before the meeting begins (though this doesn't help if you don't know in advance where the top TOP person is going to sit), pleading a draft down their necks, the glare from the sun, deafness in one ear or the other, anything in order to find what they consider to be their proper place in the circle of power.

Power circle for a meeting at a table of any shape. The second most powerful person will be at one o'clock, the *least* powerful at eleven.

A neophyte in matters of power might suppose that the seats to either side of the power figure would be worth staking a claim to, but, as we see, this is not the case. To be on his *left* (at one o'clock) is to be next to him in terms of power; to be on his right is to be nobody. The reason for this is quite simple. In ancient times, when life was more direct, it was easier to stab to your left with the dagger in the right hand, than to use your right hand in trying to stab someone seated to your right, which is almost impossible since it requires a backhanded thrust. It was therefore prudent to place a powerful guest immediately to your left, though politeness might have dictated otherwise, since in that position he could not stab you, while you were excellently placed for killing *him*. The person sitting immediately to your right would be someone of no risk to you, and hence of no importance. Although much has changed, and those attending business meetings seldom carry weapons (except perhaps for meetings in the Mafia and the police), this ancient wisdom still determines the direction of the seated power circle, while at the same time reminding us that the true measure of power is the extent to which one is feared by the person one step higher in the TOP.

There are numerous other signs to look for that may indicate where power lies. The less power people have, the more strongly lit their space or office is, the extreme of nonpower being a desk in the open, lit from above by banks of fluorescent lights in the ceiling. With each step up, the amount of light tends to decrease, the assumption being that since truly powerful people don't need to type, write or even read very much, they don't need bright working lights. In most offices this pattern is easy to observe, from the open spaces which are lit like operating rooms and the more private offices, in which a certain ambiguous dimness is maintained, to the inner executive offices, which are paneled in dark wood, have curtains instead of Venetian blinds and are lit by shaded lamps, the dark, private caverns of the powerful. In all ages, darkness has been the realm of power, and the modern office is no exception.

All such signs are useful if you already know your territory—it's simply a matter of looking at the familiar from a new point of view—but in searching for a job it may be more difficult to assess the power opportunities available and the power relationships that already exist. You need a trained eye and a certain amount of ingenuity to guess at the real nature of an organization when you're on the outside. As we have indicated, the architecture, general layout and decoration of the office can serve as useful indicators, but if you're simply interviewed by the personnel department, there isn't much you can do— personnel departments are reticent on the subject of power, and rightly so, since they have so little. Every effort should be made to avoid being hired by the personnel department, but if it can't be avoided, you should make sure to take a tour of the office on your own afterward. You can simply ask for the directions to the nearest toilet when the interview is over, then proceed to look around the office. One man I know, a perennial job-switcher, always says goodbye to the person who has interviewed him, then spends the rest of the day wandering around with a clipboard in his hand, writing down the extension numbers on people's telephones and looking preoccupied. "I don't actually pretend to be a telephone repairman," he says, "but I don't discourage the idea. Secretaries tell me all sorts of useful things. I was interviewed at one place where the personnel guy told me all about their fantastic dental plan. That was important to me, because I needed a lot of work done on my teeth, so I was interested to hear one secretary tell another that the management had decided to *stop* the dental plan because too many people were using it and it cost too much. If you can get to the area in which you're going to be working, you can see just what life is like there, how people talk to each other, whether or not they look happy. You can even ask them questions—why not? They assume you're simply curious. The thing to do is to leave your coat and your briefcase in the bathroom, so you can walk about in shirt-sleeves. Nobody distrusts a guy in shirt-sleeves with a clipboard and a few ballpoint pens in his shirt pocket. You can open people's doors, look in on meetings, study the general layout of the place, observe people at work, really decide if this is a place you want to be. I usually bring a sandwich in my briefcase so I can sit down and eat when everybody else is having lunch at their desk. They'll usually talk to you pretty freely then. I always take a careful look at bulletin boards too. They're full of useful information, and they represent a kind of office counterculture, which makes it pretty clear how the employees feel about the management, and how the management communicates with the employees. You owe it to yourself to be informed. They ask *you* questions when they hire you, but there's no way you can ask them the kind of questions that matter."

The rites, customs and traditions of power vary in different offices, but have in common the fact that people use them to "dramatize their own positions in [an] organizational scheme." [4] In learning the traditions of a place of work, you are preparing yourself

to become powerful within it. Many of these rites can
be effectively performed for yourself—as opposed to
having them performed on you—and by acute observation you can often shorten or avoid altogether the
usual initiation process. Thus, it is advisable to learn
which are the important meetings to attend and to
find a way of attending them by yourself, instead of
waiting to be invited. It is prudent to know which of
two rival executives is the more likely to win a power
struggle, before committing yourself to one or the
other, and important to know in whose power area
your office is going to be, since those within a given
executive's power territory will be presumed to be his
allies. It is not necessary to take quite so extreme a
view as did Machiavelli, who urged his readers to
"fear everything and anybody," [5] but in a competitive
world it is necessary to seize every possible advantage, and to learn how to find and secure one's own
power spot. To paraphrase "the Peter principle," [6]
one can say that people rise to a level of power just
one step beneath that which would make them feel
secure. Once we understand the nature of the power
relationships around us, we can begin to find our
security in fluidity and movement, understanding
that power is not static, but must be sought, de-
fended, increased and protected by cleverness and
originality. Once we have studied the board, we can
proceed to the moves, confident that we understand
the larger frame in which they are being played.

CHAPTER FIVE

Games of Power

A whole universe of possibilities and combinations is available to the individual player. For even two out of a thousand stringently played games to resemble each other more than superficially is hardly possible.

—Hermann Hesse
THE GLASS BEAD GAME

Kronsteen was not interested in human beings ... Nor did the categories "good" and "bad" have any place in his vocabulary. To him all people were chess pieces. He was only interested in their reactions to the movements of other pieces.

—Ian Fleming
FROM RUSSIA WITH LOVE

Once you've understood the context, you have to develop the moves you need for winning the power game. Before you can act to get yourself a raise, for example, you should know the prevailing conditions with respect to compensation, the personalities and the likely reactions of the people involved in the decision, the forces against you and potentially in your favor. But once you understand all this, you still have to know what to do. "Action makes more fortunes than caution," [1] is a piece of advice worth remembering, whenever you are tempted to do nothing. The consequences of acting are always more interesting than those of *failing* to act, and you cannot play the power game without moving your pieces (and risking them). At some point, a theoretical knowledge of power must lead to practical decisions.

The variety of plays that people use to attain the goal of power is endless, and more a matter of temperament than study, but certain moves are basic, in the sense that all others are merely variations of them. In fact, the number of basic moves available to the player is comparatively limited, the crucial division being between "games of weakness" and "games of strength." Games of weakness are much underestimated, particularly by men, since they seem to lack *machismo*. This is a pity, because they are extremely effective. The late Colonel Gamal Abdel Nasser, for example, was a master of this particular move. He was willing to bluster, bluff and talk of war, though never very convincingly, but when attacked or threatened he simply warned the major powers that he might be obliged to surrender and collapse, obliging them to rescue him. When attacked by the British, the French and the Israelis in 1956, he blocked the Suez Canal, thus cutting himself off from a considerable source of revenue and power, and announced that if he wasn't rescued by international action, he would collapse. The world at large, including his triumphant enemies, hastily came to his aid—nobody can conduct a heroic military campaign against a régime that has declared its impotence in advance. Nasser's successor has not been quite so acute—possibly the temptation to compete in terms of *machismo* has been too strong for him. It takes a really powerful man to play the game of weakness to ultimate victory.

The Israelis themselves, of course, play both the game of strength and the game of weakness with consummate skill, a rare combination. When necessary, they act with force and violence, imposing their will on the Egyptians by means of superior military power; on the other hand, when it suits them, they play the game of weakness, threatening to let themselves be engulfed by the Arabs unless they receive the arms and money they need. It would seem extraordinary for the same nation to be able to celebrate its military victories and plead weakness at the same time, were it not for the fact that our lives are full of people who do the same thing on a smaller scale quite successfully. Marriages, for instance, are frequently boards for just such a game, in which one spouse maintains power over the other by complaining that he or she has none. In the words of Lao-tse, "The soft overcomes the hard; the weak overcomes the strong." [2]

GAMES OF WEAKNESS:
"Avoid victories over one's superiors" [3]

William Hazlitt wrote, "There is nothing that helps a man in his conduct through life more than a knowledge of his own characteristic weaknesses," [4] which is certainly true, though one must of course be capable of seeing other people's weaknesses as well. The basic move in this game is to deny one has any power at all, thus avoiding the painful necessity of taking a stand on an issue. This game can be seen quite clearly when people who have considerable power are asked to get their subordinates a raise. People whose whole life and soul are wrapped up in the ability to make tough decisions, for whom "eyeball to eyeball" confrontations and "showdowns" are virtually a life-style, can be reduced to whimpering helplessness by a secretary who wants to be raised from $140 a week to $150. Suddenly, they are powerless, brought low by the specter of taking action on behalf of someone else's needs, however small. A person who has just negotiated singlehandedly a $425,000 deal and who would do anything short of physical violence at the board of directors' meeting to get a raise for himself, will plead incapacity, weariness, overwork and above all powerlessness, to avoid "going to bat" for someone else's ten dollars a week —his hands raised palms upward, elbows cocked, shoulders slumped, the Gallic gesture of resignation that signifies impotent sympathy, the instinctive body language of the weakness game.

125

When it comes to raises, *the smaller the amount involved, the more difficult it is to put through.* Raising an executive from $45,000 to $50,000 is easy enough, and it may even be felt that not giving him the $5,000 at the end of the year would be either an insult or a warning of imminent dismissal. Raising a secretary from $140 to $150, on the contrary, is sure to involve a bitter struggle, and require emotional appeals, blackmail and a personal commitment. Executive salaries, however large, are seen as reflections of the corporation, and are thus *collective* decisions, while smaller salary increases are by their very nature *personal* requests, requiring the executive involved to lay his own prestige "on the line." Thus, the same man can ask, "What do you think *we* ought to do about the vice president of sales? Don't you think we'll have to give him five?", while in asking for a raise of smaller dimensions he would be obliged to say, "I'd like to give X another ten a week. It's deserved, and it would make my life easier, okay?" The smaller the sum of money, the more personal it is going to appear, which explains why most executives are reluctant to undertake such tasks, and why the best way to get a big raise is to already be making a lot of money.

Weakness games are primarily useful as a means of saying No without actually having to say it, the question of salaries being a perfect example of an area in which weakness pays dividends. On the level above you, after all, your performance is being judged in part on your ability to hold *down* salary increases in your immediate area of responsibility, while among those below you, their loyalty to you is determined by your ability to get them what they want. In this position, the best posture to adopt is one of uncompromising toughness with one's superiors and weakness with one's inferiors. The executive who is himself (or herself) preparing to campaign for a personal raise can only do so by holding back everybody else. The more people who *don't* get raises, the more he or she will deserve one. It is therefore worth remembering that the structure of our society makes it fairly certain that the person one has to go to for a raise can only get more money himself by refusing to give it.

Denying power can be fruitful in many other ways. Any competent negotiator knows it is better to curse the management, flaunt his weakness, blame everything on the computer or the board of directors, and by joining his opponent, imply that they are both victims of the same rapacious organization, negotiate a lower price for whatever is at stake.

For example, when I first went to work, I was impressed by the fact that most senior book publishing executives made something of a fetish of making decisions. The game, as it was then played, consisted of pretending that one had autonomous, as it were, unlimited, power. It was bad form to admit that one had to consult with anyone, the main idea being to imply to agents and authors that your word was *it*. This was never, in fact, the truth; the management, those nebulous figures who controlled finance and knew where the books were shipped from, always retained a veto power, but the trick was never to admit that they existed. Today nobody will admit to having any authority at all. The old pride of decision-making has been dropped in favor of an attitude that implies one cannot make any decisions for oneself, that one is in fact a kind of messenger for unseen, dark forces. This has meant the disappearance of a good deal of the zest of publishing, which used to consist of spirited personal bargaining.

Ten years ago, if you mentioned a figure, a bargaining session would begin, rather similar to that which you might overhear in any Anatolian rug bazaar. These days, an agent merely mentions a figure, $100,000 say, and the editor replies, "Well, that's interesting, I'll have to talk to people here about it. It sounds okay to me, but I don't know what 'they' will think." An hour later, he will come back on the phone to offer $25,000, with many apologies for "their" intransigence, failure to perceive literary talent and general stinginess. He may even complain about his own salary to show that he too is a victim. This would have been unthinkable in the days when editors found their *macho* in the big confrontation, but in fact nothing has changed but the style; the editors are simply willing to humiliate themselves to make the deal they want, whereas before they were in the habit of humiliating other people.

The important thing to note is that they have turned humiliation into a productive and profitable *system*. If we can inspire pity, instill in the other person the belief that we are all victims of the same system, we may get what we want for the price we all intended to pay in the first place. Pride and a public show of authority are things we simply can't afford, hence the difficulty, in modern life, of finding anyone who will admit to being responsible for an unpleasant decision—unlike the old days, when young men regarded each unpleasant decision as a way station on the road to success, and wanted nothing more than to prove they had made it for themselves, unilaterally rather than by committee.

The humiliation factor is an effective weapon in the hands of the person who knows how to use it and who doesn't suffer from the nagging itch to show his power. Take women's liberation. Faced with the demands of women for equality in the office, men first reacted by counterattacking with anger, the big stick, so to speak. When that failed, as it did in many places, they swiftly adopted a different game-plan: the fellow victim pose. With more effective results. The trick is to counter any complaint with one's own sufferings. "I'd love to talk about it, Sue, but not this week; if you could see my calendar, you wouldn't believe it . . ." "I know, I know, I think you should have more money too, but hell, things are tough for everyone, I'm going to be here until eight tonight going over these reports, I haven't had time to answer yesterday's phone calls yet, and as far as money goes, I haven't had a raise in two years . . ." "Look, this just isn't the time, I have troubles with the Board, if I try to get more money now, it just won't work, so be patient, okay?"

Men even carry this tactic to the lengths of making it a form of preventive deterrent, complaining bitterly about their lot in order to shame women into not making embarrassing and difficult demands. This subtle form of the humiliation game is easy to observe in many offices. It requires a man to sigh a great deal, to hold his head in his hands in a posture of extreme weariness and defeat, to convey a suffering that precludes any woman from adding to his burdens by bringing up *her* problems, such as the fact that she hasn't had a raise in two years. Driven by the combination of the urban condition and the unfamiliar militancy of women, a whole generation of American businessmen have schooled themselves to portray attitudes of fatigue and nervous tension, developing these histrionics into a finely tuned response, adaptable to all circumstances and demands.

A group of men can be sitting comfortably in an office, ostensibly holding a meeting. Let a woman enter the room and their feet will fall swiftly from the desk or the coffee table, their relaxed manner will evaporate instantly. As if by reflex, they will hunch over in postures of suffering thought, clench their fists in tension, take up all those primate signals of executive man under strain—remove the glasses and massage the bridge of the nose between thumb and forefinger to indicate eyestrain and mental exhaustion, close the eyes as if in deep reflection, raise the voice to show that what is taking place is important and urgent . . .

I have known one mild-mannered executive who schooled himself to smash ashtrays and coffee mugs so as to indicate that his nerves had been strained to the breaking point, another who affected a trembling of the fingers and a bad stutter to project fatigue and defeat, yet another who uses the simple, but effective, device of asking any importunate woman to bring him three aspirin *before* she has a chance to say whatever is on her mind. The trick is to get one's claim as a victim in before she can put hers in, to show that one is oneself weak, powerless, miserable, to join in her complaints rather than allowing oneself, by a show of authority, to be put in the position of having to answer them.

My friend Harry, for instance, who is as strong as an ox and whose nature is, to put it mildly, combative, has adopted hypochondria as his protective cloak. From a bad cold, he can clinch three good deals, turn down four requests for raises and shame his secretary to staying until 7 P.M. typing letters. All his instincts drive him to command, but urban life has taught him the value of appearing weak. He has mastered the middle-class urban guerrilla arts—the shuffle down the middle of the pavement, looking neither right nor left, the quick movement across the street at the sight of three studs coming toward him, the cheery evenings with neighbors discussing private police patrols, guard dogs and the merits of the Medeco cylinder lock. Being no fool, he has put his domestic experience to business use. In the office he suffers from bouts of ill health, clutching his stomach in agony, calling for tea, Bufferin, complaining of tachycardia. In the middle of a negotiation he leaves the room to throw up, and comes back to lie trembling on his sofa for a few minutes. Ask him for a raise and he inquires if you have any nose spray on you, frowning with the pain of terminal sinusitis.

Until recently, men were taught never to complain, it was supposed to be (wrongly) something women did, but method acting has become a business asset. Certain things can't be faked, other things don't do any good. A broken leg, for example, is not only troublesome to fake—all that plaster—but is generally taken as a sign of good health and sporting enthusiasm. It evokes no sympathy. Tuberculosis and the social and contagious diseases are also out, since nobody wants to be quarantined from the board meeting. All minor ailments, and particularly food poisoning, flu, severe colds, back trouble, sinus headaches, are very much in among knowledgeable game players. At the moment, asthma is probably the most popular thing to fake. One editor of my acquaintance can withdraw to his office couch in spasms of coughing at the mere mention of renegotiating a contract or raising an author's royalties, rolling his eyes and clutching his throat as if he were playing Judas in De Mille's *The Life of Christ*. By the time you have given him a glass of ice water, found his bronchial spray and helped him swallow a Benadryl capsule, it is hard to sit down and go on explaining to him the nature of your exorbitant requests.

131

POWER!
How to Get It,
How to Use It

One of New York's best-known businesswomen, a powerful lady whose appetite always seemed voracious, now carries on her thriving business from what appears to be her death bed, seldom taking or answering calls, passing down despairing messages through her secretaries, who always begin, "Well, she isn't feeling well today and isn't coming in, but I did speak to her just before the doctor came, and she said that $50,000 isn't enough, and would you please think about it some more . . ." On rare occasions when she can be reached on the telephone, she makes it clear that any disagreement on your part may prove fatal to her; you can *hondle* and argue if you like, but do you want to be responsible for killing her? Continued argument at this point will soon produce a rash of calls from mutual friends, asking how, *how*, could you have done that to a sick woman? Did you know that she was in tears when she put down the phone? Did you know she's had a relapse? What kind of a human being *are* you?

There's no winning against this kind of self-abasement. Unless you're willing to counter every suggestion of ill health with something even more drastic and grave of your own, you are lost. An English author who felt he wasn't getting enough attention from his American publisher announced by telephone, on arrival in the lobby of the building, that he suffered from a fear of elevators. Since it was difficult to hold a meeting by the cigar and news counter, his editor came down to meet him, and together they walked up fifteen flights of stairs. This reduced the editor to such trembling exhaustion that he was more than willing to give way on every point of contention, and in fact conceded most of them somewhere between the fifth and fifteenth floor, while gasping for breath and rubbing one calf against the other.

Shamelessness is the key to winning weakness games. If you have committed yourself to do something you cannot do (or simply don't want to do), soul-wracking sobs, hand-wringing—the entire repertoire of the Jewish Arts Theater—should be brought into play, the right tone to strike being roughly that of Jacob Adler in Tomashefsky's production of *Lear*. The trick is to make the other person feel guilty, the master stroke being to make *him* apologize to you because you've gone back on your word. If, for example, you have negotiated a contract in good faith and decided that it would be a mistake to go through with it, the honest thing would be to proceed with it and take the consequences, and the courageous thing would be to refuse to sign it on the grounds that you had made a mistake; the intelligent move, however, is to say that the executive committee has refused to allow it to go through, and to persuade your opposite number that you have risked everything on his behalf, and failed. This enables you to repudiate the contract easily, and acquire a reputation for candor as well.

"Nice Guys Finish First"

Perhaps because of the general brutalization of our age, we often expect power to be wielded with as much savagery and contempt as possible, as if toughness were synonymous with success. This may explain the popularity of professional football among businessmen and politicians, who like to feel that their work, while sedentary and basically manipulative, calls for the same kind of physical courage and toughness that football players are supposed to need. This is unfortunate in many ways: in business and politics the skills of a chess player or bridge champion might be more useful as guides to success than those of a football tackle, and the kind of courage that is necessary to make decisions is very different from the kind that is needed to break someone else's nose. Knute Rockne's famous comment, "When the going gets tough, the tough get going," [5] is doubtless excellent when applied to the football field, but in matters of state and business affairs, it would be more sensible to say, "When the going gets tough, the tough get smart."

We have been conditioned to expect "toughness" from those in power, and to equate it with bad manners; thus politicians are forced to prove that they're not "nice guys" if they're to win elections. Lyndon B. Johnson was not only famous for tyrannizing his staff, but ended up trying to demonstrate his toughness on the North Vietnamese, with well-known results. Both John F. Kennedy and Robert Kennedy were contemptuous of Adlai Stevenson, not because he was clever or had lost a Presidential election, but because he seemed like a "nice guy," and therefore a weakling. Former President Nixon and his advisors, with the notable exception of Henry Kissinger, a man who clearly understands the power game, were notorious for their "tough guy" rhetoric, always ready with football metaphors and addicted to "eyeball-to-eyeball confrontations" and "showdowns." For them, pugnacity, verbal abuse of their opponents and simple rudeness are the hallmarks of power. This display of toughness is curiously unconvincing in a group of middle-aged bureaucrats whose only physical exercise is lifting up telephones and, lately, holding their hats in front of their faces when appearing on the steps of courthouses to answer indictments. Nor, of course, do they think of "toughness" as the ability to *withstand* punishment; like most people who take a vicarious pleasure in sporting events, they identify with the winners, and tend to feel that the mark of toughness is how hard you can be on other people.

Although our national political style has always favored toughness as a sign of power, in emergencies, when survival is at stake, it is seldom the people who talk tough one finds running things. General George S. Patton was a master of "tough guy" rhetoric, but control of the Army was sensibly placed in the hands of General George C. Marshall, a man of great firmness, to be sure, but universally respected for his shrewdness and politeness. General Patton's superior was Dwight D. Eisenhower, a born conciliator whose tact, niceness (and ability to do nothing when in doubt) were proverbial. For that matter, American Presidents in major wars have never been rhetorical "tough guys," perhaps by lucky chance. Lincoln was a man of graceful charm, wit and tact, who would probably have been attacked as a weakling and a "nice guy" by Richard Nixon; Woodrow Wilson, though irritating, was a quietly courteous gentleman; and Franklin Delano Roosevelt was charming, devious and willing to compromise. None of them would have been foolish enough to think that there was any virtue in having their "backs against the wall," or stupid enough to find their way into that unenviable position.

In extreme cases (of which there are many) people will even provoke a dispute in order to prove how tough they are. Many business executives are secretly delighted to catch errors in their subordinates' work, or go to great trouble to create "showdown" situations so that they can win them. It is possible to set unrealistic goals for one's subordinates then lose one's temper when they fail to meet them—this is a common way of demonstrating power. Another way is to find what an executive's opinion is on something before a meeting, tempt him into exposing it in public, then force him to do the opposite of what he wants to do. Many people don't feel comfortable unless they encounter opposition—if they ask someone to do something and it's done without protest, they feel they've asked for too little. Faced with this kind of power tactic, the proper response is to cushion one's answers and present several alternative solutions to any problem.

Thus, if you are asked, "When can we ship out the first hundred thousand units of this item?" the proper answer is *not* "June twenty-first." This will merely provoke the power player into telling you, "I want them shipped by June fifteenth or heads will roll," and you are trapped. The intelligent response to this question is "When are they needed?" This places your opponent in the position of having to fix a date. It is always better to respond to a question with another question, and very important to avoid being the first to mention a specific date or sum of money. Whenever a person who has more power than you asks a question like "How much do you think this property is worth?" you may be sure that he has already decided what *he* thinks it's worth. The only answer that will satisfy him is his own, so it is best to treat all such questions as if they were rhetorical. A pipe is useful in these situations, since you can puff on it thoughtfully while staring into the smoke until your opponent is driven by impatience to say,

"I'll tell you what *I* think it's worth!" Another good response is to shift ground by asking, "Do we really need it at all?" Once the subject has been opened up into a more general discussion, your opponent may well inadvertently mention the sum he has in mind as part of his argument.

A great many people are absolutely committed to "the tough style." They simply cannot bring themselves to show the slightest weakness, and given the choice, would rather be tough than right. They are never happy unless they can force other people to do things by threats, bullying and invective, even when the people they're fighting are perfectly happy to do what they've been told. Their lives are spent in an imaginary death struggle with the rest of the world, as if one smile would kill them. They have got to prove that in a frivolous world, only they take life seriously. Even when they attain positions of great power, they are never at ease there, fearing that a moment's weakness will reveal them as weaklings.

President Nixon and his advisors, even before Watergate, were seldom photographed smiling, and when they were, never looked natural. Haldeman and Ehrlichman always seemed to be on the verge of losing their tempers—their chins pushed forward to express pugnacious determination, the corners of their mouths turned sharply down (like their Leader's), and their foreheads creased with worry lines. They represented to perfection the face of "tough power," which is designed to convince us of the wearer's absolute faith in himself and his contempt for other, less powerful, people. Eventually it becomes difficult for the person to smile at all, since his lower jaw has been fixed in a "power underbite," with the muscles forming two hard, distinctive knots just below and in front of the ears. This jowly look of threatening self-importance, with the characteristic forward set to the lower jaw, can be seen in photographs of Martin Bormann, Mussolini, Senator Joseph McCarthy, a great many newspaper executives, most motion picture producers and a high proportion of businessmen. The object is to make the face a visual warning signal, like the elaborate aggressive displays of lower creatures, which are intended to show one animal's superiority over another without provoking a real fight. When men wear the mask of toughness, they are simply adopting a signal, like a ruffed grouse in the mating season, or a surprised owl. When wolves meet, for example, the dominant animal adopts "a rigid stare, the ears are pricked forward and turned a bit outwards . . . the whole expression suggesting there will be an explosion at any moment." [6] The brows and the back of the dominant animal's nose will also swell up, the whole mask indicating that he is ready and willing to fight, and has the power to win. Since wolves are on the whole more sensible than people (despite Vanzetti's unjust comment that "Man is wolf to the man"),[7] they seldom in fact carry out their threats. These facial signals are nearly always accompanied by a characteristic and recognizable color display, either a bright red complexion, or extreme pallor, and sometimes alternating interestingly between the two. Both colors suggest suppressed rage, exasperation and the threat of retaliation, but a face suddenly gone white is generally considered to be the more dangerous, red often being confused with overindulgence in alcohol.

What is seldom noticed is that the people who *don't* talk tough very often get ahead of those who

138

do. Aggression is so much a part of our national life-style that it's hard for most people to recognize ambition unless it's accompanied by brutality. Nothing gives a person greater freedom and more opportunities than being dismissed as a serious contender for power. A great deal can be gained by simply learning to smile, an exercise which is not all that easy for many people to perform. The person who wants to use power must learn to control his facial muscles, his temper and himself, and avoid taking "tough stands" where they aren't necessary. Flexibility and cheerfulness are better weapons than brute force, and if used properly have the advantage of making your rivals forget that you're a competitor for power.

Of course you can't expect a smile to do the whole job for you. You have to understand something about hierarchies too.

Expand, Don't Climb!

People who believe in hierarchy move upward, if they move at all, by steps. Theirs is essentially a linear and static view of power, as if life were a ladder, to be climbed one rung at a time. You can't get to the top without touching every rung, which means that the rungs themselves become, in a sense, more important than the people on them, the extreme examples of such a power system being the Army and the Civil Service.

An Army division, for example, requires a major general to command it. His duties and functions are defined by the regulations, and provided he can maintain the discipline and efficiency of his unit in peacetime, and give it at least a minimal fighting spirit in wartime, no more is expected of him. He cannot turn his division into a corps. His post exists and must be filled, whether by a gifted and ambitious soldier in the style of Patton or by a nonentity—indeed the nonentity may do the better job in some circumstances. In any event, a divisional commander (and there are many civilian jobs that resemble this position) can only move vertically, and must abandon his division to gain promotion—he can aspire to become a corps commander, for instance, or to be chosen for some staff post that carries with it the rank of lieutenant general, but there is way for him to win an extra star by changing or expanding his division.

In civilian life certain departmental executives exist in similar situations. They can only rise by leaving their present job and taking on a bigger, more important one, rising step by step, either *continuously* (i.e., within the same company)—

or *discontinuously*, by changing jobs and rising upward in different companies with each change.

Note that both diagrams are identical in one important respect: upward progress can only be made
one step at a time, and each step taken means abandoning the one below it, just as you have to take
your foot off rung A of a ladder to place it on rung
B. This kind of promotion requires a great deal of
time, and the competition for each rung is severe.
Worse, you have to abandon what you have in order
to reach for what you want, thus increasing your
risk of falling off and landing back in the heap at the
foot of the ladder. And you are planning your career
in terms of an existing and rigid structure, which
means that you're playing according to someone
else's rules.

Very different is the position of those who can
expand their jobs, gradually enveloping enough people and functions so that they have to be promoted to

regularize their acquisitions, made, as it were, by reaching out arms like an amoeba, then filling in the spaces.

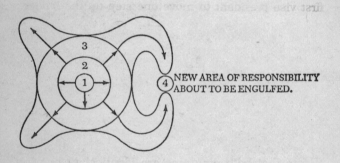

NEW AREA OF RESPONSIBILITY ABOUT TO BE ENGULFED.

Note the difference between this pattern of power and that of the "ladderer." The expander never gives up his original job or any of the ones he acquires; instead of moving upward, he expands outward, flowing like lava. He *adds* to his jobs and titles and responsibilities, trusting that he will pick up enough people on the way to make it possible for him to delegate the more onerous parts of his workload. The trick is to learn how to delegate without giving up responsibility, *until one is finally responsible for everything without having to do anything.*

The really fierce power games tend to be played by "expanding" people, as opposed to "ladderers," since the "expander" can spread out rapidly, amalgamating and absorbing whole departments, destroying old titles and creating new ones to describe his expanded functions. By contrast, the "ladderer" can only go up one rung at a time and must wait for the person above him to move. Let us assume that the "creative director" of an advertising agency, a "ladderer," wishes to rise quickly in his company. He is already a department head, so he would have to displace the first vice president to move one step up the ladder.

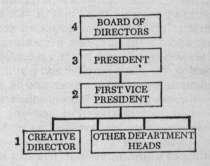

Unless the first vice president is either completely incompetent or a hopeless drunk (and even then!), this is likely to prove difficult, if not impossible, and would require the creative director to persuade the other department heads to join in a conspiracy, with obvious risks. Of course the creative director may lobby vociferously for a vice presidency of his own, but this will not change his status one bit: he is still standing on the rung below the one he covets, with three other people beside him. If he gets a vice presidency, as he probably will for the asking, the other department heads will demand the same title for themselves, which results in its immediate debasement and reduces its power significance to zero. This process, a kind of Gresham's Law of titles, has been so complete in some companies that many vice presidents refuse to use the title on their cards and writing paper, or insist on adding a second, *descriptive* title to the one they already have, as in "Vice President and Manager of Business Systems," or "Creative Vice President." Other corporations further complicate matters by creating two kinds of vice presidents (sometimes referred to in one cosmetics company as the sheep and the goats), one a meaningless giveaway to placate people who haven't received the raise they expected, the other more or less genuine, in that the recipient is a corporate officer and is authorized to sign contracts and go to jail on behalf of his employer. Hence the importance of knowing just what kind of vice president you are dealing with, the rule of thumb being that a vice president without a corner office or a sofa more than five feet long is the corporate equivalent of a Kentucky Colonel, i.e., the holder of an honorary title without power.

If our creative director gets his vice presidency, he will be swiftly followed by the other department heads. Those on the rung will simply have swollen a bit, thus making life on the rung a little more crowded and uncomfortable than it was before. Until the man above him either falls off the ladder or moves his Gucci loafers up to the rung above him and becomes president, the creative director—whatever his title—is stuck.

The "expander" has no such problem. He does not think in terms of rungs, he simply overflows, taking over bits and pieces of other people's departments, projects so boring or difficult that nobody else wants them, above all tasks which require liaison and communication between departments. Soon he will have created a complex and almost invisible system of alternative management, probably more effective than the real one represented by the first vice president, since it is closer to actual operational problems, while at the same time spreading out so widely that it will quickly be necessary to "do something for him," as the management phrase goes. A good "expander" will swallow up so many of his superior's functions that eventually nothing is left but the title, which can be discarded together with its incumbent, when he has been reduced to powerlessness. "Expanders" not only drown those in their way, but prefer to submerge all traces of the past, creating new titles to match their enormously expanded functions. Even when they have acquired the power they seek, they are careful not to reestablish a fixed hierarchy to replace the one they have destroyed. You can't knock them off their perch because they have none. Since they never relinquish any of their responsibilities, they virtually eliminate the possibility of challenge; every path in the management maze they have created leads back to them, however elaborately it has been delegated, their only weakness being a tendency to remain mired in a mass of petty detail which they can't abandon for fear of leaving a vacant area of power behind them. To the expander danger to himself always lies *within* the circle of his power, not on the periphery or the outside. Like the commander of an occupying army, the successful expander must always be on the watch for signs of revolt in his territory, constantly straining to maintain control over the vast areas of power he has absorbed.

Still, for all its inconveniences, expanding represents the surest power game of all. The promotion ladder only exists as long as people believe in it, and are willing to trudge up it. The moment somebody begins to spread out like a tide, it floats away.

The Information Game

More important still is the control of information. Almost everybody is dependent on the supply of information, yet "information input" is usually regarded as a clerical task, not much better than menial labor. Hours are spent in discussing major questions of policy, but the information on which these decisions have to be made is sought after in the most casual way. An executive planning a promotional campaign that may cost a hundred thousand dollars is perfectly capable of turning to a person whose salary is under two hundred dollars a week and saying, "Listen, check the production people to see when the product is coming off the lines, and make sure sales and shipping get the stuff into these cities so it's there before the ads run, okay?" For the next two hours, he may debate with his subordinates the merits of print vs. television, the right color for displays, whether the model in the ads should be sexy or motherly, whatever else is on his and their minds, but the only important thing has been delegated to someone who may well be a secretary.

By the same token, information always comes from below, and the more important it is, the farther down one has to go to collect it. If the same executive wants to find out how much money was spent on a comparable campaign a year earlier, he will ask his secretary to find out, and she will ask the advertising manager's secretary, such routine matters being beneath his attention, and together they will go back to the files and add up whatever figures they can find. Because they are not privy to high policy, there may be hidden items they know nothing about, with the result that their meticulously collected figures will be entirely misleading. Nevertheless, six well-paid executives will base their assumptions on these figures unquestioningly. Almost all requests for information are burdensome and involve someone in tedious research, particularly since information is seldom kept in the form it has been requested. If you want advertising figures for a specific product over one year, you will be sure to find that they are kept by city for all products, or simply as a yearly total, or broken down into a series of figures so meaningless as to be useless. The person who has to bend these statistics to produce an answer to a specific question must therefore use judgment and imagination.

Years ago I was assigned to examine a book publisher's list of books over a five-year period and break down the total output into several categories—"religious," "fiction," "belles-lettres," "history," "biography," etc. The object was to trace on a graph the percentage of books in each category, so that the executive committee could plan ahead for purchases of manuscripts according to the number of novels or biographies or works of poetry needed. My companion in this unwelcome task (now the editor in chief of a major publishing house) knew as little about the company's past history as I did, and both of us were at the very bottom of the hierarchy—nobody with any power would have undertaken such a tedious job of information collection. Unfortunately, the categories were hopelessly selected. It was impossible to decide, for example, whether a work of mysticism by a Greek poet should be listed under "poetry," "philosophy," "belles-lettres" or "religion." If we listed it under all of these (which would have been correct in the literary sense), our total count of books published in that year would be inaccurate, since we would be counting one title as five books. If we assigned one-fifth of the book to each category our survey would be hopelessly cumbersome. Our choice was to toss a coin, or list the book as a "translation," or chuck it into "miscellaneous," along with four-color wall charts of the herbs of the world, a teaching machine for beginning bridge players and a pocket calorie-counting dial. Despite our literary scruples, we listed it as "miscellaneous," a category which soon included about fifty percent of the list. Not having read the books, we found it difficult in some cases to guess from the titles where they belonged, and when it seemed to us that the number of novels published in a year was unreasonably low, we simply transferred some of the more doubtful "general nonfiction" books to the "fiction" category, where they probably belonged. Our task was to produce a neat graph in a week, interestingly colored, broken down into preset categories; the fact that these categories made no sense was no concern of ours.

Needless to say, our labor was accepted with enthusiasm, and formed the basis for "planning" at the highest level for some time thereafter. Years later, the percentages of various categories we had worked out even found their way into textbooks on publishing, and took on the special aura of "second-degree information," that is to say information that has been given to someone outside the company, put in printed form as a book or magazine article, then fed back into the company in this new and far more authoritative form. People who doubt the figures in their own files will accept them as gospel when they come back from the outside in a magazine, forgetting that they provided the magazine with the information in the first place.

Of course we failed to use our task as a power game, being then comparatively innocent. We took the praise for our work and used it to push a number of avant-garde French novels onto the list. Had we taken our chart seriously, we would have produced a system of information so complex and ambitious that only *we* could have explained it, with the result that the executive committee would then have been obliged to consult us on publishing decisions. Instead of simplifying, we should have elaborated.

Those who play the information game know better. They not only obtain and control information, they know how to make it practically incomprehensible. Their object is to render the information at their disposal as mysterious and inaccessible as possible, compiling it in such complex forms that only they can explain what (if anything) it means.

The advent of the computer has made their task much easier, not only because most computerized information is printed in odd ways on forms that fold like an accordion and tend to slip off the desk onto the floor in a hopeless jumble, but also because any information produced by the computer needs interpretation. Whatever the question, the computer is likely to provide several responses, none of them in quite the form that will answer the question easily, and all of them leaving out the essential knowledge of just what facts were fed into the computer in the first place. The person who controls the computer is thus in a singular position of power, and all the more so since he is in charge of an extremely expensive piece of machinery. Once a corporation has invested several million dollars in a computer system, it is obliged to pay some attention to the information the computer produces. To ignore it is to admit having wasted a fortune.

The information game is seldom played successfully at the level of "information input," though there are examples of companies that have been taken over by the expert in charge of the computer, who has succeeded in devising a system of information and accounting so complex that the only way left to run the organization is to hand it over to him. In most cases, however, those who process information are pawns. The master players simply attempt to channel as much of the information as they can into their own hands, then withhold it from as many people as possible. If the weekly sales figures and the profit-and-loss sheet are regularly circulated to a dozen people in an organization, an executive who wants to play the information game will first devise some new way of reporting these figures, arguing that the old way was meaningless (of course the new way will be meaningless too, but that doesn't matter).

Once he has taken over the responsibility for creating a new form of reporting, which his colleagues will be willing to let him do, as a rule—most of them being content to tick off their initials as the sheets pass over their desks—the power player is then free to cancel the old distribution list. The information is now fed to him, and he controls access to it.

At first, nobody is likely to notice or care, but gradually the person who controls information can use his monopoly to good effect in any discussion. Faced with disagreement, he can say, "You're speaking from opinion; I'm speaking from facts!" This device (your *opinion* vs. my *fact*) is remarkably effective. In the first place, nobody can get at the "facts" once all the information has been channeled to one person. In the second place, the "facts" are now reported in a form that only one person can understand. Even if you can persuade the executive who controls the information to show you the figures, you will have to ask him to explain what they mean, which automatically increases his power over you. Finally, any protracted argument about these "facts" would mean challenging them, which implies an exhaustive study of the information system itself. Nobody in his right mind cares to do that, and the possessor of "facts" is therefore in a fairly invulnerable position.

The amount of information that can be subject to one person's control is virtually unlimited. Once you have taken over certain key reports, you can begin to expand by asking other people to report their information directly to you, which they are usually happy to do, since nobody else has ever shown the slightest interest in knowing how many typewriters there are in the office and what their insured value is, or the number of letters that pass through the mailroom in a single week (not counting those lost). The possession of this information not only gives one power in arguments, but also gives one a certain authority over the people who are submitting the information, even though they may not be in one's official area of responsibility. It is important not to throw away any report, however trivial, if this authority is to be confirmed. The proper move is to return every report to its sender marked "Noted," with one's initials and the date below. This meaningless courtesy will quickly be accepted as standard practice, and with a minimum of effort you can begin to argue that the reports are not "approved" until you have initialed them. The fact that nobody authorized you to approve them in the first place and that they don't need authorization anyway can safely be ignored. A power custom will have been born, and only a major change of some kind can shatter it.

This move, simple though it is, can be used in many ways. Let us assume that all the department heads in a company send in a weekly report to a major executive, with copies to three other key executives. These reports are mostly meaningless and time-consuming. For the person who compiles the report for his department it's a tiresome chore, only useful because it proves the department exists; for the people who receive the report, it's virtually inter-office junk mail, and goes straight into the waste-paper basket. Assuming there are such things as accurate figures, they will come from the accounting department in the form of quarterly reports, so it's a waste of time looking at the weekly reports. An ambitious executive, however, will ask to receive copies of these reports on the grounds that he's trying to improve "the flow of information." Since this involves nothing more than making an extra Xerox copy, nobody will object. But instead of throwing the reports away, like his colleagues, he initials them and returns the initialed copy to each department head. Unless the department heads object—and they are unlikely to do so, since they have other things on their minds—the executive will have established "initial rights" over this system of reporting. He has created a new area of power for himself, and can now proceed to use it as a base from which to establish his right to control the department heads in other, more important, ways.

Controlling information has an additional advantage as a game of power. It tends to make the person who controls it seem indispensable—and the indispensability game, though risky in the long run, is an excellent secondary move in acquiring and holding power.

"Nobody Is Indispensable!"

All struggles between management and personnel are contained in the problem of *indispensability*. The employee must consider himself indispensable, even if he or she doubts it, while the management must hold the opposite view. Many people spend their working lives attempting to make themselves indispensable, a search for absolute security which seldom pays dividends. First of all, the management point of view is basically correct: nobody *is* indispensable; however important you are, replacing you is at worst a question of inconvenience, expense and time. People who attempt to prove their indispensability are obliged to expand at a geometric rate—they can never have enough tasks, titles, duties and responsibilities to establish their indispensability to their own satisfaction, just as nobody who requires love to feel secure can have enough love. To expand in order to get more power, or more money, or more prestige, is a feasible ambition. To expand until you are *secure* is impossible. In every corporation, the people who think themselves indispensable, and are generally regarded as such by their colleagues, eventually get fired. The reason is simple, but seldom accepted: no corporation can afford to believe that its existence is dependent on the health, sanity and good will of a relatively small number of people, especially if it's true.

One of my dearest friends set out to make himself indispensable to his company, and almost did so. Not only were his projects enormously profitable, but he gradually extended a kind of moral control over the entire office. Important files were locked away in his drawers, totemic pieces of furniture were removed from their places in the middle of the night and carried to his office, so that the ancient mahogany boardroom table appeared one morning as his desk; he had the lock to the lavatory on his side of the office changed, so that nobody could go to the bathroom without coming to him for the key. Constantly fatigued, harassed and complaining, he involved himself in every problem, from the company picnic to the typography of the annual report. What is more, he had mastered the most important strategy of indispensability, which is to create an outside legend: a good part of his time was spent in giving interviews, going to parties and appearing on television, and since any management prefers to believe what they hear and see from the outside rather

than what they can observe for themselves, his claim
to indispensability went unchallenged.

As one of his colleagues says, "For three years we
lived with this legend. All the power gravitated
toward this guy, and if you objected or argued, he
would explain how tired he was—he had this thing
of taking off his glasses and massaging the bridge of
his nose to show that he was exhausted—then he'd
tell you that he wasn't sure how much longer he
could go on carrying all these burdens people were
heaping on him. 'How much more can flesh and
blood bear?', he would ask, but if you tried to do the
smallest thing without asking him, he would quietly
undo whatever you'd done, and make you do it his
way. Nothing could stop him—if you pushed him too
hard, he'd lie down on the floor and suffer from
tachycardia until you went away. You couldn't win.
If you got in at eight in the morning, he'd tell you
that he'd been in on Sunday for hours, if you came
in on Sunday, he'd tell you that he'd been up to four
in the morning trying to make sense of other people's
work, and wasn't sure just how much longer he
could carry on, and it was *true*. He made a practice
of making at least one change in *everything*, however minor, so he could always tell you that he hoped
you wouldn't mind if he added 'the finishing touch,'
and so he could say to other people that whatever it
was made no sense until he'd 'saved' it. Then one
day he walked out to take another job, and it was
like the end of the world. It wasn't just that nobody
could be sure what was in the files, or what it meant,
we couldn't even *find* them. Everything was so centralized that when he took away his little pocket
address book, we couldn't find the telephone numbers of our customers—we hardly even knew who
they *were*. Then I realized what made him power-

ful: we were lazy. We'd been happy to let him take over. It simply meant less work for us, and better than that, no responsibility, because after all he wanted to be responsible for everything. We'd made him a monster, and within a couple of weeks it was as if he'd never been there. Life went on; it was a lot better in fact. We didn't go bankrupt, and we didn't go to pieces. But I realized one thing: *nobody is indispensable*, it's really true, and it's not just management paranoia either. The moment you think you're indispensable, you're doing too much work for what they pay you. It's a loser's game."

The more you try to prove how much you're needed, the more you are likely to attract the attention of people who wonder whether your job is necessary in the first place.

Someone who tries to make himself indispensable is like a swimmer clinging to a piece of flotsam in a raging storm when it might be safer to let go and swim. The world is full of people who will work a fourteen-hour day to hold a job that could easily be done in seven hours, exhausting themselves and irritating everyone above and below them in the useless struggle to prove that life couldn't go on without them. It's better by far to make it clear that a great many other people could probably do your job, some possibly even better, but that for the moment *you* are doing it.

No-Power

The ability to say No can be pyramided into a position of unique influence and authority. This power is usually financial, and manifests itself as a kind of "Scrooge power" in most organizations, in which every request for money, whether it is an investment, an expenditure or a raise, is automatically turned down at least twice, however reasonable, even profitable, the request may be. This attitude is perfectly represented by Ms. Mildred Pearlman, a New York City civil servant in charge of reclassifying the city's 3,600 job titles: "You start by saying No to all requests," says Ms. Pearlman, "then if you have to go to Yes, okay. But if you start with Yes you can't go to No."[8]

Power and money await anyone who can manage to say No all the time, nor are such people easy to find. Almost everybody likes to be thanked and loved, no matter how powerful they are, and saying Yes is therefore a constant temptation for most people. The true "no-sayers" like Mildred Pearlman are incorruptible and invaluable, nor do they mind looking ridiculous. Their mode of operation is simple: they say No to everything until overruled, secure in the knowledge that they are likely to be right at least sixty percent of the time and forgiven for the other forty percent.

A talented "no-player" can rise very fast, since most executives are happy to find someone who will say No for them. How much easier it is to listen to an impassioned plea for a new project, or a $5,000 raise, or an expensive marketing survey, or a new Xerox machine, and say, "Yes, you're right, it makes good sense and I'm for it. Just clear it with X first on the budget side, and we'll go right ahead . . ." X's job, of course, is to listen in stony silence and say No, immune to pleas, threats and common sense.

The most important thing for those who want to play the "no-game" is to be consistent—the moment you start saying Yes to some things, making value judgments, acceding to certain requests because they're reasonable, you've become simply another decision-maker.

People who can say No are usually penurious by nature, and the "no-position" requires a certain reverence for thrift if it's going to be carried off successfully. Most "no-players" have a minimal sense of proportion, and can spend endless time saving paper clips, or worrying about the number of times a single sheet of carbon paper can be used, or issuing directives on the re-use of interoffice envelopes. Their value to the management lies in the simple fact that paper clips are as important to them as anything else; they will say No to a plan that might double the company's profits with the same firm lack of passion as when they refuse a request for a new box of paper clips.

Paper clips, in fact, are a potent symbol to "no-players," and when you see someone hoarding old, bent and worn out paper clips, and forcing them back into shape for one more use, you can be sure that a "no-game" can be expected from him. Or *her*, since a great many "no-players" are women, perhaps because of some atavistic sense of housewifely thrift, or the feeling that all men are showoffs and spendthrifts, while women are cautious and realistic. Whatever the reason, women frequently make excellent "no-players," treating every request for money as a wife might the pleas of a drunken and self-indulgent husband who has a weakness for playing the horses. I know of one powerful woman who used to turn toward any man who came to her with a request for money and say, "Mister big spender!" Like most players of the "no-game" she believed that conserving office supplies was a worthwhile and profitable occupation, and indeed the test of corporate efficiency. It was possible, though not wise, to drive her to distraction by twisting paper clips into bracelets while talking to her.

Lights are another potent "no" symbol. People who like to say No are usually compulsive about turning off lights; indeed I once knew an executive who insisted that no work done after five-thirty could possibly make enough money to justify the waste of electricity, and used to walk through the office as he left for the day turning off the lights, even where people were working. Needless to say, he said No to everything—no matter how tempting and profitable a deal was, he would listen in silence and then reject it. His power was unshakable, and he retired to a condominium in Arizona, heavy with honors and money.

Certain physical signs can be discerned in "no" people, the most obvious being the ability to remain unmoved by enthusiasm, passion and excitement. Most "no" people prefer huge, heavy desks, which serve as barricades, and usually place the chair for a visitor so that you're obliged to face them directly, looking right into their eyes. Since they know in advance what they're going to say, they are usually very polite—indeed politeness is often a sign that the person who is talking to you has already decided what to do.

*   *   *

Closely allied to "no-saying" and indispensability is the use of *responsibility* as a power game. It consists, quite simply, of feeling and appearing to be responsible for everything, as if by showing concern for the things that *don't* come under your control, you can excuse the state of the things that *do*. Just as everybody is a perfectionist about other people's work, everybody is entitled to worry about the things they aren't responsible for, and take a grave view of problems they don't have to solve. It is a basic rule of power players that when they look worried, they're worried about what *you* are doing, not about what *they* are doing. People who play the responsibility game almost always appear more worried than the people who are actually in charge, their goal being to show that they *care*, at the very least; and, if they're lucky, to qualify themselves to take on the job of worrying about really important things in a corner office. Just as there's a place for someone who can say No, there's also a place for a person who can manage to look worried even when things are going well. Constant pessimism can be irritating to those in charge, but events will almost surely justify pessimism sooner or later, so the pessimist, if he is patient, will eventually gain a reputation for good judgment.

Games of Manners

At first glance, the world of power seems to contain nothing but "savage men, and uncouth manners,"[9] but the social games of power are in fact complex and various. The most obvious is the use of bad manners to emphasize one's power, and indeed many men, and not a few women, compete in terms of profanity and "uncouth manners" in order to prove that they are powerful enough to humiliate those who have to listen to them. Extreme profanity has a certain shock value, as if one were saying, in effect, "I know you don't like this kind of language, but you're in no position to object, and the fact that I'm using it shows just how little I care about what you think." There is also an implied threat in profanity, a kind of vicarious *machismo*.

Until recently it was much used by men to keep women in their places, but with the advent of Women's Liberation and the arrival of a new generation of young women who can perfectly well answer back, returning profanity for profanity, the charm of this game has dimmed. Profanity remains, however, a very distinct claim to power. Anyone who has ever attended a meeting will remark that there are certain rules governing its usage. The person running the meeting may use profanity to show that he (or she) is tough, serious and has power, but those in inferior positions do not use profanity until the most powerful person present has opened the way for them. At the same time, the introduction of profanity into any meeting leads to an automatic escalation of obscenity, since everybody wants to outdo the previous speaker. The ability to swear becomes synonymous with seriousness and power, and nobody wants to be left behind—which explains why one can sometimes find agreeable middle-aged women executives and well-bred Harvard graduates using language like cavalry troop sergeants at meetings, while remaining perfectly well-spoken in private. When used sparingly profanity can establish one's superior position instantly, but as a style it is of limited use and has the disadvantage of debasing conversation throughout the office to the point where the whole place sounds like a barracks, and swear words no longer have any meaning.

Other examples of bad manners, while less extreme, may sometimes be more useful, and frequently take on bizarre and complicated forms. Perhaps the most interesting is the reverse by which people in positions of power imply that any knowledge or ability which they do not share is both unimportant and ridiculous. This popular game has never-ending variations. Thus, an executive who needs the advice of a lawyer to help him draft a clause in a contract, will put down the lawyer as being cautious and lost in details, whereas he has in fact asked the lawyer to come in precisely to supply caution and a grasp of detail. Early in my own pre-publishing career, I learned to hide my knowledge of foreign languages, since I found that every time I was called upon to make use of them I would then be subjected to ridicule. "I can't read this crap," I would be told, "what does it mean?" or I would be introduced to others as "a guy who speaks a lot of languages," with the implication that a knowledge of languages was proof positive of my powerlessness, one of those effete educational accomplishments that either meant I was a refugee or a failed professor.

Powerful people are inclined to believe that anything they don't know or can't do has to be useless, and a sure sign that the other person is a technician or a specialist, unable to grasp "the broad picture." They instinctively develop a number of tricks to keep their superiority afloat when asking for help, phrases like "I don't know anything about these details," or "Don't give me all that jargon, just tell me, will it work or won't it?" The best trick is simply to call the "expert" in, whatever the nature of the expertise, and make fun of him or her in front of other people.

Humor is an unreliable means to power. People who like power take themselves seriously, and distrust humor in all but its most savage forms. Besides, people who have a great deal of power get accustomed to hearing other people laughing at their jokes, so even if they *do* have a sense of humor, it tends to atrophy from a surfeit of unwarranted appreciation. Many powerful people see jokes, in any case, not so much as a humorous diversion but as a means of dominating the conversation. Thus, if six people are engaged in a discussion, a person trying to emphasize his position of power may say, "Listen, before we go any further, I've got a funny story to tell you," and proceed to tell it at great length, not to amuse, but to prove he can interrupt the discussion on a whim. An excellent clue to power personality can be found in the use of such phrases as "You're going to love this," or "I'm going to tell you something you'll find hilarious," or "Listen to this, you'll *die!*" Jokes and "funny" stories that begin with a command are almost always weapons of power, and not to be confused with good fellowship or humor.

Precedence is of course a gold mine of power games, the basic technique being to call people into your own office, rather than going to theirs, which implies giving up your power spot and entering theirs. This is simple enough, but ignores the complexities of territorialism. Many powerful people, particularly the aggressive ones, *prefer* to go to other people's offices, since they are then invading the other person's turf. Thus a man who wants to establish his precedence over another may go into the other person's office, sit down, and put his feet on the desk, thus infringing on the intimate territory of his inferior. These small signs of conquest are numerous, and include using objects as ashtrays when that's obviously not what they were intended for, giving orders to somebody else's secretary, spilling coffee, and even lying down on someone else's carpet to do back exercises when the other person is seated at his or her desk. The important thing in such games is to simultaneously establish territorial rights and appear more casual than your opponent, giving the impression that you believe *his* office belongs to you by making yourself at home there. Generally speaking, people playing the power game on subordinates will call them into their own power spot to give orders, and go into their subordinates' offices to issue warnings, threats and denunciations. A special situation (though doubtless familiar to many) is that of calling a meeting in your own office and making sure there aren't enough chairs, thus obliging people either to go and carry their own down the hall or sit on the floor. This establishes one's power by making people uncomfortable.

*   *   *

While hysteria may not seem a likely source of power, in fact it is an effective weapon in the right hands. All things being equal, a person who has acquired the reputation for being hysterical, thin-skinned and oversensitive will usually get a raise or a larger office more easily than a placid worker, for the excellent reason that nobody wants to provoke a nasty scene. If your work is needed, it is quite possible to acquire a good deal of power by behaving badly, crying and going into brooding, somber rages. As one executive told me, "We've got a person here who goes berserk at the slightest opposition, and I imagine in the long run it's paid off, in terms of raises when nobody else was getting anything. Somebody like that will never get to the top, but providing they deliver, they can get more little privileges than you'd believe, and carve out a whole world of their own. When you've got to treat somebody with kid gloves all the time, you pay more attention to them than you would to somebody else, and in the long run they *get* more. It's unfair, but that's the way it is. Of course it's not without dangers. It's like the theater: people who do star-numbers had damned well better *be* stars."

The theatrical side of power is often overlooked, perhaps because most people in business want to be thought calm and conventional in their behavior, and rational in their decisions. However, the element of theater exists, and not just in the kind of tantrum that is usually associated with Broadway rehearsals and dressing-room feuds. Since office life is often dull, the ability to produce drama is a helpful element in acquiring and maintaining power, in much the same fashion as the later Roman emperors were obliged to provide both bread *and* circuses to keep the mob quiet and busy. A dull executive, who lacks the talent for dramatizing his own career and the work of people around him, is bound to lose popular support. Astute power players know just how to create and publicize epic crises in order to get the credit for solving them, and how to predict catastrophe just before announcing good news in order to make the good news sound even better. In fact, if this game is played properly, even *bad* news can be made to sound like a triumph—it's simply necessary to make the predictions so terrible that anything short of bankruptcy will come as a relief.

A command of such games eventually gives a person a certain mythic quality as a "miracle worker" or, in the currently popular phrase, "a trouble-shooter." Nobody is likely to notice that the "trouble" was either imaginary or self-created in the first place. If you have a good reason to believe that the monthly figures for your department are going to be down $200,000 from last year's, the correct thing to do is not to waste time inventing excuses, but to go into action with the news that catastrophe has struck, that the figures will be down at least $400,000, that "heads are going to roll." It should be noted that the first step is to imply that it is *other* people's heads which are at issue. The best way to do this is to call your staff into your office and stage a scene appropriate to *Othello*, accusing everyone of betraying you and threatening dire reprisals. Once you have established that you are not at fault, you can move to the next position, which is to take responsibility for disaster in a noble and self-sacrificing manner. Your superiors will have heard of your attack on your subordinates, and having indirectly established that they are at fault, you can now quietly announce that things look bad for the month and that you're willing to be made the scapegoat. It is okay to offer your resignation if you think there's a good chance it won't be accepted, which is usually the case. By now, you will have prepared those above you for the worst, reinforcing their fears by sending out calamitous memoranda, and by staying in the office until everyone else has gone home. It is also useful to see as much as you can of the higher management executives. The more you involve them, the more *your* problem becomes "our" problem, and the responsibility for it is spread above you as well as below you. When, at the proper moment, you announce that the loss is "only" $200,000, it will be thought that you have worked a miracle, and with a little bit of effort you can extract as much credit as you would have from an *increase* in the figures. What you have done is to make a prosaic failure into a full-scale drama, with yourself as the hero. Since everybody is happy to watch a drama unfolding, and even happier to be able to play supporting roles in it, the figures themselves will soon seem unimportant and meaningless, and any judgment that is being made on your career from above will be based on the exciting quality of your performance. Months later people will be talking about the way you "weathered the storm," and you will be congratulated on your courage in the face of disaster. "He didn't panic," they will say. "He was down some fantastic amount, five or six, I forget what, and he got it down to two."

Creating artificial catastrophes is a game that can be played at every level, and is particularly useful in making other people feel guilty, and in warding off unwelcome requests. You can usually keep your subordinates in their places by making their mistakes into major dramas. I have heard an executive say, "This is the worst day of my life," sitting slumped at his desk in an attitude of despair, only to discover that he has been struck down by a misplaced file. Exaggerations of this kind not only contribute to a heightened sense of drama, but serve to make everybody around you feel guilty, even if they're not involved. The logical extension of this kind of game is the man who returns home after a perfectly happy day at the office and drops into his armchair with a sigh. If his wife asks, "Did you have a bad day?" he can say that it was indeed so terrible that he can't even begin to explain it; if she doesn't ask, he can complain she doesn't care. In either case, he wins. In its nondomestic form, this game can be used to discourage people who want raises, emphasize the stress involved in one's own job, evoke sympathy, and prove that one's salary is justified. After all, the more we suffer, the more we have the right to ask for a raise, and impose our wishes and demands on other people. All that anybody asks is that the suffering be dramatic and interesting. Nobody respects a person who suffers silently or, worse yet, boringly. The trick is to suffer in style.

One of the most profitable behavioral power games is *transference*, in which a discussion of a specific fault or mistake of one's own is opened out into a more general conversation. The object, of course, is to spread the guilt among so many people that one is no longer individually responsible.

Thus, if you are criticized for lateness, you should not protest or argue—instead you shift the conversation to the general question of office discipline, as if you were part of the management. You *join* them—

MANAGER: You were late again. We have rules here, you know.

YOU: I know. And we need them, too. You can't run a place like this without rules. A lot of people are coming in late, leaving early, taking long lunches . . . It's bad for everybody.

MANAGER: What people?

YOU: I don't want to name names, you understand, but I think what we have here is a morale problem. I've been giving it a lot of thought lately, and I have some ideas on it. Do you want to have lunch someday soon, whenever you're free, and talk about it? Something has to be done, and worrying about individual cases isn't the answer.

The important thing is to move as quickly as possible from the specific to the general, and to side firmly with the person who is giving you a hard time. Most people in positions of power would rather talk about general problems than deal with the matter at hand, and given an opportunity, will be happy to speak at great length about their own pet theories of management. This is particularly true if you can manage to have such interviews take place immediately after lunch or late in the afternoon, both of which are low-ebb periods for action and decision-making. Not everybody can hope to emulate a friend of mine who worked for a large conglomerate and managed to parlay a discussion about the lunch bills on his expense account into the management of the company's newly acquired restaurant and food division, but on a smaller scale, it's a game everybody can play.

CHAPTER SIX

Power Exercises

Those engaged in the struggle forever over-
estimate it, forever glorify their own enter-
prise—but it is nothing but brutal, bestial,
material power they seek . . . this age old
stupid scramble of the ambitious for power
and the climbers for a place in the sun . . .

—Hermann Hesse
THE GLASS BEAD GAME

I'm a compromiser and a maneuverer. I try to
get **something.** That's the way our system
works . . .

—Lyndon B. Johnson
NEW YORK TIMES, December 8, 1963

In the business world, it is possible to lead a full, rich life without ever having to hire, fire, retire or promote others; and indeed some corporations keep "hatchet men" on the payroll just in order to spare senior executives these difficult tasks. To the person who seeks power, however, these are acts that must be accomplished.

At some point power must be put to the test, and it can only be done by exercising it on other people, seldom in ways they will appreciate. Some enjoy this direct application of power, but very few; for most, it is the unpleasant but necessary price of success. For example, almost everybody prefers to find a way of firing someone indirectly, rather than in a face-to-face confrontation, perhaps because we can all too easily imagine ourselves what it would be like to be fired, and sense with a certain gloomy foreboding the uneasy caprices of fate. In much the same way that the death of another touches most people with a sense of their own mortality, the presence of someone about to be fired troubles and unnerves even the most powerful executives, most of whom are half inclined to fear that failure may be contagious. In our age we have come to terms with death, on the private level by hiding it away in "funeral homes," and on the public level by making mass murder a media event or a historical curiosity. What we fear is not so much death as failure, as though failure were a kind of premonition of the larger and more final loss of power to come. The deaths of our contemporaries do not, if we could tell the truth about our feelings, shock us as much as the news that they have lost their jobs or been forced into unwilling retirement. By comparison, death is sometimes treated as if it were a welcome release from impotence and failure. After all, once you have lost your power, what else is there left for you to do but die?

"I'm Afraid I Have Bad News for You . . ."

Firing people is comparatively simple, provided you can first persuade yourself that the person is being fired either because of incompetence or because he has committed an outrage so great that firing is virtually an act of mercy. It is always interesting to see how those in power tend to work themselves into a rage against someone they have to fire, and how they quickly become fond of the same person once the act has been accomplished, simply because they're relieved to have it over with. Half the trick in firing people efficiently lies in inventing for yourself reasons why they deserve to be fired, the most persuasive reasons being, of course, personal and irrational. People who have to do a great deal of firing steel themselves to it by a careful inventory of the victim's annoying character traits, physical characteristics and clothes, and search for forgotten grievances and slights. The actual reason may be inefficiency, corruption or stupidity, but such valid causes are seldom

173

sufficient for the person who has to do it. He needs to find something *personal*. The victim may have lost every important file in the office or been responsible for the loss of thousands of dollars, but in the end it is the fact that he wears brown shoes with a blue suit, or crunches ice cubes from his drink, or has shifty eyes, that makes it possible to get rid of him. People are never so closely watched as when they're about to be fired. If someone who has quietly done a job in comparative obscurity, without attracting much attention or offending anyone, finds the importance of his job suddenly inflated, it may well be a sign that dismissal is imminent.

One senior executive tells of an assistant department head, a congenial and respected young man, whose somewhat nebulous job seemed like a good place to start making economies when the order came down from the top to "cut back." "Everybody liked Martin," he said, "but nobody knew exactly what he did. You couldn't say he was doing a bad job because nobody could explain what the job *was*, except that it consisted of keeping a lot of magnetic wall charts with colored markers, and generally reminding people of things they'd already done or had already left until too late. The moment the management committee began to consider him as 'firing material,' his job was magnified into a major management function, as if this poor son-of-a-bitch, who was making twelve or fifteen thousand, was responsible for all the troubles of a multimillion-dollar company. Martin was made into the scapegoat without even knowing it, and top brass, who didn't even know who he was, were suddenly tracing every error in the past two years back to Martin's wall charts, which nobody had ever looked at before. Up to then, he'd been a guy

most people liked, but pretty soon people were complaining about everything from his scuffed shoes to
the shape of his face. All the habits that had en-
deared him to people, or at any rate made his presence tolerable, suddenly irritated them. Martin had
always been a calm man, a positive trait so long as
he was wanted there, but he was now accused of being lazy and indifferent. He'd always been punctual,
and one executive complained that he was just the
kind of guy who comes in on time to make up for
the fact that he doesn't do anything. He had never
been pushy so now he was 'stand-offish, a lousy
mixer, a neurotic who can't get along with people.'
By the time it was necessary to give him the bad
news, everybody on the management committee had
persuaded themselves that he was some kind of mis-
fit or psycho, which made it easier to can him. Nobody ever paid as much attention to him as they did
in the weeks before they gave him the ax."

Nobody likes firing people, which explains why
every business is full of people who clearly *ought* to
be fired by any rational standards of efficiency or
common sense. A friend of mine, not normally a
superstitious or unkind man, once explained to me
why he didn't want to sit next to a colleague whose
dismissal seemed inevitable. "I don't want to get too
near him," he said, "in case the bad luck rubs off on
me." This fear is quite common, and the first sign
most people have that their further employment is
being "discussed" is that they're quarantined and
ostracized. People greet them a little too heartily, but
while doing so, carefully cross to the other side of the
corridor in order not to get too close. A hush descends
when they enter a room, and there is a certain reluc-

tance to take the chairs on either side of them at a meeting. "I knew I was through," one executive told me, "when I was waiting for an elevator after work and a man I knew came out, saw me standing there, and said, 'I have to go back and get something I forgot,' rather than share an elevator with me. I started phoning around for a new job the next day."

The Mythology of Meetings

It is not so much the fact that we care in human terms about the people who are fired, nor even that we empathize with them, so much as that there is a ritual significance to a firing. There is a quality of exorcism about it, the hope that sacrificing one person will somehow cause the gods to smile upon the rest. When things are going badly, people are let go not so much to cut back on overhead (they will almost certainly be replaced by others brought in from the outside at higher salaries) as to fulfill this need for a ritual sacrifice, like the tanists who, in ancient times, were slaughtered at midwinter, their sprinkled blood serving to fructify trees, crops and flocks, in the hope of plentiful spring harvest.[1]

The act of firing, therefore, has awesome potency far beyond the fate of the individual concerned, or the justice of the decision, and tends to make the person who is empowered to commit the firing a tribal shaman in the eyes of his subordinates. Like the ritual priestess of pre-Hellenic Europe, the "firer" must perform the sacred act himself, and on his choice of the right victim lies the survival of his tribe or group. Just as the victim used to carry with him to his death the symbols of all the guilts, crimes and misfortunes of the preceding solstice, so that these might be borne away with him, cleansing the tribe, the person to be fired, as we have seen, tends to grow in importance prior to his dismissal so that he or she can be made responsible for everything that has gone wrong.

All power is ritual and myth, as it always has been, and those who seek power must be prepared to enact the rituals of power and take their place in the local mythology. Certain events have totemic significance. A meeting called by one person for a specific purpose exists for its own sake—or for his. But fixed meetings, whether of committees that meet at regularly appointed times, or board of directors' meetings, meetings which do not occur at one person's whim but take place by schedule, automatically become invested with magic significance. On one level, they represent meetings of the tribal elders, whether real or self-appointed; but on another, deeper level they symbolize the soul and the continuity of the tribe, which is why it is so hard to change their timing or their place. It is not necessary that such meetings be productive, or even that substantive questions be discussed; it is only necessary for them to *take place* so that the rhythm of tribal life is maintained in an unbroken pattern. Without such routines, life would seem chaotic, unorganized, and there would be no calendar of events to give form to work.

Those who play the power game are aware of this, even if unconsciously, and take every measure to transform the meetings held under their control into regularly scheduled ones as soon as possible. With habit, even the most spurious and useless meeting becomes a rite, investing the person who "owns" it with the status of a tribal elder. From the point of view of power, it is much less profitable to hold casual meetings whenever they're necessary, however urgent and productive they may be. The important thing is to create a purpose for which a meeting may legitimately be required, then to make sure that meeting takes place at the same fixed time and in the same spot, and is firmly marked on everybody's calendars, whether there's any business to be discussed or not. Since all those who are called upon to attend the meeting are obliged to consider it important (if it weren't, what would *they* be doing there?), there will soon be any number of people eating their hearts out in bitterness because they weren't invited to attend, which gives the person running the meeting the chance to award favors and establish his or her own authority by inviting certain people. There is a limit to the number of people who can be invited to a meeting—once it has lost its exclusivity, it has lost its power—but there is no limit to the number of separate meetings, for different purposes, that can be created by an imaginative person. Sooner or later, everybody can be a member of *some* meeting, and of course some people will overlap so many meetings that they will have little time left for anything else. The number of meetings such people attend will ensure that they are always thought of as important, both by themselves and their superiors, yet never have enough time to become rivals to those in power. It is also a perfect way of keeping one's eye on potential rivals or malcontents.

Participation in group rites represents a form of initiation into the tribal power structure. People can work for years without receiving this initiation, which can come in many different forms. Being elected a director (not an outside director, of course) is a form of initiation into the central, symbolic power circle of the tribe, and is generally regarded as such. Meetings to discuss other people's salaries represent initiation into real power, and confer special prestige, as do certain kinds of policy meetings and some conventions. Perhaps the most jealously guarded privilege in most corporations is that of talking to people on the outside, particularly the press, but the power in this case does not attach itself to the people whose legitimate job it is. They are merely message carriers —real power is the right to by-pass them and deal directly with the press on matters of "corporate policy" or the occasional scandal. A pipeline of your own to the media, even if it's only the appropriate trade journals, gives you enormous leverage, and will certainly lead to initiation into the power group— unless the power group decides to fire you for not going through authorized channels.

All forms of initiation are designed to "separate the men from the boys," even when the boys are in fact girls, as is so often the case today. At meetings, powerful executives will sometimes brief a junior to attack someone else's proposal or plan, so that the "man of power" can pretend to be impartial, listening to two juniors debating a question without having to acknowledge that one of them is putting forward the predetermined view which has to succeed. This kind of delegation involves initiating the junior executive into the ways of power, while at the same time actually suborning him. It is particularly effective as a device for tormenting older executives on the verge of retirement. By getting younger people, with less power, to oppose them, it is possible to make older rivals feel that they're being ridiculed and belittled, while maintaining a calm façade of impartiality oneself. Where an open confrontation with one of the tribal leaders might fail, it is always possible for the aspiring warrior to persuade younger members of the tribe to make fun of the older man, until his position has finally been eroded by disrespect from below. Because it's beneath a senior executive's dignity to argue with younger and more junior executives, he has no way of fighting back: he can only retaliate against an equal adversary, and none being offered to him, he is bound to be destroyed.

The ritual aspect of such struggles for power is always the important element, not the consequences themselves. Many a man could rise to power without eliminating his rivals, but his power would not be confirmed in ritual terms if he *failed* to eliminate them. A sacrifice is required to legitimize a promotion, and without it the act is incomplete, just as some tribes require a young warrior to smear himself with the blood of his vanquished enemies. Merely killing them would not be enough—the young warrior must add their strength to his if he is to be truly powerful, as the aborigines of the South Seas used to eat the flesh of their enemies to become stronger and more powerful themselves, and as the American Indians of the plains collected scalps to protect themselves with the magic of those they had killed. Since most people on the rise do not want to collect the scalps of weaklings and nonentities, they are bound to exaggerate the power of those over whom they have triumphed, which explains why office mythology is full of legends about the cunning, ruthless and predatory executives of the past, who, if they had truly been that powerful, would never have had to leave in the first place. Their reputations must be glorified to make the victories of those who defeated them meaningful.

The Rituals of Power

Meals, and food in general, offer further examples of ritualization. Here the religious significance is strong and obvious: a meal shared together is supposed to establish a sense of unity, as if an expense account luncheon were a kind of Eucharistic transubstantiation. We "break bread together," "*share* a meal," "have a bite together," in obedience to ancient laws of ritual in which hospitality plays only a small part. It is not so much that people want to eat lunch

181

with suppliers, colleagues, rivals, inferiors, superiors, agents, salesmen, lawyers, accountants, inventors, authors and public relations experts, nor is there any real belief that you can buy agreement for the price of a meal—rather there's an unconscious memory of the *significance* of eating as a gesture of peaceful intentions. In many tribes, and in most cultures, a stranger must share something to eat with a member of the tribe before being accepted. From the tribe's point of view, he has been offered hospitality and an obligation has therefore been placed on him; from the stranger's point of view, he has announced his peaceful intentions and accepted those of the tribe. An exchange has taken place, but it does not involve food, except in the ritual sense.

The question of *obligation* is central to such rituals and can be seen in its most extreme form in the traditional culture of Japan, and in the determination of most men to sign an expense account lunch check. The point is to show civility and friendship, while at the same time forcing the other person to incur an obligation to you. Seen in these terms, picking up a check at lunch—seemingly prompted by a generous instinct—is, in fact, a concealed act of aggression. In Japan, this notion of obligation was elaborated into a complex code of behavior, or *On*, in which the repayment of these obligations was precisely defined and made into a schematic formula.[2]

A rigid system that defines exactly one's obligations toward state, friends and family may well have made life easier for the Japanese by relieving them of all the tedious doubts and questions that plague Western social intercourse, but it is possible to see behind the imposing facade of their code of manners

the bare bones of a complex game of social black-
mail similar to our own. *On* is very precise about the
manner in which obligations are to be repaid, and
even the amount of time allowed, but it also makes
it clear that the man who accepts an obligation is
the loser. The dialogues of *On* are perfect examples,
on a ritual level, of the kind of struggles we go
through all day long in attempting to obligate others
while refusing to accept obligations in return. Hence
our notorious inability, as a culture, to settle the
question of who goes through a door first, which in
other, more codified societies might be settled by a
precise order of precedence. Five men leaving an office
together will not only go through extraordinary con-
tortions to find the proper order, bumping into each
other, missing their turns in revolving doors and
holding up other people, but will repeat the same
confused jockeying for position on the way back. In
a democratic society, no solution to a social problem
is a permanent one, so the order will have to be
worked out again at each door, and will offer no clue
to behavior tomorrow, if the same men have lunch
together then. What is more, the complexities of *On*
in a case like this are infinitely difficult to solve. In
principle, the senior man present, in age or authority,
should be offered the chance of going through a door
first, and this is usually the case. As a rule, however,
he will refuse this honor to show his modesty and
place an obligation on someone else. If this person
also refuses to go through the door first, the senior
man may give way and allow himself the luxury of
going first. More likely there will be a short struggle,
consisting of a series of subdued taps and squeezes
on the shoulder, between the senior person who is

refusing the right to go first and the person he is trying to push through the door instead. The latter, of
course, is attempting to show his unworthiness of
such an honor, and trying to refuse a gift which will
effectively put him under an obligation to the senior
man, and possibly attract the hostility of the other
men waiting as well. If he allows himself to be
pushed through the door first, he will jockey for position at the next door to make sure that the senior
person goes through first this time, then wait until
the others have gone through so that he can enter or
leave last, thus canceling out the obligation placed
on him at the first door. Since this same struggle is
being repeated in the rest of the group, each man
trying to get behind the other, or *ahead*, in the case
of a very few aggressive and ignorant souls, the possibilities for confusion, collisions and delay are excellent on even the shortest journey.

Some people make a fetish of avoiding obligations
—on the simplest level, they are eager to do favors
for people, but wily and determined in refusing to
accept favors in return. They simply *cannot* allow
other people to sign restaurant checks, open doors
for them or lend them a newspaper, as if accepting
the normal social civilities would place them under
some ritual obligation to those offering them. Unfortunately, they are not altogether mistaken—the whole
purpose of social civility is to place others in a position of obligation with a gesture that costs the offerer
little. Nothing makes a power player more nervous
than a favor he or she is unable to refuse, or repay
on the spot. Power players live by a system of *On* of
their own, its rules often personal and obscure, but
absolute for all that. Beat them to a restaurant check
and they will move heaven and earth to invite you to

lunch at their expense as soon as possible, or to perform some small, unwanted favor on your behalf that
will, in their eyes, if not in yours, cancel out the debt.
What is more, these repayments are carefully graduated in master players' lives. In keeping their own
personal score of favors received and repaid, they
attach a value rating to each transaction. Let us say
that in the mind of the man whose lunch you have
bought a meal at the Italian Pavillion counts for 5
on a scale that runs from 1 to 10. You have won by
picking up the check, and you are ahead 5 points on
his mental scale, a situation which he cannot allow
to continue, because you have acquired *On,* or power,
over him. He must find a way of repaying that obligation by some favor or act that will not only pay
back the 5, thus canceling out the exchange and
freeing him, but try to increase the score in his favor.
If it's your birthday, he may send you a bottle of
champagne, which might count for 8 points on his
scale, in which case he now feels you have an *On,*
or obligation, toward *him* of 3 points. He can now
rest easy, so far as you are concerned, though instinct
will drive him to increase the value of the obligation
as much as possible, until he feels you owe him so
much *On* that you can never repay it. For the power
player, the accounts must be balanced if possible,
but if they can't be, then nothing must be owed.

The receiving and giving of presents is another example of *On* behavior—very few people can accept a
gift without immediately worrying about how it can
be repaid. It is no accident that people say, "You
shouldn't have!" when confronted with an unexpected gift, or that at Christmas-time, the exchange
of presents reaches a neurotic intensity. The instinct
not to place ourselves in another's debt is as strong

among us as it is among the Ik tribesmen of Uganda, where a man tries to build his house secretly at night, if he can.[3] Politeness and custom obliges his neighbors to help him erect a house, and in turn, he is obliged to offer them food as repayment for their help. Since the Ik live at starvation level or below, a man's neighbors can fulfill their social obligations to him and starve him out at the same time. The social contract has been fulfilled by their help, but the last thing the prospective Ik householder wants is to assume this unwelcome, indeed fatal, obligation. He cannot afford gratitude or the acceptance of favors, and is able to see very clearly the motives behind the "generosity" of his neighbors. Most of us do not feel that we are better off in this respect than the Ik, though affluence allows us the luxury of pretending otherwise. The worst news at Christmas is the arrival of a gift or a card from someone to whom we have sent nothing, especially when it's too late to buy the return gift that will cancel out the obligation. An *On* obligation has been placed on us, and we know it. Even an expensive present sent to the people in whose debt we now are will not altogether cancel our *On* to them, and we may find ourselves bitterly exchanging presents for many Christmases to come, or simply deciding never to see them again.

In this sense, all social customs consist of concealed aggression carried out as politeness, much as Clausewitz defined war as diplomacy carried out by other means. We shake hands to prove that we are not carrying weapons in our right hands (a custom which explains the bad reputation of left-handed people for treachery), we rise to our feet at the approach of a stranger to our table, not out of politeness, but because our ancestors couldn't draw their swords from a sitting position, and if we believe that the elderly and the respected should go through the door first, it is simply because in ancient times only the most powerful and courageous warrior would take the lead, in case of ambush, with the result that it became an honor. The exchange of obligations is at the very heart of our relationships to the rest of the world, and can be seen at work in almost every situation in which power is involved.

"... None Will Sweat But for Promotion ..."[4]

"I like the Garter; there is no damned merit in it,"[5] Lord Melbourne once said about the most ancient and exclusive of English honors, a view which applies to promotions in general. Almost everybody in the world feels that they deserve to be promoted to some higher estate, no matter how high they may already have risen. Since the number of positions declines as the level of power increases, most of the world is automatically doomed to live in disappointment and envy. This system has many advantages, chief among them the fact that if it were not for the hope of rising, few people would do any more work than is necessary for survival. It is important for people to believe that work will lead to promotion, but, as Melbourne pointed out, merit is in fact something that most people in power dislike.

From above, merit merely confuses the issue: the reasons for promoting someone that have nothing to do with merit are always the most persuasive ones, if only because they're easier to notice and remember. Those who hang on, get up. Most promotions are based on a system of rewards for faithfulness, rather than on any real attempt to assess merit. It has to be remembered that nobody can be promoted to a job until the person who occupies it has left, a fact which is simple, but often forgotten. If that person is about to be fired, then it is sensible to make yourself as different as you can from him; if he is about to be promoted, then it makes sense to pattern your behavior on his; if he is about to retire, you're on your own. After all, if he is in danger of being fired, then his superiors will be looking for "somebody different"; if they're thinking of promoting him, they will be looking for someone as much like him as possible, not only because they think highly of him, but also because as "promotion material" he will be asked for his advice on replacing him, and will naturally recommend someone like himself; in the case of someone who is about to be retired, the management will be unable to decide what they want, and may even be willing to consider the dangerous expedient of "bringing someone in from the outside." It never does to forget that managements, like individuals, get bored with what they have, and since they are not anxious to replace themselves for the sake of change, they can only change by shaking things up below them. As one executive said of another, "He likes to stir the pot from time to time, just to show he owns the spoon."

To those in power, promoting people is second only to firing them as an exercise in the use of power. As games go, it has the advantage of involving many people—after all, you can only fire one person at a time, as a general rule, but there may be a dozen people who want to be promoted to a given job. The opportunities for playing one person off against another are endless. What is more, such occasions present an excellent chance to gauge the loyalties of those beneath one. As the aged Emperor Franz Josef of Austro-Hungary said, when a minister was recommended for promotion on the grounds that he was a patriot, "Yes, but is he a patriot for *me?*" When people are being interviewed with a view to promotion, the person doing the interviewing, like old Emperor, is looking for *personal* loyalty, trying to determine the extent to which the interviewee will be obligated, in the event he or she gets the job. This is normally a delicate dialogue; very few people can bring themselves to say, "I'll swing the job your way if you'll agree to join my camp," yet the underlying rationale of promotion is much the same as that of medieval vassalage, each executive trying to build up a small army of supporters who owe their livelihood to him. These people comprise his feudal levy in time of need, and the higher up he is, the more of them he will want; but the more of them they are, the harder it is to support them. Like a medieval army, they must be clothed, fed, housed and provided with rewards and booty. Their leader belongs to them as much as they belong to him, and his obligations to them are as demanding as theirs to him. These groups exist in every corporation, and the urgent need to provide them with promotions, titles, work they can do and raises explains much of the endless activity and intrigue that makes office life so fascinating. Since there is always pressure from below, and the need on the part of every executive to build up his ranks of loyalists, the temptation to create openings at every level is always strong, and naturally leads to a good deal of the unnecessary firing and job-changing that characterize corporate life.

A good rule for those who have the power to promote others is to ensure that they maintain absolute control over the process. Many executives insist on being the bearers of good news, with sound reason, and not a few are addicted to creating false rumors, building people's hopes and generally fogging up the issue, in order to keep everyone in suspense and dramatize the final decision. The more nervous people are about getting a promotion, the more they will appreciate it if they do, and many people are flattered at even being included in the rumors. By giving the maximum number of people the chance to believe they may be selected for a job, even if you have already selected the person for it in your mind, you can focus everyone's attention on your power while at the same time making an exciting event of a one-horse race. Besides, as a management friend says, "You don't want a guy to become too cocky, even if he's the only logical choice for a job. Make him sweat a little. He'll be just that much more grateful when he gets it, and it gives you a chance to show him who's boss."

For those who want to be promoted, there are certain rules worth observing. In the first place, propinquity helps. If you can move your office closer and closer to that of the person whose job you want, he or she will not only feel threatened (or that you are the logical successor for the job), but you will also create a certain feeling of inevitability in the minds of the people who will decide on your promotion. It is, therefore, always worthwhile to move from where you are toward the corner of power you covet. By the time you have taken the office next to the one you want, most people will assume that the next step is yours by right of succession. Ordinarily, the executive nearest to the one who has to be replaced will be first in line, so every opportunity should be taken to move in the right direction. Power people walking in and out of an executive's corner office will see you sitting next door, and will naturally assume that you are being "groomed" as the executive's successor, whereas the person who is most qualified to succeed to the job (in other words, the one with merit) may be four offices down, and thus comparatively invisible.

A promotion should always involve a change of office, if it's to do you any good in the larger scheme of things. It does little good to change jobs or receive a new title if you stay in the same office, no matter how important your new responsibilities are. To stay put always seems static. Shifting offices, by contrast, gives people around you a sense of dramatic change, as if by moving sideways you were in fact moving upward. Even for the most important and successful players, the promotion that means the most to them is likely to be the one that involved a major change of office (to a corner or to the "executive" floor, for example), however many new titles and promotions they may have acquired afterward. It is the *geographical* change that gets celebrated, because it is both visible and symbolic. A promotion may be an important move in a person's career, but if it merely involves ordering new cards and stationery, its effect on most other people will be minimal. What counts is a new office. Few people know or care what an executive's new title is, or can work out what it means in terms of power, whereas a new office can be compared to other people's in terms of size, desirability and decoration. I know of one man who worked his way up the ladder of promotion, eventually reaching quite a high position and title, without ever acquiring any real power over other people, or being taken seriously by his colleagues. Unfortunately for him, he had inherited a large and comfortable office early in his career, when he was not strictly entitled to two windows, a tufted leather couch and a designer desk in Jacaranda veneer. Already comfortable enough, he had no desire to move, and in any case there was no larger office to move him to. As a result, all his promotions seemed like empty formalities, and were dismissed by others as meaningless; eventually they even began to seem meaningless to him, and he complained constantly that his career had "bogged down," though in fact his rise in terms of promotion was impressive and swift.

It is quite possible to simulate promotion by moving one's office, provided the move is accompanied by sufficient ceremony, and doesn't look like a midnight flit or mere restlessness. It is as in certain Indian tribes, where the size of one's tepee, and its place in the encampment, determined one's social standing. Some Indians were notorious for attempting to take advantage of each move the tribe made to a new location to alter the place of their tent.

Promotion by side-effect is a more difficult game, but quite effective. This can take many forms, but the most familiar is to work out a specific relationship with another executive, preferably one who is ambitious and bound to rise. If you can establish that your proper relationship to him is one position behind, then you are quite likely to be promoted whenever *he* is, in order to keep the same distance behind him. Thus, if you are able to persuade people that you belong one rung below X on the ladder, you go up one rung whenever he does, your only risk being that X turns out to be a non-starter. A great many promotions are determined by this or other schemes designed to preserve a balance between people, and once locked into them, it is possible to make one's way quietly upward with little or no effort. Nothing is more useful than an ambitious executive, especially one brought in from the outside, since almost everyone will have to be "adjusted" to compensate for what it has been necessary to give him in order to acquire him in the first place. Thus, the arrival of an outsider who has to be given a good title may well lead to the inflation of everyone else's titles, just so that nobody's feelings are hurt. In cases where the turnover of outsiders is high, the people who remain may find themselves promoted upward with dizzying rapidity, until it's hard to even invent new titles for them. One man I know has stayed in the same place for ten years, placidly doing the same job, while the entertainment conglomerate he works for has nervously hired and fired executives in a reflexive, twitchy attempt to create a new image for itself. By now, he has acquired a certain power, being one of the few people who has been there long enough to remember where everything is and just what it is the company manufactures, but with each change of executives, he gets a new and more sonorous title "to keep him happy." "Happy?" he says, "of course I'm happy. What's not to be happy about? Every time they bring in some hotshot, they come to me and they say, 'Listen, we don't want you to worry, we need this guy and we had to give him a title to get him, but just to show we love you, we're making you deputy creative director, or senior vice-president, or whatever.' Everybody says that these are just phoney titles, they don't mean a thing, and in a way it's true, but you can always use them to get an extra thou or two at the end of the year. I mean, they're pretty embarrassed to have to admit that the titles don't count for anything, and they usually figure if they've given you the title, they may as well give you a little cash as well, just to make it okay. Anyway, if they've given you a new, bigger title, it's hard for them to fire you. Somebody would be bound to ask why they made you a vice president in 1974 if you were doing such a lousy job that you had to be fired in 1975, you know? So you've got them, really. By me, they can bring in people from everywhere, anytime, and promote them over my head. When they come in, I go up one notch without any effort, and if they keep on doing it I can see myself being president and chairman of the board in five years."

The astute power player should be able to make good use of other people's promotions, rather than resenting them, as many people do. Every promotion means another job or title open, and most promotions can be used as a good reason for promoting *you*.

"Money and Sex Are Forces Too Unruly for Reason . . ."[6]

What is true of promotion is equally true of raises; the two are inextricably linked, with the major difference that one is public, the other almost always secret. There would be no point to a secret promotion —by definition, it has to be a public event—while

raises are generally shrouded in mystery, the innermost secret of any given business tribe. This is as it
should be, of course. Money is what all business is
about, and therefore it retains all the power of the
central mystery of a religious cult. Most people will
tell you anything about themselves except what they
earn, and most corporations approach the task of
deciding upon salary increases in an atmosphere of
secrecy, intrigue and conspiracy suitable to a CIA
plot. The problem of money raises is common to
every organization, and it is not surprising that
among the documents purporting to prove that Martin Bormann, *Reichsleiter* and Deputy-Führer of the
Third Reich, is still alive, there exists a letter refusing
Adolf Eichmann a larger pension, on the grounds
that the other Nazi refugees would be clamoring for
more money if they ever heard about it.[7] It is not
necessary to be alive and well in Argentina to have
heard this argument a thousand times before—"if
we gave you what you want, and it leaked out, we'd
have to give it to everybody, then we'd be out of
business." It is always difficult to win—ask for a big
raise, and you will be told it can't be done because it
would set a precedent; ask for a small raise, and you
will not only lose respect, but be told that the management refuses to be "nickled-and-dimed to death."
In no single area of adult life do the rules of childhood apply so strictly as in raises; arguments having
to do with money duplicate on both sides the baffling
dialogues that take place between children and
adults. If you ask how much someone else is getting,
you will be told, "That doesn't apply," or "It's not
your business," just as something other children
were permitted to do was never a sufficient reason
for being allowed to do the same thing ourselves.
You will also be told to "be reasonable," "be patient,"

and to "try and understand our problems," advice liberally given to children by parents, teachers and headmasters, and designed to make them feel guilty for even asking. All else failing, there is the private school approach, an appeal to one's sense of community—"Look at it from our point of view, it's a big organization, we have to think of the receptionists, the secretaries, everybody, you're not the only one, after all."

Very few executives know what they're worth, given the general secrecy about money, and most have some slight suspicion that they might well be worth a good deal less than they're already being paid; few management people can bring themselves to say no without wrapping the refusal in explanations and justifications. "Money," in the words of one executive, "is the bottom line," but because nobody wants to talk about it, managements find it easy to separate promotion and power from money, giving people responsibility, authority and titles with a lavish hand, while at the same time arguing that none of these things justifies a raise. It is easy enough to co-opt people by promoting them. The more power they have, the more responsible they are for the corporation's profit, and the more responsible they are, the more restrained they have to be in their own demands. There is no better way to discourage people from asking for a lot more money than promoting them to the inner circle of power and then appealing to their sense of responsibility.

Most employees cannot be sure whether they're being overpaid or underpaid, a situation which explains a great deal of their *Angst*. It's another of the crosses the respectable middle class has to bear. Union workers know exactly what people in other trades get an hour, the officers of a corporation can find each other's salaries in the annual corporate report, but the vast multitude between these two extremes lives in ignorance. Nor, of course, do they understand that salaries form a power structure, in which the actual amounts of money involved are in fact of secondary importance. Nobody minds giving secretary X another ten dollars a week, or executive Y another thousand a year—the problem is what X's raise would do to the delicate balance of relationships between all the other secretaries, and the same for Y, on a higher level. As one experienced advertising executive put it, "There's a *system* to salary. There's a subtle relationship between yourself and other people, and when you ask for more money, you're fighting the system. Let's say it's *established* that you make, say, twenty-five, and your colleague makes twenty-seven-five. If you go to twenty-six, you've narrowed the gap between the two of you, and that gap was created for a purpose. So your thousand is going to cost the company twice that, because they're going to have to give something to your colleague if they give something to you, or accept a change in the balance, which upsets everybody's position on the power scale. It isn't *money* or overhead* that's at stake: it's the integrity of the power structure. So what I do is simple. I encourage everyone around me to ask for more money, even the highest executives, who decide on raises. What the

---

* "Overhead" is a common enough word; its counterpart, "underfoot," is less well-known, but represents an essential management fact of life. "Underfoot" is the amount of work a person or a department needs to justify overhead. Most people in any large organization are producing underfoot to sustain an increase in overhead. Neither word has any connection with "profit," a very different concept.

hell, they think they're underpaid too, so the best thing you can do is to tell *them* they deserve more. You also have to do everything you can to encourage raises for people *below* you. That's important! A lot of guys have a 'dog-in-the-manger' attitude toward money; they get itchy and nervous when people below them get raises. That's foolish. So long as you can keep your position on the power scale, they're going to have to adjust your salary upward when the people below you get raises, and when the people above you get more money, they'll pull you along, in order not to widen the gap. At the moment, the number one man here makes $100,000, and the number two man makes $75,000, and I make fifty. Fine. I don't waste my time asking for a raise—that would threaten them, right? I try and persuade number one he deserves at least $125,000. If he gives that to himself, we'll all go up proportionately, without my having had to ask for anything at all. It's the way the system works. From above, salaries don't represent money, except when they're all added together on a yearly basis. They represent a kind of points system which indicates everybody's importance and their position vis-à-vis each other in terms of power."

"Stand Not Upon the Order of Your Going, But Go at Once"[8]

Although not generally recognized as such, quitting is an art.

It obviously requires no great intelligence to walk

out of a job in a fit of rage, because one hasn't been promoted, or given a raise, or simply because one doesn't seem to be getting anywhere. This is the equivalent of ending a chess game by conceding.

For people who know *how* (and above all *when*) to quit, it can be the most rewarding move of all. Most experts at quitting are people who are determined to rise meteorically; at the least sign that their rise is slowing down, or being obstructed, they make a spectacular leap to another company, usually gaining one step up the ladder in the process, and continue from there. Each time they change jobs, they try to reach a new level of power and money, thus getting a good jumping-off point for the next move. "The important thing," as one executive said, "is never to stay too long. When they hire you for a good increase over what you were getting, there's a honeymoon period. The trick is to quit while you're ahead."

Best of all, in the words of one successful quitter, is "to quit on a high." There is a certain power in leaving a job when you're on top, both because it's dramatic, and because it shows that you control the situation. "It's partly shock therapy," explained one quitter. "You bring off a big *coup*, and they expect you to come in asking for money, and instead you come in and say, 'I quit,' and leave them with egg all over their faces."

Quitting is an *action game*, rather like dancing over sword blades. The player is required to leap quickly and unerringly to the next job without ever missing his footing. One slip, and he loses. Once his upward momentum has gone, he becomes just another of the unemployed, and it is always harder to look for a job when you don't have one than when you do. The job you have gives you the power to get the job you want, but without that power you may find that people's interest in you ebbs swiftly. Power players know this, and conform to the etiquette of quitting. Job interviews, for example, can only take place after-hours, over drinks; if they take place during working hours, they are a breach of etiquette toward the company you're currently working for. The mystique of loyalty must be preserved to the very end, and even the people who are thinking of hiring you will be alarmed if you fail to do so. In playing the quitting game, it is therefore necessary to lavish praise and respect on those whom one is about to quit, while at the same time emphasizing one's desire to leave. Nobody wants to hire a person who is contemptuous or disloyal to his present employer. There is a bond that links all those who have power, even when they're in competition, and it is wise to respect this.

"Men Must Endure Their Going Hence . . ."[9]

Difficult as it may be to exert power by quitting, it is even more difficult to take a powerful approach to retirement. To most people, retirement is the ultimate loss of power, a fear intensified by the fact that it is usually accompanied by a sharp drop in income. The most interesting power games are often those played to postpone retirement and those designed to speed an aging executive on his way.

The best way to postpone retirement is to do nothing. A last-minute, desperate burst of activity not only attracts attention to you, but is also likely to make people feel you are a menace to their plans and ambitions. It is better to cultivate the relaxed and confident demeanor of an elder statesman: write no memos, enter no arguments, acquire a reputation as a "peace maker" and, if possible, take up pipe-smoking. It is prudent to join as many industry groups as possible, and to serve on every committee, board and association you can, making speeches whenever possible. It is always difficult for a company to get rid of an executive when he has become a public figure "on the outside," and since such activities are mostly meaningless, they threaten nobody at home. The art of delaying retirement lies in securing the *appearance* of power while giving up its *reality*. To hang on to real power is pointless and self-defeating—it merely makes it necessary for younger, ambitious people to drive you out. By conceding real power to them voluntarily you can not only keep the appearance and the perquisites of power, but give up most of the worry and work that usually accompanies them. Those who fear that their power to retain the comforts of business life—a corner office, a secretary, a liberal expense account, business travel—is threatened, are usually mistaken; it is their power to make decisions that arouses antagonism, or to be more exact, *their power to limit other people's growth to power*. For this reason, the best way to avoid retirement is to give up any influence one may have on other people's salaries, promotions and careers, while holding on to every possible title and honor.

Needless to say, from the opposite point of view, the best way to *speed* an executive's retirement is to keep him involved in power decisions which no longer concern him, and can only cause him trouble and aggravation. Ambitious people who want to get rid of an aging power player are usually reluctant to attack his prerogatives. It seems brutal to scrutinize the expense account of a man in his sixties, or withdraw his credit cards, or prevent his flying to Hawaii for a convention. Company presidents and chairmen are usually fairly near the retirement age themselves, or past it, and have a natural sympathy for people of the same age, however much they may dislike them or wish them gone. The sight of a man in his sixties being shorn of his privileges can only alarm them; they may agree to his being deprived of power, but they will not, as a rule, be pleased to see him humiliated or relieved of his comforts and self-esteem. Past the age of fifty, every man, however powerful, is inclined to feel, "There, but for the Grace of God, go I." [10]

It is therefore much better to lavish respect on anyone you would like to see retired, while at the same time drawing him into every decision and difference of opinion, then shifting the final responsibility to him. At the same time, he can be isolated by setting up committees which will in fact determine whatever happens, but of which he is not a member.

The first step in such a game is to suggest that there are all sorts of "day-to-day" routine matters which the victim doesn't need to be bothered with. Many a man has discovered too late that a whole new set of meetings has been taking place on a regular basis, without his having been invited to join them. "Oh," he will be told, "we didn't think you'd want to be bothered with all that stuff . . ." In some cases, such meetings are held informally, over a drink after five-thirty, say, which restricts the power group to those who are willing to stay on late at the office. This is an effective tactic, since those who work on into the evening not only get a reputation for hard work, but also form a kind of inner power circle. A man who doesn't want to be retired should beware of people collecting for "a little chat" at just about the time he is leaving to catch the commuter train for home. They are usually his executioners.

Other, more subtle, signs can indicate to a man that his time has come. Promoting his secretary is a move that never fails to indicate the erosion of his power. It is also possible to produce anxiety by rapidly changing all the forms and procedures of the office, so that everything looks unfamiliar to him, including the labels and the letterhead. New reports, expense-account vouchers, contract forms and information sheets can quite easily undermine the confidence of an executive nearing retirement age, and when all else fails, it is always possible to change everybody's telephone extension number so that he's always dialing the wrong one.

It is often useful to put a man on the verge of retirement in charge of such things as pension schemes, profit-sharing plans and employee benefits. In the first place, such irritating and time-consuming responsibilities are likely to make him *want* to go, and the sooner, the better. But at the same time, a man about to retire is apt to take a more generous view of company benefits and retirement policies than a younger executive would, and will therefore do his best to improve things from the employee's point of view, particularly if he's likely to benefit from it himself, while the nature of these tasks is sure to make him think about his own retirement.

In the words of one veteran, "When a man reaches sixty, and the people around him and below him are in their thirties and forties, there's bound to be pressure to get him out early. He has power, they want power. It's as simple as that. If you own the place, you can fight back. But if you don't, the only thing you can do is to trade power for comfort. A guy who's willing to become a figurehead can go on forever, but the trouble is, not many people are content to be figureheads, or know how to enjoy it. They eat their hearts out because other people are making decisions, formulating plans, *acting* on things. It's crazy, but a lot of quite smart guys would rather be kicked out than kicked upstairs."

Exaggerated deference and extreme rudeness can both be useful in making a man think about retiring, and it is also possible to make him feel uncomfortable by constantly referring to pop music stars he has never heard of, dances he has never learned and restaurants he has never been to. People under forty discussing things which are absolutely unfamiliar may go far in persuading a man who is over fifty-five that he's hopelessly out of touch. It is possible to talk in a very low voice in an effort to make him believe he is going deaf, though some prefer to shout in a loud voice as if they were already convinced of the victim's deafness.

The important thing is to keep the candidate for retirement constantly on the defensive. If he can be persuaded to talk about the past ("Well, the way we used to do it was . . ."), let him ramble on, then point out that things are now different. Once you have him *defending* the past, you have won. We live in an age when only the present and the future are of interest, and any reference to past events qualifies a man above the age of fifty for "the chop," particularly since the errors which took place in the past are easy to discern, whereas those in the present and future are as yet invisible.

Astute power-seekers should beware of openly attacking the position of a man who is close to retirement. The important thing is to get rid of the individual without destroying the power of his position. If his position is totally eroded, there is nothing left to inherit, and therefore, no point to having driven him out. It may be wiser to exaggerate his importance, in fact—by making his duties seem more necessary and vital than they really are, it is that much easier to suggest that he's too old to fulfill them. Many a man suddenly finds himself being taken seriously at the age of sixty, after a lifetime of relative obscurity. Everyone nearing retirement age should beware of a last-minute inflation of his importance; it is the beginning of the end.

CHAPTER SEVEN

Symbols of Power

At last he had attained his goal. The battle was won. It had been a great labor to subdue this elite, to drill them until they were weary, to tame the ambitious, win over the undecided, impress the arrogant.

—Hermann Hesse
THE GLASS BEAD GAME

There was a sameness to these men . . . They ate in the same restaurants, wore the same suits, wore Gucci loafers.

—Zan Thompson

Foot Power

You might not think that feet are symbols of power, except in those paintings of ancient tyrants putting one foot on the chest of a vanquished enemy, or resting an armored and spurred foot negligently on the tail of a dying dragon, but sometimes feet tell the whole story. Most people will only expose the soles of their shoes when they feel themselves to be in a position of protected power or superiority, not because they fear they may have holes in their shoes, but because the sole of the foot is a particularly sensitive portion of the anatomy. Even the toughest person will hesitate before walking barefooted over gravel or hot sand, and most of us are extremely ticklish—and therefore vulnerable—in this area. When men cross their legs, they have a tendency to lower their toes, as if they were protecting the soles of their feet, despite the fact that this places considerable strain on the muscles and tendons of the ankle. It's a reflex action, an indication of the fact that we are at our most comfortable with both feet on the ground, firmly planted, ready to spring up if we have to.

Watch an executive in action, talking over a problem. He sits back, one leg crossed over the other, apparently self-assured and relaxed. At the moment when the discussion becomes serious and difficult, he will almost always uncross his legs, place both feet on the ground, and lean forward with his hands on his knees, assuming his position of maximum power. At this point, the other person has two choices: he can do the same thing, in which case they will now be hunched forward toward each other in a mutual combat position, or he can cross *his* legs and lean back, expressing indifference and lack of fear at the other's power stance. Oh yes, our feet give us away: they swing back and forth, showing impatience or doubt; we tuck them out of sight under the chair in moments of timidity and fear; we place them solidly before us to indicate that we're not going to budge or change our minds; we turn the toes toward each other in a position of maidenly deference when talking to a very powerful person, and place them far apart, with the toes pointing outward at a forty-five degree angle to show our contemptuous superiority.

Power people are very sensitive about feet, perhaps because the question of what to do with them has only recently re-emerged. In the past it was a matter of careful etiquette, but the advent of the box-like desk in the nineteenth century, which protected a man from his visitors and employees like a wooden Maginot Line, made foot-behavior and foot-signals a lost art. Now that desks have become mere tables, often just a plate-glass or wood shelf on thin chrome legs, feet are once again painfully visible.* Few people know what to do with them, though most power-

---

* Desks can be useful in determining their occupants' style. Many people feel more comfortable and secure behind a huge, heavy wooden desk, and it is always easier to do business with such people if you can tempt them out from behind it and get them to sit on a sofa or chair in the open. If you can't, then put your hat or brief case on the desk if you want to make them nervous. Note that people with old-fashioned desks that serve as barriers almost always leave them to say "yes," and sit behind them to say "no." Once they have taken refuge behind five-hundredweight of mahogany, you can't argue with them.

ful people prefer to leave them on the floor, where they belong, and to keep them as still as possible.

What to put on them is another problem. When they were hidden behind a heavy desk, it was possible for everyone to wear black boots, sturdy and practical objects, guaranteed to keep the wearer's feet snug and dry, and indicating power and class only by the quality of the leather and the perfection of the shine. J. P. Morgan's boots were not very different from those of his clerks, except that he had a valet to shine them and make sure that the heels never wore down. It was, in this sense, if no other, an age of equality. Today, with feet once more out in the open, they can be used to mark all sorts of social distinctions and to emphasize a variety of claims to power.

One thing is basic: power people have their shoes polished, or do it themselves. In all shoe-wearing cultures, and in every age, a dirty shoe is sign of weakness. Latin American gentlemen of the old school spent hours sitting in the streets having their shoes shined, and the best place to see important people lined up is at the shoeshine stand in any big office building at about nine in the morning. Many powerful people have a second shoeshine after lunch, when the shoeshine man makes his afternoon visit to their offices to restore the morning's gloss. At night, when they go home, they can afford to get their shoes dusty and scuffed, since they are leaving the world of power. This explains why there are no shoeshine stands at commuter stations, and very few open after five—nobody needs a shine on the way home.

Powerful people generally wear simple shoes— Peal & Co., Ltd., five-eyelet shoes from Brooks Brothers, for example, and always put the laces in straight, not crisscrossed, and use round, waxed shoelaces. Shoes that have square toes, or high heels, or large brass buckles, or stitching in odd places, or are cut like jodhpur boots, are all definitely not power symbols, and to be avoided. The investment of sixty or seventy dollars in a good pair of shoes is a sound move for anyone interested in power. Since people go to great lengths not to look at other people's faces, or expose their own to direct scrutiny, they tend to see a man's shoes more than any other part of him, and when they think of the person, the image that stays in their minds is that of his shoes.

Recently, loafers with little brass snaffle bit buckles have become fashionable, and these are all right if they genuinely come from Gucci's, in New York. Imitations are subtly recognizable, and absolutely out. David Mahoney, for example, wears black patent leather Guccis, with a red-and-green cloth stripe and a brass snaffle bit across the instep, and these are strong symbols of success and confidence, though like all fashionable objects, they may already be out of date by the time you have bought a pair. For the moment though, they are acceptable. I recently heard two businessmen talking in the King Cole bar of the St. Regis Hotel in New York, and one of them said to the other, "Listen, don't forget you promised to take me to Gucci and help me buy a pair of shoes." The second man, wearing his Gucci loafers, of course, nodded wisely, and replied, "Well sure, I *will*, but if you need help maybe you're not ready for Guccis. You can't put Guccis on Florsheim feet, you know."

Florsheim shoes! The ultimate foot put-down, along with people who wear anklet socks, exposing unsightly stretches of skin every time they cross their legs, almost as terrible as wearing shoes of crisscrossed, plaited leather in the summer. You understand, the right shoes won't *make* you powerful, but you may as well start somewhere in learning to read the symbols of power, and shoes are basic.

"Phone Me in the Limo"

In simpler societies than our own, the symbols of power are instantly recognizable, whether they consist of a necklace of glass beads or a crown and scepter. When there is only one visible power structure, the symbols of power are generally easy to read. Such relatively simple hierarchies exist even within our larger, more complex society—in the Army, for example, everyone's relative power is clearly marked, and every soldier and officer can instantly tell the position of a complete stranger. In the armed services, a man's career is summarized on his shoulders, his sleeves and his chest, for all to see, and the same is true for officers of the law, uniformed postal workers, firemen and teen-aged youth gangs. This is a simple way to mark differences of power, like the eagle feather headdress of a Pawnee Indian chief, the gold spurs of a medieval knight, the brown shoes that used to distinguish naval aviators in summer tans from ordinary line officers, and a thousand other peculiarities of dress and tradition.

In our everyday world, the marks of power are necessarily more ambiguous, and a good deal of the anxiety that is evident in modern life derives from the constant struggle to *guess* other people's relative positions of power. Since we cannot wear stripes on our sleeves or stars on our shoulders, we are obliged to invent more subtle distinctions, and can only hope they will be recognized for what they're meant to be.

The problem is that one person's power symbols may be meaningless to the next person: it's all a matter of guesswork, and as a result even the smallest things become important to someone. One executive I know has a firm, if unreasonable, prejudice against French cuffs, another despises people who wear buttondown collars, still another, a major figure in book publishing, believes that no man who wears a belt instead of suspenders can be trusted. Most of these prejudices are totally irrational, though when all is said and done, it is probably just as sensible to promote a man because he shares your taste in shirts (or imitates it) as for any other reason. However, the important thing is that these prejudices do not form a system that can be readily deciphered: the seeker after power must guess what the significant signs are, and guess right. Since most people's fixations in this area are based on dim, ancestral memories of what their fathers used to wear, or what they were taught to wear at school or college, or the notion that anything that doesn't come from Brooks Brothers is flashy and untrustworthy, power signals outside the armed services are often baffling, and in an age when women are beginning to fill positions of power, sometimes even incomprehensible.

Because they are baffling does not mean they do not exist. David Mahoney's enormous office, with a view of the midtown Manhattan skyline and both rivers, is a symbol of power, and an obvious one, but so are his carefully cut blue suit, his Gucci loafers, his midwinter tan and his command of a limousine. The "limo" syndrome is, in fact, a very common barometer of power. On one level, a limousine is of course a comfortable and desirable way of moving around town, one of the obvious prerogatives of success, but on another, it is important because it clearly and instantly defines your rank. As one senior executive told me, "When I get into the limo on a rainy evening in December, and look out the window, it isn't speed that I think about. For God's sake, the subway would be faster. No, I say to myself, 'Those people out there are getting cold and wet, and I'm in here warm and dry.' I had to go through a lot of shit to get where I am, but when I look at people waiting for a bus in the rain, it makes it all worthwhile. They know I've made it. I know I've made it. You can't beat a limo for that."

Even among those who have limousines, there are distinctions of power. Rented limousines are less prestigious than ones which are owned, Rolls Royces carry more prestige than Cadillacs, and nothing quite equals a Mercedes 600 with the chrome painted black and the rear windows tinted to make the occupant invisible. Telephones in limousines have become so commonplace that they are no longer a significant power symbol, though it is interesting to note that several radio supply companies offer dummy radio-telephone aerials at $19.95 for your "limo"—they aren't connected to anything! The "limo" game is much like any other, after all. One businessman I know rents a limousine whenever he needs one, but always finds out the driver's first name and slips him ten dollars. He then will say, "Listen, Harry, I think we'll take the Midtown Tunnel today, right?"— to imply that it's *his* car and chauffeur, not a rented one. He also sits up front, which tends to give him an air of proprietorship, as well as the illusion of familiarity with the driver. With power symbols, it's attention to detail that counts. I have myself seen a respectable businessman tip the bartender of a big hotel five dollars at lunchtime, with the instruction that when he returned in the evening, the bartender was to say, "Good evening, Mr. X, you'll have your usual?"

Not being in the armed services, we have to manufacture our own system of power signals, using whatever opportunities and materials are at hand, searching for ways to prove that we are, in the words of a West Coast producer, "very important people."

The symbols of power are all around us, crying out to be recognized, changing with each new fashion in dress and decoration, becoming more widespread and complex as more people reach for power. When I first began to work in publishing, one telephone was considered ample for each person. In the case of very busy and important people, the instrument itself might have a row of buttons, allowing the user to buzz his (or her) secretary and to have two or three extra lines. Over the years, the telephone has blossomed as a power symbol, and in the same office that used to contain one instrument, unobtrusively planted on the desk, there are now four—one on the desk, one at either end of the sofa, and a bright red push-button private telephone, that doesn't go through the switchboard, on a stand beside the desk. The number of lines available has not increased, unless you include the unlisted private phone, nor is there any real increase in efficiency, but the sight of all those telephones certifies that this is a "power center," where instant and constant communication is necessary and available.

Telephones are not necessarily a convenience—for many they are a prop. I know a good many people who arrange to have their secretaries call them at lunch so that a telephone can be brought to the table and plugged in, and what's more, won't eat in a restaurant where they can't have a phone at the table. One top executive in New York has a private bathroom with a telephone on the wall next to the toilet, which is certainly a convenience for a busy man, but not a very public symbol of power. Another major corporation executive has telephones concealed in small green, rustic boxes attached to trees on his estate, so that he can make calls and receive them even when he's walking to the pool or the boathouse, the insistent ringing rising above the gentle woodland noises of the birds and the wind. Once people have associated telephones with prestige, there's no end to what they can do. There are radio-telephones built into handsome leather briefcases, which sound a soft, distinctive hum when you're being called, and sell for just over $2,000—well worth it in case somebody rings you on your way from your office to your "limo." More plebeian telephone addicts carry rolls of dimes, fresh from the bank, in their pockets, and set up shop in telephone booths, desperately anxious "to keep in touch" at all times.

The telephone is a perfect example of how we make do with what we've got to create power symbols. What was invented as a mundane and unattractive convenience, we have made into a complex mark of status and power, as if by instinct. If we have a visitor in our office, we can demean him by accepting telephone calls while he's talking, or impress him by saying, "Excuse me, it's the chairman of the board calling"—or the President of the United States, or "the Coast" or a call from overseas—and finally, if we want to flatter him, we can say, "Hold *all* my calls, whoever it is." Nothing puts a person in their

215

place better than carrying on a dialogue with a man who has a telephone receiver cocked between his ear and his shoulder, and who says, "Keep right on talking, I'm listening, I just have to take this call."

The telephone can effectively establish your power over the people in your presence particularly since the instrument is in *your* hands. They are limited to talking to you, or filling in the time by making whispered small-talk between themselves, while you can be connected to anyplace in the world, or place calls to people far more important than your visitors. You don't even have to *place* the calls. You can simply tell your secretary, "No calls, but if Henry Kissinger calls me back, put him through."

Years ago I was invited to lunch by a world-famous motion picture director who had expressed "interest," as a fleeting and ill-informed whim is called in the trade, in an idea of mine, and had vaguely suggested I might like to fly to Los Angeles and "develop" it. He summoned me to lunch at The Four Seasons restaurant in New York at twelve forty-five, together with his lawyer, my lawyer and two studio flacks. At the appointed time, the five of us were seated by the reflecting pool, but our host was conspicuously absent. A captain arrived from time to time to bring us bulletins—"He's on his way," "He's due any moment," "He says to have a drink"—and to bring us fresh rounds of drinks. By one-fifteen, everybody at the table was glazed with fatigue and alcohol, and any appetite they might have had was quenched by having consumed several baskets of rolls, breadsticks and croissants and a pound of butter. Nobody, however, had had the courage to order.

When the great man finally arrived at one-thirty, unapologetic and cheerful, he sat down, and before saying a word to us, ordered a telephone to be brought to the table. As soon as it was plugged in, he had himself connected to his chauffeur, then cruising the midtown streets in the "limo," and proceeded to give a series of animated directions, most of them having to do with suits that had to be picked up from the tailor, or taken to the cleaners. Communication from his luncheon table to his limousine having been established, he placed a call to the West Coast, and then, cradling the receiver to his ear, appeared to notice us for the first time. "Say," he said, "have you guys ordered yet? I just have to phone my wife, but why don't you all have another round of drinks?"*

Few power symbols are as versatile as the telephone. Let us say that it is necessary to show a business associate that you are still alive and employed, but that for various reasons you do not much want to talk to him, perhaps because he will then pin you down to a lunch date. Or perhaps there's a deal you don't want to say No to, can't make up your mind to say Yes to, and don't want to lose for lack of having expressed interest. By means of the telephone, you can keep your options open for a considerable period of time—you simply telephone the other person at a time when he or she is guaranteed to be out, lunchtime for example, leaving a message to say you called.

* A refinement of this game is now available to patrons of New York's La Borsa di Roma restaurant, which provides the services of a secretary, Ms. Diana Danar, at no additional charge. Customers can dictate letters, place overseas telephone calls, make airline reservations and order birthday presents for their wives right at the table, without, in the owner's words, "letting the tortellini get cold." There's no end in sight. Yesterday I saw two men lunching together, and each had his own telephone plugged in at the table! One wonders why they bothered to have lunch together at all.

You are now in the position of having initiated a telephone exchange; whatever happens, you can now say, "I've been trying to reach you." When the other person calls back, you do not accept the call; you ask your secretary to say you're already speaking to someone and will call back shortly. You then return the call the next day, once again choosing a time when you can be sure the other person won't be there—say, five minutes before he or she gets to the office in the morning. When your call is returned, you are, of course, in a meeting. With very little effort, this exchange can be kept going for at least a week without the two parties ever making verbal contact, yet nobody can accuse the initiator of the exchange of not trying. On the contrary, as the person who started the series of calls, the initiator gets credit for attempting to open communication, even if it never takes place. The person who receives a telephone call is always in an inferior position of power to the person who placed it. This explains why people with a sense of power do not like answering services or mechanical devices. People only have to phone and leave a message, and you become responsible for getting back to them. The proper power response to a call you don't want to take is to have your secretary ask the caller to try you at home after six-thirty, then make sure that nobody is at home to take a message. The moment a message has been taken, the ball is in your court, and all further responsibility for completing the exchange is yours.

As a general rule, the power game in telephoning is to have the maximum ability to place telephone calls together with the minimum possibility of receiving them—the flow, in other words, should always be outward. When input equals or exceeds output, there is a loss of power. This is not as difficult a trick as it sounds. The more telephone calls you make, the less time is available for people to reach you. By carrying this procedure to its extreme, it is possible to delay almost any matter until it has ceased to be of importance to either party without ever being accused of negligence or indifference.

One peculiar aspect of telephone power is the fact that a touch of the dial or buttons defiles. Among power-conscious people, it is all right to pick up a telephone receiver, but not to actually place a call. No matter how hard the telephone company's researchers work to make dialing easier (and with area codes, direct dialing and push-buttons, it could hardly be easier), there is still a general feeling that you lose power unless you can have someone else do the fingerwork. In part this stems from the power player's traditional reluctance to pick up the receiver until the party he or she is calling is actually on the line and waiting, a power game so familiar that we hardly even notice it any more, but there is also a slightly subliminal feeling that dialing a telephone is manual labor of a kind. With rare exceptions, power people do not dial telephones, use Xerox machines, add up figures themselves, type or sharpen pencils. The first sign of a rise to power is often creeping helplessness—people who have dialed their own telephones for years, or rushed to the Xerox machine to run off a copy of a letter, not only *won't* do these things any more, but even claim not to know how. As one secretary told me, "We had a guy here, an assistant manager who started in the mailroom, where one of his jobs, actually, was looking after all the copying machines. When they didn't work, you phoned down to the mailroom and he came up and fixed it. A few days ago he was promoted, and the next thing I know, he's standing by my desk holding a piece of paper and he says, 'Could you run off some copies of this for me? I don't know how to use the machine.' He's forgotten how to dial a telephone too. Until his new secretary arrives, he wanders around asking people to place *calls* for him. He's not so dumb. The less you have to do for yourself, the more power you have."

Status Marks—"A Gold-Plated Thermos Is a Man's Best Friend"

The more elaborate and expensive pieces of office machinery are seldom power symbols—merely knowing how to use them, or even where they are, indicates a low power rating. Electronic pocket calculators, when they were first introduced, had a certain *cachet*, and it is still possible to use them in negotiations by performing what appear to be complicated problems in higher mathematics whenever money is being discussed. When turning down someone's request for a $1,250 raise, for example, it is useful to do a quick calculation on your pocket machine and ask if he or she has any idea what percentage of the present salary the raise would be, a question which is irrelevant, but unanswerable by anyone who doesn't have their own calculator at hand. Slide rules serve much the same purpose, and have the advantage of taking longer to use.

If calculators never quite caught on as power symbols, it is partly because they seem related to adding machines, and thus associated with supermarket checkers and accounting clerks, and partly because people in power aren't much interested in mathematics—they're interested in winner-take-all, not profit-and-loss. If they can force you to agree with their view of a situation or a deal, they can usually rely on having someone else work out the details and be pretty sure of making a profit somewhere along the way. An obvious attention to mathematics seems to them small-minded and self-limiting. "Once a guy pulls out a calculator," says a well-known negotiator, "I know I've got him. He's interested in the mathematics of the deal, which means he's already sold on the idea and the substance of it. Guys who do that never stop to think whether the deal is worth making in the first place. They're too busy working out how much money they can make, or what it's going to cost."

An office calculator on the desk is therefore a sign of weakness and overattention to detail. On the other hand, Presidential example has turned yellow legal pads into power symbols, cheap as they are. By sitting back and writing everything down on a yellow legal pad while the other person is talking, you are in the position of keeping the record, of *having the facts*. Nothing is more inhibiting than the sight of someone carefully writing down everything you say, and many quite powerful negotiators are thrown off-balance when faced with an opponent who calmly nods and writes away industriously. A further advantage to the use of yellow legal pads is that they provide you with a perfect excuse to avoid looking at the person who is talking, thus hiding your own reactions—so long as your eyes are on the paper, you give nothing away. What is more, you can punctuate the discussion by tearing off a page when you've come to the end of it, a noise which serves as a warning that the meeting has gone on for too long or no longer interests you.

People who use yellow legal pads in power games nearly always cross one leg over the other and sit well back, so as to hide the surface of the pad. Secrecy is essential to the proper use of the pad, all the more so if it is merely being used for doodling or calculating one's income tax during a contract negotiation. Gifted power players have long since learned that when a man who has been assiduously writing on a yellow legal pad *stops* writing, he has made up his mind. This is the moment to shut up. Noah Levine, a well-known labor lawyer and a gifted negotiator, has developed the use of the yellow legal pad into a fine art. "Look," he says, "on one level, it's just a working tool for lawyers, right? But on another, it's a weapon. Everyone is talking away, and you're nodding wisely and writing on your pad. If the other guys aren't writing things down too, pretty soon you're in control of the situation. When someone *else* is writing things down, I watch his pencil. If it's moving fast, he's interested, but not very; if it slows down, he's getting more interested; if he begins to underline things heavily, he's either getting angry or preparing to say no; if the pencil moves erratically, in circles or zigzags, the guy has lost interest altogether, he's doodling, he's just letting you talk yourself out, jerking you off; and if he *stops* writing, he's decided what he's going to do. It's important to watch for that moment. You may have a guy ready to sign, but if you go on presenting your case after his pencil has stopped, you can blow the deal. It's like the old salesman's saying: 'When you've made the sale, shut up.' Another thing: if two guys are negotiating and they both have legal pads, it's a Mexican stand-off.

Nothing gets done, because both parties are busy protecting themselves. When you're selling or persuading, you just don't use it—you have to go in empty-handed. It's a classic defensive weapon."

Dictating machines are in a somewhat different category; at one time they had a certain prestige, since their presence on a desk implied at least that the person had the use of a secretary and needed to answer a good deal of correspondence. They can no longer be said, however, to confer any real prestige. A recent IBM advertisement shows three "executives" (interestingly enough, a middle-aged white man, a young woman and a black man) sitting at identical desks in a row, each dictating into a small microphone. Two young women at smaller, less impressive desks, are busily transcribing their dictation, by means of a centralized system. The office contains no status marks of any kind, except that the woman executive has a bowl of red carnations on her desk. Far from serving as power symbols, the "dictating input system" more or less puts the "executives" and the secretaries on the same level, and indeed the only happy, smiling face in the picture is that of one of the secretaries—everyone else looks like a zombie. In real life, of course, each executive would manage to have distinguished his or her desk from the others' in some way, and one of them would be leaning on the smiling secretary's modesty-paneled, formica desk, persuading her to type *his* memo first. Nobody in the picture seems to have a pencil or a yellow legal pad or a chair for visitors—it is an egalitarian view of executive work, far removed from any recognizable reality.

The only IBM product that serves as a power symbol is the IBM Selectric II typewriter, provided that it's used by the executive's secretary, of course, and also provided that it's equipped with a carbon ribbon and Bookface Academic type. Letters typed on such a machine have more authority than those which are not, and most executives would far rather fight to get their secretary the right kind of IBM typewriter than a raise for her. In some companies, the use of such machines is restricted to very senior executives, and certain typefaces are reserved for the most powerful people—the chairman of the board or the president, for example. Such small signs as these are quite often reliable indicators of power. A woman I know, who had asked for a $10,000-a-year raise, was offered $5,000, an IBM typewriter for her secretary and the right to have her name printed on her office stationery. "I accepted the deal," she told me, "silly as it sounds. Above a certain level, they can only give you so much, and a lot of what you're offered is symbolic. All the little things, like your own letterhead, or the right to fly first-class, or a private telephone, count for something. The trick is to find out what's important to the people who are at the top. If the people who make up the inner power circle all use Pica Elite type for their letters, then you can be sure it means something when they take away your secretary's typewriter and bring back one with Pica Elite. It's not just a sign of acceptance, it's a kind of marker, a promise that you're being thought of, and will eventually get what you want in terms of money, even if it can't be done right away. You have to read the signs.

"The first place I worked, the power symbol was a gold-plated water Thermos. Some people had them, some people didn't, but you couldn't just go out and buy one. That would have undermined the system, it would have been an insult, an act of revolution.

At a certain point, the office manager simply put a gold-plated Thermos on your desk, with a little tray and two glasses, and that was that. I never found out who gave the order—maybe she just *knew*—but a guy who hoped for a big raise, say $5,000, and deserved it, and who only got let's say, $2,500, would get this Thermos, as if the management were saying, 'Don't worry, we'll take care of you as soon as we can, here's our marker.' Other places, it used to be the key to the executive washroom. That was a very big deal in a lot of places in the fifties, and I remember that my ex-husband was ecstatic when he found an envelope on his desk one morning with *the* key in it. That wasn't all. Once you had the key, the head of the mailroom put a clean towel in your desk drawer every day—no more paper towels from the dispenser! These days, the executive washroom bit has pretty much gone out of style, maybe because it automatically excludes women, maybe because in the new office buildings the real power sign is your *own* bathroom, with a shower.

"Nobody is immune. I know one guy who owned his own company and was being wooed by a big conglomerate. They offered him everything they could think of, stock, a lifetime seat on the board of directors, use of the company plane, a limo—he turned it all down. Then they offered him one thing more: a couple of floors in a new building, with a private bathroom—a bathroom with a real bath, and a shower, and a heated towel rack!—and a private elevator. That did it. He accepted. Afterward, we were talking and he was a little sad. 'It's as if I'd sold my own child,' he told me, 'but I couldn't help it. It wasn't so much the money—I'm already a rich man, and in a real sense I'll have *less* power, because they'll have control. But there was something about the

225

idea of a full-sized elevator all to myself, an elevator with just one button in it that only goes to my office, that I couldn't resist. It was like being offered the chance to play God.' "

At the top, the chance to play God is perhaps the greatest reward of all. Nobody imagines that a corporation's profits will be significantly increased by using a helicopter to transport the chairman of the board from his home in Connecticut to the midtown heliport and back, nor can it be argued that the convenience of such an arrangement is worth the enormous cost. As a symbol of power, however, it can hardly be improved upon. "I didn't know how rich and successful I was," commented one company's chairman, "until I got into our new helicopter and took off from my own lawn."

For others, the symbols of ultimate power are less grandiose. One company president realized he had "made it to the top" when he put down his brief case, never to pick it up again. "When you're in management," he says, "you carry a brief case to meetings, and the brief case, in a funny way, is more important than you are. You go there with reports, contracts, documents, files, information, and your role is to interpret them or deliver them. Someone else could take the same brief case full of material; you're really a kind of thinking messenger boy at $100,000 a year. But when you have real power, all they want is *you*. You come with nothing in your hands because what you're bringing isn't expertise, or information, but the right to say yes or no. The guy who has the power is the one who walks in empty-handed. The ones with the attaché cases are spear carriers—they can argue the facts, present the case, set the parameters of the deal, but the guy without one has the power."

Of course there is a progression in the significance of brief cases as there is in anything else. The bulkier the case, the less power its carrier usually has, the lowest power status being that of a salesman's sample case, a big, boxlike piece of luggage in heavy vinyl. Attaché cases that open up to reveal a complete desk, with files and a blotter, are only useful for impressing elderly ladies on airplanes. Elegant, thin attaché cases, however expensive and magnificent, always look like somebody's birthday present to a young executive on the make. Brief cases with embossed patterns on them, whether genuine Vuitton or not, are meaningless as displays of power. All one can say is that a man making less than $50,000 ought to carry an ordinary leather brief case that opens at the top and has two handles, and that it should be old, battered and much-traveled; a man making more than $50,000 but less than $100,000 should carry a thin leather portfolio, the simpler the better; a man making more than $100,000 should never carry anything. As Richard L. Simon, the publisher and co-founder of Simon and Schuster, once said to an editor who was struggling home with a heavy brief case full of manuscripts and contracts, while Simon stood empty-handed in the hall, waiting for the elevator, "You editor; me publisher." When in doubt, it is best to carry anything you need in a plain manila mailing envelope; this suggests that you don't normally carry anything at all, but have been obliged to take some documents along with you at the last moment. By contrast, a brief case, even when it's empty, suggests that you make a habit of lugging bulky work around with you like a donkey.

It should be noted that women executives nearly always carry brief cases. Theirs is a different position—having only recently emerged as a power group, they feel the need to carry an unmistakable masculine symbol of authority. A woman with a brief case is automatically accorded executive power status, provided she does not also carry a handbag.

One widespread use of symbols in business is as incentives to better performance. An excellent example is Ewing Kauffman's system for encouraging his salesmen to expand their sales of Marion Laboratories' products. Kauffman, whose maxim is "Produce or get out," is a master salesman himself, who has pyramided a $5,500 investment in a pill for alleviating fatigue into a vast corporation and a personal fortune in excess of $150,000,000—a fortune built up in part by the idea of grinding up oyster shells discarded by food processors to make into a calcium supplement pill, but mostly on an instinctive knowledge of how to motivate people to perform. Although he sometimes calls executives in and tells them that before they leave his office one of three things will happen—they will be fired, will quit or will change—Kauffman's real genius in getting people to deliver for him lies in making them accept a system of symbolic rewards as finely structured as those of a European monarchy.

Fortune reported that "Many of the rewards for performing at Marion have as much symbolic as monetary value. A man who increases his sales enough to win a big bonus also wins a Marion signet ring. If he wins rings for two years, plus a national or regional sales award, he becomes a member of the Marion Eagles. The dozen or so salesmen who are Eagles are entitled to special blazers, stationery, and calling cards, as well as extra holidays, and a company-purchased Buick Centurion (run-of-the-mill salesmen drive Fords, Chevrolets, or Plymouths). An

Eagle who wins *three* rings can become eligible to enter the even more lofty ranks of the Marion M Club, which also has about a dozen members. M Clubbers drive Oldsmobile 98's and are entitled to other perquisites, including the "bumping privilege," which allows them to take the seat of any Marion officer, including Kauffman, at company banquets and other functions."[1]

These marks of approbation are duplicated, in varying forms, in almost every large company. At National Liberty Life Insurance, there are invitations to "Inspiration Breaks" in the company cafeteria, at which astronauts, sports champions and evangelists encourage the executives to "Come to Christ," and explain that the company's "senior partner is the Lord"; special status attaches to meetings in what amounts to a secluded prayer retreat, where, as one executive put it, "When we have a problem, we pray."[2] At Holiday Inns' corporate headquarters in Memphis senior executives are presented with "great sign lapel buttons" (replicas of a Holiday Inn signboard), a greenbound book on "Attitudes," listing 104 "positive personality traits," and invited to attend "executive fellowship breakfasts" on Wednesdays at 7:30 A.M., presided over by what may be the only "corporate chaplain" in American business, The Rev. W. A. ("Dub") Nance.[3]

Furniture

Office furnishings have strong symbolic value. Take
file cabinets—in themselves, they are meaningless.
Most executives, in fact, place them out of sight, in
their secretaries' offices or cubicles. Put a lock on the
filing cabinet, however, and it becomes a power symbol, however unsightly and bulky. When you want to
take a file out, you have to walk over to it and un-
lock it, the implication being that it contains material of great importance and confidentiality. Given
a lock, the filing cabinet can become a central power
symbol, well worth having in your own office, no
matter how much space it takes up.

Furniture can tell one a great deal about the person. A *New York Times* reporter remarked of one
tycoon that "Callers, suppliants and salesmen who
make their way to [the chairman's] 42nd floor office,
get swallowed up and find themselves peering between their knees at him,' helplessly sunk in
deep, soft chairs.[4] This is a fairly common power
game, and can be observed in many offices. One
young lady, job-hunting, noted that almost every senior executive in the publishing business had a low
sofa. "You go in," she said, "and they ask you to sit
down on the sofa, which is about four feet lower than
his desk chair, so he's looking down at you, and
you're looking up from nowhere, with your ass practically on the floor and your knees up in the air. You
couldn't arrange things better to make a person seem
really unimportant."

This is not altogether true. There are more elaborate ways of making people feel unimportant. Harry

Cohn, the tyrannical president of Columbia Pictures, designed his office in imitation of Mussolini's, a huge, elongated room with the desk at the far end, raised above floor level. "The portal to the position of power was a massive sound-proofed door which had no knob and no keyhole on the outside. It could only be opened by a buzzer operated from Cohn's or his secretary's desk . . . In later years Glenn Ford noted discoloration of the door jamb at mid-level; it had been soiled by the sweat of innumerable palms of those who had passed through to an audience with Harry Cohn."[5]

This is a somewhat extreme example of power decoration, but even lesser power players will usually arrange their offices so that their visitors are obliged to sit in as much discomfort as possible. It is particularly helpful to make sure that all the ash-trays are just slightly out of reach so that visitors sitting in low chairs and unable to rise have to stretch awkwardly to dispose of their cigarette ash.

The disposition of furniture is a better indication of power than the furniture itself. Some offices run to luxurious decoration, others do not, but the scale of luxury is more likely to be dependent upon the management's whim than the occupant's status. At *Playboy*'s Chicago headquarters, for instance, even the junior editors have "plush, cork-paneled hideaways, many equipped with soft chairs, stereo sets and stunning secretaries,"[6] an atmosphere of sybaritic luxury that emanates from Hugh Hefner's vision of himself, rather than from any power they may have.

Power lies in how you use what you have, not in the accouterments per se. All the leather and chrome in the world will not replace a truly well-thought-out power scheme. A large office is pointless unless it is arranged so that a visitor has to walk the length of it before getting to your desk, and it is valuable to put as many objects as possible in his path—coffee tables, chairs and sofas, for example—to hinder his progress. However small the office, it is important to have the visitor's chair facing toward you, so that you are separated by the width of your desk. This is a much better power position than one in which the visitor sits *next* to the desk, even though it may make access to your desk inconvenient for you. When a small office is very narrow (and most are) it is often useful to have the desk placed well forward in the room, thus minimizing the space available for the visitor, and increasing the area in which it is possible for you to retreat, at least psychologically. Thus, in a typical small office, the alternative desk/chair relationships would look like this—

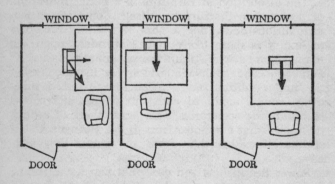

Of these possibilities, number three is by far the strongest power position for the occupant. Behind his desk, he has left himself plenty of room, so that he isn't likely to feel that his back is against the wall when arguing with a caller or a colleague, while his visitor is tightly enclosed, with little psychological space and breathing room. In drawing number two, the visitor is placed in an aggressive position, having more space than the occupant, and being further forward in the room. In drawing number one, the occupant has no power position at all, and is obliged to turn to his right at an uncomfortable angle to talk to the visitor. Power, let it be remembered, moves in direct lines. (Attempts to do without desks altogether, though popular in the recording and the broadcasting businesses, have never caught on. The desk performs a useful social function in power terms that is hard to eliminate.)

In larger offices, power arrangements are more varied. Most people prefer to divide their offices into two separate sections, one containing a couch, which can be used for informal, semisocial discussions, where decisions do not actually have to be made, and the other containing the usual desk and chair, for "pressure situations" and confrontations, in which the whole object is to reach a firm decision. In entering such an office, it is therefore very important to notice in what area the occupant wishes you to take a seat. If you have come to negotiate a deal, and he moves toward the sofa, you can be fairly sure that he has decided to stall you; if he asks you to sit at his desk, you can be equally sure that he is ready for serious negotiation. At the same time, you can influence *him*. By firmly seating yourself at the desk, you make it clear that you want an answer; by sitting on the sofa, you demonstrate that you are not eager to conclude the deal. A certain tug-of-war is often evident when the two parties have different goals in mind, the "host" trying to push the visitor toward the sofa, with the plea that he will be "more comfortable" there, the visitor obstinately making his way toward the desk, or vice versa, of course.

Some people are past masters at this game. When he comes to my office, a well-known lawyer of my acquaintance always manages to sit on the sofa between me and the telephone on the end table when he wants to persuade me to do something I would just as soon not do. In the first place, he has trapped me in a semisocial position, by getting us both on the sofa; in the second place, he has effectively cut me off from the telephone, so that I can't be interrupted by a call. In this position, he has me at his mercy— we are seated side by side, at the same level, both facing the window and away from desk and telephone. When he wants to *sell* me on something, he sits on the chair in front of my desk, then gradually works it around until it's beside mine, so that he's moved to my side of the barrier, so to speak. There are several ways in which he assures himself of this position, the first being to put his portfolio, hat and coat on the sofa, so that we *can't* sit on it, the second being to plead mild deafness, so that he has an excuse to come to my side of the desk, which implies an invasion of my territory. An attempt to prevent his moving closer by buying an armchair so massive and heavy as to be practically immovable failed; he pleads a bad back and asks the secretary to find him a simple, straight chair, which he then places exactly where he wants it.

This subtle use of space can best be understood by seeing how the two different areas, the semisocial and the pressure, relate to each other spatially—

Typical office divided into "pressure area" and "semi-social area." If the occupant is intent on serious business, he should try to place his visitor in position A, squarely facing the desk. If he wants to delay or placate a visitor, he should try to place him in position D on sofa. An aggressive visitor will either move his chair to position B, or assume position C on sofa, forcing the occupant to sit at D, cut off by an intruder from his own telephone. Chair E is the weakest power position, and is reserved for unimportant third parties. Note that the coffee table separates one area from the other, and that the sofa should be as low as possible.

Still larger offices are sometimes divided into *three* areas, one end being set aside for a large conference

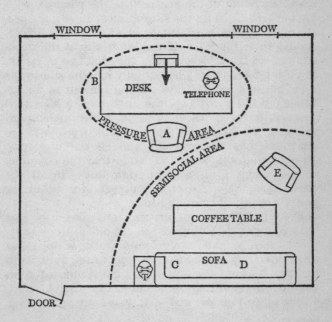

table, with chairs around it. This is frequently the case with the offices of chairmen of the board, and is usually a sign that they want to maintain control over the board by holding its meetings on their own territory, rather than having them in a separate board room. As a general rule, boards that meet in an office a corner of which is used as a board meeting area have less power and autonomy than those that meet in a separate board room, and are to that extent less valuable to be on.

Board-room tables, it should be noted, are almost never round, since it is necessary to have a very precise gradation of power, and above all, imperative that the most important person, usually the chairman, should sit at the end next to the window, with his back to it, while the second most important person, usually the president or chief executive officer, should sit to his right. If the latter sits at the opposite end of the table (playing "mother," so to speak, in dining-table terms) he not only has the sun in his eyes, but is almost always placing himself in an adversary position vis-à-vis the chairman, a sign that there is either a power struggle going on between them, or the likelihood that one will develop. If the chairman has an armchair and all the rest have straight chairs, it is an indication that the company is run along firm, authoritarian lines. If all the chairs are the same, the prospects for acquiring power are probably much better.

Even bathrooms can matter. It is obviously best to have a private bathroom in your office, second-best to be close to a bathroom, and worst to be miles away from one. As one literary agent said, in explaining why he wanted a best-selling author moved from his present publisher to another, "He should have a nice office to come and visit, you know, someplace where he can sit down in a social way when he wants without feeling he's in an *office*. The bathroom should be in the same office, you know? If it's in the hall, it's a little less good. Where he is now, he has to go down the hall to wash his hands when he visits, it's not so nice."

Desks can tell us a great deal about people's power quotient. The objects most people place on their desks are not there by accident, after all, and usually give some clue to the power status of the occupant. One successful conglomerator was described as having "his desk peculiarly arranged—with a window at the back—so that outdoor light all but blinds the visitor while striking two polished glass paperweights on his desk, giving an impression that you have come under the scrutiny of two translucent orbs, that your thoughts are being read and your capabilities assayed in a second or two."[7]

Desk sets—usually a pen and pencil set in a marble or onyx base—used to be potent power symbols, perhaps because of their phallic appearance, but they have been eclipsed, partly because of the popularity of the ubiquitous felt-tip marker pen, and mostly because too many people finally acquired a set. Framed diplomas are definitely out as power symbols, and so are stuffed fish, family photographs, children's paintings, mezzotint engravings of Harvard Yard in 1889, all posters, Audubon prints (unless they're originals), 37mm. cannon shells converted into paperweights, anything made of plastic or lucite and ashtrays stolen from famous restaurants or hotels. Simplicity is the best way of suggesting power. It's also useful to maintain a certain amount of clutter, just enough to make it clear that you're busy, but not so much as to suggest you're a slob. A nice touch is to leave out two or three red folders marked "Confidential" and to push them out of sight once any visitor has noticed them. Stacks of magazines give a good impression, particularly if they have slips of paper inserted in them, as if for future reference. Care should be taken, however, to ensure that they aren't such magazines as *Playboy* or *Penthouse* —*Foreign Affairs* carries considerable prestige, *Psychology Today* suggests an interest in alternative lifestyles, a large stack of *Fortunes* looks very good, and *Forbes* gives the impression of a serious interest in money, never a bad thing. Television sets have become popular as power symbols, perhaps because the late Lyndon B. Johnson had three of them in his office (so he could see himself on all three channels at once). A television set in the office is supposed to connote a burning interest in current events and world affairs (nobody assumes the owner is watching reruns of *I Love Lucy* during office hours), and also implies that the occupant of the office works at odd and irregular hours, always a sign of power.

Indeed, semidomestic furnishings are very good power symbols, since they suggest the office is a kind of home away from home, not just a place in which one comes to work from nine to five on weekdays. Even people who go home religiously at five-thirty like to give the impression that they often stay to eight or nine at night, which explains the popularity of radios, clock radios, bars, small refrigerators, blenders, heating pads, exercise poles and Health-O-Matic scales, all of which I have seen in people's offices. Electric hot plates, on the other hand, are out, since they imply you haven't enough authority to send your secretary out for coffee.

A special category of office furnishing would have to be established for my friend Tim Hennessey, a successful sales executive who had a convertible sofa bed installed in his office. This was a doubly potent power symbol, since it suggested at once that he had to work late enough to spend the night in the office, and that his sexual successes with the office staff justified his having a sofa bed handy. To the best of my knowledge, it was never opened, but he acquired a valuable reputation as a hard worker and a daring cocksman, and became, overnight as it were, a legendary figure. Hennessey also had a lock fitted to his private telephone, a nice, small touch which certainly impressed many people, and a rheostat switch under his desk so that he could dim the lights, partly because he believed it would make it easier to carry out a seduction, partly because he liked to think he could persuade the more elderly executives that they were going blind by alternatingly dimming and brightening the lights during a meeting. He was also the first person in publishing to have three wall clocks, one for New York time, one for California time, and one for London time, suggesting an international scope to his job which was purely imaginary.

Time Power

Clocks and watches are in fact the ultimate power symbols; for time, in a very real sense, *is* power.

For people who make an hourly wage, time is money in a direct sense. Analysts, for example, inevitably see the day as being divided into so many hourly sessions (fifty-five minutes actually) at so much an hour. Freudian analysts tend to maintain a certain power over their patients by not having a clock visible—the patient knows when his hour is up when the analyst tells him it is, thus intensifying the analyst's control over the patient, who can hardly look at his watch and is therefore kept in suspense, unsure of how much time he has left to drag out a boring dream or compress a whole, rich life experience into a few minutes.

The greatest compliment a busy executive can pay to a visitor is to take off his watch ostentatiously and place it—face down—on the desk. It's a way of saying, "My time belongs to you, for as long as you need me." Alternatively, taking off your watch and placing it face *up* on your desk is a way of announcing that you're a busy man and can't spare much time for your visitor's business, that he'd better damn well state his case in a hurry and get out. I personally am such a taker-off and putter-on of wrist watches that I have to go into Cartier's at regular intervals to have my watchstrap retightened, and often manage to leave it behind on my desk, or even on someone else's (leaving it in somebody else's bed is, generally speaking, a dangerous thing to do and leads to bad scenes and divorces).

One executive I know has a huge outdoor pool clock with numbers 2 inches high on the wall, and a second hand that clicks to signify passing time. It is arranged so that it faces his visitor squarely, thus announcing that his time is more important than yours, and has the same effect on most people as the writing on the wall at Belshazzar's unfortunate feast ("God hath numbered thy kingdom, and finished it"). This somewhat oppressive effect can be reinforced by arranging to have his secretary come in at regular intervals to announce that he's running behind schedule, or that Edward Bennett Williams is waiting outside to see him, but the consummate time player shouldn't need anything as obvious as this to fluster a visitor and give him the terrible guilt of wasting a busy person's precious time.

Lawyers, who usually charge on the basis of time, have their own ways of establishing their importance. At the lowest level, they have clocks that face toward them, status being set by the kind of clock it is. A round, wedge-topped battery-operated clock that sits flat on the desk and is only visible to the lawyer himself seems to be this year's favorite, though I greatly admire one lawyer who has a complicated Swiss "Atmos" clock in a glass case on his desk with the dial facing him, leaving the client to become mesmerized by the restless swing of the brass pendulum and the endless clicking of the gears and wheels—without ever being able to see what time it is. At this stage of power, the lawyer wants to know how long the client has been there, but would just as soon the client didn't know. More important lawyers announce that their time is expensive by having the clock face the client, digital clocks being favored by corporation lawyers and ancient, noisy grandfather and railroad clocks by the more traditional old-line lawyers. The *most* important lawyers have no clocks at all, the implication being that everyone they see is on a retainer basis anyway, and if they're not, there's a secretary outside to keep the log. Divorce lawyers, who have to listen to endless personal *Angst* from their clients, like analysts, seem to have no clocks and often no watches either, though one lawyer I know wears a Mickey Mouse watch which he never winds, on the grounds that it makes him seem like a simple, unthreatening figure, rather than a symbol of authority or a husband.

Just as there are fashions in clocks, there are fashions in watches, which can tell you a good deal about the people who wear them. The West Coast watch-power symbol is to have the letters of your name painted on the dial instead of numbers, though this only works when your name has twelve letters, like Ernest Lehman, the producer, unless you can abbreviate your first name, like Irving Mansfield, the late Jacqueline Susann's protean husband, whose watch reads "Irv Mansfield." This fashion does not seem to have made it to New York, where the status watch is still the old Cartier tank watch, with one of those Cartier hinged gold buckles that is almost invisible except to the connoisseur, who *knows*. On the whole though, watch wearers are divided into two basic categories: those who like watches that are impossible to read, either having no numbers or four almost invisible dots, and those who like the kind of watches astronauts, pilots and skindivers wear, with enormous luminous dials and bezel rings that allow you to compute how much air you have left or what GMT is, in case you need to know. One executive I know wears a watch that actually tells the time in London and New York simultaneously at the push of a button, but my own experience is that the less powerful the executive, the more intricate the watch. The lowest power rating goes to those who wear little miniature calendars on their watchbands, thus indicating both that they can't afford an automatic date adjusting watch and that they need to be reminded what day it is. A complicated watch like a Rolex "Submariner" usually shows the wearer is prey to extreme time anxiety, and thus fairly far down the scale of power. More powerful executives wear watches that hardly even show the time, so thin are the hands and so obscure the marks on the face. People who are really secure in their power sometimes show it by not wearing watches at all, relying on the fact that nothing important can happen without them anyway.

Styles of wearing wrist watches are pretty limited —after all, we only have two wrists—but I have noticed that a good many men now wear their wrist watch on the *inside* of the left wrist, an affectation that puzzled me for some time. In my youth it was one of those mysterious British military customs, like a rolled up handkerchief in one's right coat sleeve, and indicated membership in the professional officer caste. I think officers wore their watches on the inside wrist so that the luminous dial wouldn't be visible to the enemy at night, or possibly so that you could look at the time while keeping the reins of your horse in the left hand (most military affectations are cavalry inspired). None of these reasons seemed to me to apply to modern businessmen, who could hardly have been inculcated in the sartorial traditions of Sandhurst and Cranwell, but close observation has shown that this habit has its purpose in the modern world. A man with a watch on the inside of his left wrist can put his arm around a woman and kiss her while looking at his watch, which will then be facing him at about the level of her left ear, invisible to her. This custom can be observed in a great many midtown bars and restaurants at lunchtime, when men are making the difficult decision of whether to stay and suggest an afternoon in bed or go back to the office and answer their telephone calls. It is obviously callow to look at one's watch openly; still, at a certain point, say, one forty-five, or just about the time one is thinking of ordering coffee, it's necessary to know what time it is and move accordingly. An arm around the shoulder and a kiss will quickly establish whether a proposition is likely to succeed and simultaneously, if one's watch is in the correct position, whether one has time to follow through.

Time has its own rules, its own victories and defeats, its own symbols. In a city like New York, Chicago, or Los Angeles, you can see the losers every day at lunchtime, if you care to, sitting at restaurant tables (usually too near the entrance—winners sit as far away from the door as possible), glancing at their watches and trying to look as if they had all the time in the world or intended to eat alone. They are the people who arrived on time for a luncheon and are going to be kept waiting for at least half an hour because their guest or host is still on the telephone in his office while they're already on their fourth Rye-Krisp, and wishing they had brought a magazine along.

Lunches, of course, and meals in general, are very much connected to time concepts. The late M. Lincoln Schuster, for example, used to fit as many as four lunch dates into one day's lunch, arranging to meet several different people at the same restaurant, taking soup at one table, main course at the next, dessert at the third and coffee at the last. Had he been a drinker, he could no doubt have managed a cocktail at the beginning of the meal with a fifth person. To get through this kind of gastronomic relay race takes an iron digestive system or a total indifference to food. Still, it can be done, and allows one to have as many as twenty lunch dates in a five-day work week.

The power trick in lunch dates, apart from making sure that you're never kept waiting (even if this involves lurking in a telephone booth to watch the doorway of the restaurant), is winning the preliminary battle to fix the meeting at a time of your choosing, and in many businesses, particularly those in large cities, a great deal of the morning is spent in determining whether to meet at 12:30, 12:45 or 1:00; the point being that the person who proposes to win must not only establish the time but arrange to arrive last.

Whether in a restaurant or elsewhere, the most important aspect of the time game is making people wait, the most familiar example being the old one of not speaking on the telephone until the other person is already on the line, a power struggle which can occupy many otherwise unproductive minutes in a busy executive's day. "Buzz me when X is on the line," says the power player, while X is naturally telling *his* secretary to buzz him when Y is on the line. Some people play another form of this game by answering all their telephone calls themselves, asking the caller to wait "just one second," then putting everyone on hold, until they have three or four people backed up waiting to speak to them.

Those who play the power game seriously can never be free from the tyranny of time, and don't even want to be, since a tightly packed schedule not only gives them a sense of importance, but is a perfect excuse for not doing whatever it is they don't want to do. A full calendar is proof of power, and for this reason, the most powerful people prefer small calendars, which are easily filled up, and which give the impression of frenetic activity, particularly if one's writing is fairly large. One of the best power symbols is a desk diary that shows the whole week at a glance, with every available square inch of space filled in or crossed out. It provides visible evidence that one is busy—too busy to see someone who is anxious to discuss a complaint or a burdensome request. At the same time, one can confer a favor by crossing out an existing appointment and, in the current phrase, "penciling in" the name of someone who has requested an appointment. A close inspection of such diaries often reveals that a good many of the entries read "Gray suit at cleaners" or "Betsy's birthday—present?," but the effect from a distance is awe-inspiring.

Many executives stroll to work in a leisurely fashion, stopping to look in shop windows and pausing to glance at pretty girls, then, as soon as they pass through the revolving doors of their office buildings, gather themselves up in a kind of Groucho Marx crouch, as if they wanted to run but felt constrained to hold themselves down to a fast, breathless walk. By the time they reach their offices, they are moving at top speed, already giving dictation while they're struggling out of their topcoats. Men who could quite easily allow themselves a good hour to get to the airport for a flight will happily waste time until they have to leave in a dramatic rush, shouting out last-minute instructions as they run down the hall and pursued to the elevator by people with telephone messages and letters to be signed.

Standing-By

Another excellent tactic is to allow half an hour for meetings that are sure to last at least an hour, so that the people who have to see you afterward are obliged to wait without knowing quite when they'll be called for. This is the familiar "stand by" game, in which people are warned to "stand by" for a meeting that was supposed to take place at 10 A.M. and probably won't begin until noon, or may even be postponed until next week. In the meantime, of course, they are more or less obliged to stay close to their phones, and may even have to cancel their lunch dates. The busier you can make yourself, the more you can impose your schedule on other people; the more you impose your schedule on other people, the more power you have. The definition of power, in fact, is that more people inconvenience themselves on your behalf than those on whose behalf you would inconvenience yourself. At the very summit of power —the President of the United States, for example— almost everybody will wait, go without lunch, "stand by" or give up dinner with a beautiful woman on your behalf. One doubts, for example, that everyone in the White House necessarily *wants* to rush through lunch in order to fly to Camp David in the Presidential helicopter at the last minute, canceling their weekend plans and their golf dates. But when power beckons, most people follow, at whatever cost to their comfort and private lives. The important thing is to keep moving and drag as many people along in your wake as possible.

A tight schedule is a guarantee of power, as anyone can tell from the description of David Rockefeller's departure from his office. "The man who runs the garage at the Chase Manhattan Bank Building has been keeping watch. When he saw David Rockefeller leave the Federal Reserve Bank of New York . . . he shouted, 'O.K., Chester!' [8] No sooner has Chester pulled up the maroon Cadillac limousine than Mr. Rockefeller is into it (his aides are already waiting in the car, presumably having been sitting there for hours in the underground garage to be ready for the moment), and opening his scarlet folder marked 'For Immediate Action,' he proceeds to give his orders for the afternoon on the way to a waiting helicopter, its rotor blades already turning, which will carry him to a cocktail party in Albany."

One might well ask whether a cocktail party in Albany is worth this kind of mobilized effort, but worth it or not, the elements of time power are perfectly illustrated in Mr. Rockefeller's breathless rush to the helicopter, involving the time of the pilot, Chester, the chauffeur, the aides who have been waiting in the car, the garageman who gives Chester the warning, and presumably a host of other people at both ends of the journey, all of whom are at "stand by" for hours in order to convey one man to a party. David Rockefeller's power would hardly be emphasized if he had strolled out of his office with time to spare, whistled at a passing girl, bought himself a Hershey bar and a copy of *Penthouse* and left himself plenty of time to walk to the Wall Street heliport. The higher up one goes, the more valuable one's time must appear to be.

Closely allied with time, is the ability to make other people perform the small demeaning tasks of life for you. Men do not necessarily ask their secretaries to get a cup of coffee for them because they are lazy, or because they are male chauvinists, or even because they don't know where the coffee machine is. Getting one's own coffee is a sign that one's time is not all that important, that it can be wasted on inconsequential personal chores. People who are power-conscious would rather sit at their desks with their eyes closed "thinking" than get up and go for their own coffee, or collect their own dry cleaning, or fetch their own mail. In extreme cases, they insulate themselves from *any* trivial task; as John Z. DeLorean, the flamboyant former general manager of General Motors' car and truck division, put it, "I don't think the heads of state of many countries come close. You travel like an oil sheik." G.M.'s senior executives travel in private jet aircraft, limousines carry them to and fro, teams of PR men fly in a day or two before their visits to ensure that everything is in order, and check the hotel suites "to make certain, among other things, that flowers are in place." [9] One PR man, *Fortune* reported, found what seemed suspiciously like semen stains on a sofa in the suite reserved for the president of G.M., and spent the afternoon before the great man's arrival cleaning the furniture off with his handkerchief.

Not everyone can aspire to this kind of insulation from everyday life, but it represents the ultimate symbol of power in our culture, the notion that one has no time for mundane details and that one's comfort and convenience are the responsibility of other people.

In the words of one executive, "I've always somehow associated power with cleanliness, maybe because at heart we're all afraid of falling back into manual labor, of having to get our hands dirty, like our fathers or grandfathers. Right from the beginning, I've always noticed that powerful people *never seem to get dirty*. You take a rainy day in the city, when everyone arrives with wrinkled, wet trousers and wet shoes, powerful people appear magically with knife-edged creases and shiny, dry shoes. How do they do it? I don't know. I can't even imagine it, which is the reason, I suppose, that I'm down here on this floor, and they're up there. Do they change when they arrive at the office? Do they walk around sealed in plastic Baggies? Is it just that they don't have to take the subway or stand waiting for the Fifth Avenue bus in the rain? Who knows? But it's true—they have this magic gloss to them, they don't sweat, you don't see them coming in after a taxi has splashed muddy water all over them. I know, deep down in my rational mind, that it isn't altogether true, and that a lot of it has to do with limos and company planes and things like that, but for me, powerful people are forever defined as those who can walk to work without stepping in a puddle. When all is said and done it's like the old vaudeville routine about sex appeal—'Some people got it, some people don't got it. I got it.' "

CHAPTER EIGHT

Women and Power

It is customary in the Province for the daughters of the citizenry not to marry early.

—Hermann Hesse
THE GLASS BEAD GAME

Nature has given women so much power that the law has very wisely given them little.

—Samuel Johnson

At first sight, the largest visible group of people who "don't got it" consists of women. It is not so much that women do not *have* power—in many ways they do, and many of them are beginning to take on power roles that until now have been traditionally masculine—as the fact that the symbols and the mythology of power are predominately male-oriented. Our ultimate image of power is the President, a man surrounded by men in a male-oriented world and sustained by the artifacts and trappings of a masculine society and technology—soldiers, lavish jet aircraft, secret servicemen, helicopters . . .

The main reason why women find it hard to break into the world of power is not so much that men put obstacles in their way but rather that power is thought of as being essentially male. The rituals of power are those of a male-bonding group, and however *successful* a woman may be, it is difficult for her to project a corresponding degree of power. "Power people," in the words of one woman executive, "tend to be father figures. Their whole approach to life is patriarchal, like a demanding, difficult, stern father, who can reward or punish as he pleases. At our agency we have a new executive, a very powerful man who can't be more than thirty-five years old, and the first time he collected us all together, he took off his glasses and said, 'Well, kids, let's review the situation.' Some of the people sitting there were forty or fifty, but nobody seemed to notice how odd it was. He was the person with the power, and we were his children, to be judged, rewarded, loved or punished. He was just what everyone expected a power figure to be, a dominating father who is difficult to please. A woman would have had to have extraordinary physical presence to establish her power and authority as easily and quickly as he did, and would have had to find a style of her own to bring it off successfully. Most of the successful women I know either try to charm or nag because they haven't found the authentic voice of power."

In part, the problem lies in the fact that "the authentic voice of power" we are used to hearing is of course that of a man. From childhood on, at every level, the symbol of ultimate authority tends to be a man, in one guise or another; the President of the United States is a man, most judges are men, when we think of the police, we see them as men, even in schools where the teachers are women, the chances are excellent that the principal is a man, even that special figure of power in the popular culture, the Mafia don, is not only a Godfather but a father. Wherever we look, men, as one woman puts it, "have the keys," both figuratively and literally. In banks, a woman may process your application for a safe-deposit box, but the person behind the bars who lets you in to open it is a man in a dark business suit, with a bunch of keys: he has symbolic authority, as do doormen, security guards, train conductors and most other uniformed figures. During the televised hearings of the Ervin committee on Watergate, a stranger to this country might have supposed that American women were still imprisoned in the circle of *Kinder, Kirche* and *Küche,* so conspicuous was their absence on both sides. The stern figures of authority were all men, the lawyers were mostly men, and the subpoenaed witnesses, from Cuban burglars to Presidential advisors and former members of the Cabinet, were men. The faces of power and authority that appeared daily on the television screen, whether as interrogators or delinquents, were men to a man. This is true at almost every level of our national life. The justices of the United States Supreme Court are

men, the governors are men, the big corporations are
run by men, and while black men have begun to take
their place as big-city mayors, few women have yet
to do so. Though the president of the Washington
Post is a woman, Mrs. Katherine Graham (her father
bought the *Post*, and until his death her husband was
its publisher), and though Mrs. Dorothy Chandler is
an executive of the Los Angeles Times Mirror Co.
(which her family owns), the newspapers of America are controlled by men and most of the major
political commentators are men. It is therefore not
surprising that in nearly 1,300 companies required
to file proxy statements by the Securities and Exchange Commission there were 6,500 officers and
directors earning over $30,000, of whom *eleven*—
that's right, eleven—were women! [2]

Under the circumstances, the odds against having
to deal with a powerful woman during the course of
one's career still remain very high, though of course
they are decreasing at lower levels of power and in
certain industries and professions. At the top, however, men still retain power, and their view of power
and the ways in which they symbolize it, continue to
determine the picture that most of the people below
them have of power itself. As one successful woman
vice president told me, "The biggest thing I have to
fight against is that people assume the *real* power
and authority in my job is somewhere else. I've got
the job, I do it well, I make the decisions, but because
I'm a woman, men tend to feel, 'Oh yes, she's a vice
president and all that, but she probably reports to
some guy who really makes the decisions.' And of
course the guys above me feel that too, they really
believe they're responsible for whatever I've done. I
make a lot of tough decisions, and I make them myself and carry them out myself, and I think I'm pretty

well respected for it. But men still feel that they're
in touch with power. I make a decision and they'll
nod and accept it—they have to. But they want to
have it confirmed for them by another man, in a
power situation that they can understand—a 'man-to-
man' confrontation. What they get that way they
believe. What they get from me, whether it's Yes or
No, they're not quite sure of."

Women are constantly confronted with demands
to "review," "discuss" and "finalize" their decisions.
Men will go to extraordinary lengths to invent power
structures that exist primarily to deprive successful
women of their autonomy. In any organization that
contains a successful woman executive, the committees, meetings and "decision review structures" magically proliferate, as if the male power hierarchy were
throwing up spontaneous defenses to protect itself.
Enormous efforts are made, for example, to deprive
women executives of the right to adjust the salaries
of those who work in their departments, since the
ability to deliver raises is essential to any executive's
firm control of a department. A man who has a
woman department head working under him is likely
to give her the hardest possible time when the end
of the year comes by and it's time to deal with raises,
or worse yet, to insist on calling in members of her
department to talk money behind her back. The important thing is to undermine her by suggesting to
her staff that promotion and money are controlled
elsewhere—by a *man*. In microcosm, this is part of
the basic male-chauvinist game against women at
work, which is to suggest that anything "serious"
must be handled by a man, particularly questions of
money—as a rule *"serious" questions are those that
get settled at a level immediately above the most successful women in any organization.* Whatever women

cannot decide themselves, or are prevented from deciding, is by definition "serious." Thus, if a woman is running a department that involves millions of dollars annually, and has the right to make decisions about six-figure contracts, these matters automatically become "unimportant" matters of day-to-day business routine, whereas the things she *isn't* concerned with, salaries, or shipping, or billing, for example—become grave and weighty matters of the utmost importance. Any job a woman does is downgraded the moment she has proved she can do it. If a woman were elected President and chose a male Vice President, we would doubtless see the Vice Presidency transformed into a position of serious responsibility and power, while the Presidency was downgraded until the President and Vice President could be treated as if they were a "team" of equals.

The means by which men tend to exercise control are many, but the need is constant and almost instinctive. Take committees: the moment a woman is appointed to one, there is a natural tendency to downgrade its importance, and to transfer whatever executive functions it has to a new and smaller subcommittee on which, by some strange coincidence, there will be no women. This explains why the nomination of one woman to a committee—however much it is hailed as a triumph—is often followed by the arrival of a great many more women. It is not that an act of sexual equality is taking place—far from it, the men who run the committee are simply abandoning it to women, and replacing it with another, more exclusive one. This is a very common procedure, with endless variations. Let us assume we have an eight-person committee for the purpose of "developing long-range goals." The committee has a chairman, a secretary and a vice chairman, and these people naturally form an inner power group, effectively controlling the committee by establishing the agenda and preparing the minutes.

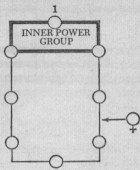

An eight-person committee on plans, with an inner group of three, about to be increased by the addition of one woman member.

Let us assume that it becomes necessary to add a woman to the committee, either to prove that the organization isn't male chauvinist, or simply to accommodate a successful woman who wants to join it. We now have a nine-person committee, run by the same three men. They are still in control, but in their eyes it is no longer a meaningful power group, since a woman has joined it. Their solution will be easy and natural—since several more women would like to get on the committee, the power group decides to take on four more committee members, three women and one man.

The committee has been "democratized," but at the same time it is now possible to argue that it is too large to function effectively in making decisions or recommendations. The inner power group will now re-form itself, perhaps beginning in an informal way, with the intention of becoming an "executive" com-

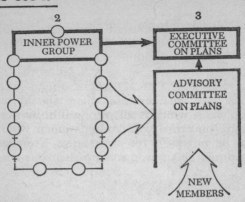

In 2 and 3, we see the new committee of 9 members expanded to 13, at which point the inner power group re-forms as a new, separate committee, opening up the old one to so many people that it becomes powerless.

mittee. They will argue, quite rightly, that a small group is always more efficient, without pointing out that they deliberately diluted the original committee. They are now free to turn the enlarged, original committee into an "advisory group," allowing so many people to join (which, by the way, is an easy means to repay old debts) that it becomes a "talking shop." Overgrown and reduced to an impotent advisory role, the committee will sink of its own weight—meetings will be held less frequently, busy people will fail to attend, and it can be allowed to vanish into obscurity. This tactic is repetitive: if it ever becomes necessary to add a woman to the new "executive committee," then it too will expand until it's too big to serve any useful or decisive function, and the inner power group will once again abandon it to its fate and resume business as the same three-man team under some new title.

"I've seen it happen again and again," said Jane
Shields, a major magazine executive who has made
her way up to a corporate vice presidency in an organization that has never been lavish with titles for
women. "It's a kind of *Totentanz* around here. The
big issues are whether researchers should have to
answer phones, which is all very well in its way, but
is entirely concerned with young women who don't
want to be mistaken for secretaries. Everybody is
willing to talk about 'women's problems' in terms of
twenty-two-year-olds, but when it comes to giving up
real *power*—forget it! We had one executive committee that was very important, and when I got my
vice presidency, I said I wanted to be on it. Well,
there'd never been a woman on it, but the vice president I was replacing had been a committee member,
so there was a precedent. First they told me I couldn't
be on it because some of the members would feel
embarrassed discussing important financial matters
in front of a woman! I said *bullshit* to that! Then
they explained that the meetings were held in a private room at a club that doesn't allow women in at
lunchtime. Well, I fought that too, and it was moved
to a room in the restaurant upstairs, which was a
little less luxurious, but what the hell.

"Then, all of a sudden, the meeting began to get
larger and larger. They were making it so big that it
wasn't a distinction to be a member of it any more,
and we moved to a conference room because there
were so many of us, and had food ordered in, which
was messy, and gave the men an opportunity to let
the women do all sorts of catering chores and worry
about who gets what sandwich. By the time the committee had reached the chaos point, the original
members were beginning to meet again by themselves
in their old private club, and every woman who had

ever wanted to be a member of anything was sitting in the conference room with us. When I got on the committee, the men sank the committee by letting everyone in. And afterward they even went around saying that you couldn't expect anything else once you opened something like that up to women!"

Jane, a handsome woman in her late forties, shakes her head and lights a cigarette, tapping the end impatiently on the back of her hand, a male identification gesture from the 1940's which she must have picked up somewhere along the way, along with a gunmetal Zippo lighter. Jane is a tough, experienced lady, who put in a lot of time to get from a secretary's desk out in the hallway to this office high above Manhattan, with primrose yellow walls and a deep red carpet and three yellow telephones. She runs a tight department, and watches every penny, even though she knows that these characteristics are held against her by men on the next rung up the ladder, who describe her as "a housewife looking for bargains, a real penny-pinching broad, who'd rather save a nickel than make a dollar." Jane can't help it. She's been earning her living since she was eighteen, and spent most of her life on a low salary—a woman's salary. Easy attitudes toward money don't come naturally to her, and never will. Like a great many successful women, she has learned to do her job supremely well, but still knows very little about power, and can never quite understand why she always ends up being controlled by men who work half as hard as she does and earn twice as much. Committees, meetings, the precise editing of minutes, the delicate process of "stroking lunches" at which new power alliances are formed, all these things bore her; she wants to get on with her job and be left alone, to be paid and respected for work well done.

"They're all playing games up there on the floor above," Jane says, pointing a finger at the ceiling. "Me, I don't play games. I work."

Unfortunately for Jane, playing the games is as important as doing the work. Men are trained to know this; they learn it in team sports, in the Army, at school. It's part of their make-up, a sense of power is natural to them if they have any intelligence and ambition. Some of them make the mistake of assuming that power is enough, that you don't need to work at all, but most of them learn, somewhere along the way, to live with power. And since they think of power as a male prerogative, their fiercest games are fought with women.

These games are sometimes very subtle indeed, and need consist of nothing more than an adroit use of sex at the proper moment. Accomplished players can easily put down a woman and flatter her at the same time, and the use of sexual signals is a basic tactic in a whole series of complex power games that have nothing to do with sex. Flirtation, flattery, seduction innuendo, all can be turned into a technique of control.

In office life, such signals have a *specific* function: they establish a sense of intimacy, which by its very nature becomes conspiratorial. Because of this, sexual signals in office power games often tend to be played from the bottom up, organizationally speaking, and can even be used by women against men. We thus picture an office meeting that has been called in order to permit a senior executive to give his "staff" a pep talk about their failure to follow through on certain contractual details. Ten people are placed around his desk in various positions of discomfort, since there aren't enough places to sit and most of the chairs will have automatically been taken (Male Chauvinism, of course) by the more senior male members, who feel that by sitting comfortably in a chair, as close to the desk as possible, with their feet firmly planted on the ground, they will appear to be part of management—that is, they will seem to be part of a subgroup, of which the senior executive is merely the spokesman, rather than part of the larger group which has been called in to be criticized and told to get on the ball. For this reason, they all wear their jackets and smoke pipes reflectively, anxious to have it seem that they already know what is going to be said and agree with it. The women, of whom there are four, stand, or lean against the radiator grills by the window. The senior executive takes a quick phone call, in order to show that he has more important things to do than talk to his "staff," and that he can make them wait if he wants to, but while speaking he waves to them, to indicate that he is also one of them and that they have to understand the demands that are made on his time and therefore be sympathetic even when he's about to chew them out.

He hangs up, and proceeds to his subject. "Listen," he says, "there's no excuse for not getting these forms through on time. I'm going to go over the steps you have to take one by one, and from now on it's going to be done, and done *right*. Understood?" He glares at the men seated by his desk to show them that they're included (to their discomfort), then looks at the women standing by the window, all of whom look down at the floor but one. She stares straight back at him with fixed and rapturous attention, then fingers a gold chain around her neck, hanging as it were on his every word, admiring the power of his delivery. Being a man, he cannot fail to notice, and as he launches into the subject, he occasionally looks back at her, then, almost instinctively, signals *his* sexual interest by removing his glasses and chewing at the end of one sidepiece (an obvious oral display). A tacit bond has thus been established, a kind of secret communication, and before long the executive has turned his attack on the men seated before him, pouring the blame, the threat and the scorn on them, much to their surprise, since they are unable to realize that in fact their tormentor is now performing for someone else. He has effectively been diverted from an attack on the group as a whole and from any fundamental attempt to solve the issues at hand into making an empty show of power.

In the hands of an experienced player, the sexual signal can be very effective in power games, and has the enormous advantage that it needn't be followed up. It's understood that neither party is obliged to escalate a signal into an affair—it merely serves to produce a momentary feeling of intimacy and understanding, thereby deflecting an attack or an unwelcome piece of work onto someone else.

In most cases, when women use sexual signals, they are weapons of defense; when men use them they are weapons of attack. What is more, most men *expect* women to use their sex as a weapon; it's part of their ingrained distrust of women in general. A man is not expected to play what is generally thought of as a "feminine" game, and therefore gains the advantage of surprise when he does. Nor is it difficult: a man can easily become a father figure (thereby making the woman he's talking to a surrogate daughter), or a husband figure (which gives him a spurious right of intimate authority), or a lover (in which role he will attempt to replace tangible benefits with charm, affection and understanding). The main thing is to establish one of the existing *social* male-female relationships as the basis for a business or professional relationship. Hence, men flirt outrageously with their secretaries in order to make it difficult for them to ask for a raise or refuse to perform an unwelcome chore. They will show a "fatherly" interest in a woman executive's work so that in any disagreement they will have the advantage of parental authority. It is sufficient to get the woman to think of her role in the organization as the equivalent of her role in the outside world. A woman who puts up with a domineering husband may soon find that she has a second one as a boss; a woman who wants protection, love and flattery will soon get it from men at work, at the expense of raises, titles and power. Men are adept at forcing women to become stereotypes.

Let us take an example: A distinguished consultant on financial matters in an office is called in to a meeting by a very hot-shot whiz-kid executive who wants to get rid of the consultant so he can operate more freely within the company. There are several people around the table, including an attractive young woman. The consultant expresses his opinion about the first item on the agenda, and the executive makes no comment. Nor do any of the other men, of course, since they neither want to expose their lack of original ideas, nor commit themselves until they know who is likely to emerge the victor from this particular power game. On the second item, the consultant explains his point of view and the executive turns to the young woman, and asks her to say what *she* thinks. At the same time, he nonchalantly takes a cigarette from her package and lights it with her lighter, flipping it back to her casually and looking straight at her, very intently, as he exhales. A signal!

But the sexual signal is not the point (though it is worth noting that the borrowing of objects, particularly when they have an oral significance, is very often a display intended to suggest further intimacy).

In this case, male chauvinism being what it is in managerial circles, the distinguished consultant is being put down, shown that in the executive's eyes a young woman's view counts for as much as his, which will lose him status among the other men at the table, while at the same time he can't help thinking that if there *is* a sexual or emotional link between the executive and the young woman, he would do well not to get into a vehement argument with her. It should be enough to throw him off-balance, which is all that's needed, and to reduce the effective hammering out of ideas between the two principal opponents to a confused and polite discussion, which can afterward be used by the young executive to argue that the consultant is slipping, that he no longer has forceful ideas or presents them forcefully. Note that the young woman doesn't even need to be aware of what has happened. A very high proportion of sexual power games are played out between men, with women not even realizing that they're part of the game, that in fact they're being *used*.

Examples of this abound. It is very effective for a man to bring in a young woman to make a presentation, and to imply, by a host of small attentions and an air of familiarity, that there is some kind of attachment between them. If the presentation is successful, it will be thought that he allowed her to present it because they're having an affair, and since every man understands this, he can still get credit for the success. In addition, the more he insists on giving *her* credit, the more other men will assume that the ideas were his, and the more they will respect him for being generous to the woman he's involved with. A man I know recently went to a meeting to present a graphic design for an advertising campaign to a group of male executives, and took along with him the young woman who had in fact done the work and whose idea it was. As they came into the room, he put his arm around her shoulder casually, and said, "Gentlemen, this is Jane. I'm going to let *her* present this project to you, and I want you to know that it's her project, and I think it's terrific." Every man automatically assumed that the intimate gesture (the arm around the shoulder) implied a close relationship between them, and inferred from that the project was in fact his.

Note that if the project should fail to please, the man has already established an alibi for himself—it was *hers,* not his, and he can then join in rejecting it, perhaps murmuring to one of the other men, "Yes, I can see you're right, I had some doubts about it myself, but I wanted to give her a chance, you know how it is with women. What the hell, we can always try something else . . ."

This game of providing oneself with a fall-guy—or rather, a fall-gal—is very popular in all the so-called "creative" businesses. It perfectly illustrates a way in which men prevent competition from women by seemingly making them accomplices. Radical feminists are thus right in questioning the purpose of the traditional man-woman courtesies in working situations. A woman would do well to be on her guard when a man who is a colleague at any level goes out of his way to praise a dress, admire her appearance, open the door for her or make a thing of lighting her cigarette. Many men use these small courtesies to emphasize to their male colleagues and to themselves that the person they're dealing with is in a category apart, so that deference to a woman becomes a means of excluding her from the group. This is particularly true at large meetings. The men are all sitting there, coats off, hard at whatever work they're doing. A woman comes in and they rise to their feet, pull up her chair for her, someone lights her cigarette: it looks like politeness, no one can accuse the men of excluding her—on the contrary, they have behaved with perfect courtesy, made all the correct socio-sexual gestures, but have effectively segregated her all the same.

One sees the more extreme forms of this kind of put-down taking place still today, despite women's liberation. I have watched men reach over and gently pat a woman's hair to emphasize their agreement or their approval, or put their arm around her when going into a meeting or a restaurant, as if to show her that there's nothing to be afraid of, or even pat her on the cheek. If these sexual signals were designed to lead to intimacy one could not reasonably object to them, but their purpose in working life is much more likely to be that of reducing the woman's importance in the eyes of other men, of implying that there is a protective role between oneself and the woman, that the old biological differences transcend the job. A sound rule of thumb would be to ask whether a man would offer comparable gestures of intimacy to another man in the same situation— would he pat a male colleague on the back to indicate approval, would he shake hands to mark his agreement? Usually, the answer is No. Gestures of physical intimacy are very rare on a man-to-man basis at work, which isn't to say that men don't *make* them—it's just that they're considered more appropriate to the sports field, the party and the bar, where physical

contact between men establishes a certain sense of
solidarity, and of course equality. At work, this kind
of physical familiarity is used only to emphasize that
the fellow who is being touched is a subordinate. A
vice president may make his point by playfully tapping his finger against a man's chest, but he is in
effect pointing out that he is the superior, that he
can touch the other man's person without being
touched back. A senior executive may put his arm
around a male colleague's shoulder to indicate approval, but the subordinate can hardly do the same
to him. Such gestures are either patronizing or threatening, and the great master of them was the late
Lyndon B. Johnson, who used to squeeze his subordinates' knees, punch them, stab his finger in their
stomach, and generally use every physical means to
show just who had the power.

Of course, many women fight back with sexual-signal
games of their own. In certain industries and businesses, they have great power and wield it ruthlessly.
I well remember the woman editor of a major magazine, who had developed over the years the authority
and the sense of command of a Borgia Pope. Her
office was designed to startle men—to make them
feel as if they had blundered into the ladies' room by
mistake with their flies unzipped. The carpet was
imitation leopard-skin, the walls were covered in
bright, flowered paper, great bowls of lilies were
placed on every Parsons table, and the tables themselves were covered in snakeskin. She had no desk—
just a large, circular rattan and glass garden table,
and all the chairs were small, delicate objects of
bamboo and lime velvet, the kind of things on which

most men sit gingerly, afraid of breaking them with their weight. A small woman, she had all the furniture cut down to her size, a fact that was not at first apparent to anyone entering the office, but which tended to give any man over 5'2" the hallucinating feeling of being out of scale, as if he had suddenly been changed into a clumsy and grotesque giant by the wave of a magic wand. A non-smoker herself, she had no ashtrays in her office, so that a visitor who lit a cigarette would find himself searching hopelessly in the clutter for a place to put his match or ashes, while the lady affected not to notice his predicament. Every square inch of table space was covered in bric-a-brac—bird's eggs, sea shells, crystal bowls full of glass beads, porcelain, carved animals, Battersea boxes, dried flowers pressed in plastic, carved ivory fish swimming in jade ponds, icons, swatches of fabric, small green enameled frogs (her trademark— everything she owned, wrote on or gave away was marked with a small green frog) and crystal paperweights. The only working space was the table area immediately in front of her chair.

Both her secretaries sat *in* the office, rather than outside, at lime-green desks, with lime-green IBM typewriters (they had been specially sprayed) and lime-green telephones. They were always present during any meeting or conference, which tended to give male executives the feeling that Mrs. Lynch (as her name was during her marriage of that time) feared rape at their hands, and wanted to have two female witnesses to any conversation or interview, like the matrons who stand by during a police interrogation of a female subject. In moments of stress, Mrs. Lynch would turn to her secretaries and say, "I don't think we can do that, do you, girls?" and they would reply in chorus, "No, Mrs. Lynch!" It was enough to freeze the blood of any man, and most male executives felt about an interview with Melissa Lynch as a French aristocrat might have about meeting Mme. Defarge and the *tricoteuses*.

Like most magazine editors, Mrs. Lynch had limited power; her control of the magazine itself (and its staff) was absolute and dictatorial, and for that matter, unquestioned. On the other hand, she had little or no power in the corporation that owned the magazine, which was composed entirely of well-connected men, without exception members of the University Club, the Metropolitan Club and the Coffee House. Tyrannical though she might be over the layout of her magazine and its content, Mrs. Lynch was merely a corporate employee like her secretaries. Above her there was a corporation, with an executive committee, a financial committee and a board of directors, all made up of men whose fathers had shared rooms at Groton and Harvard. On the whole, Mrs. Lynch was content to leave them to their business, whatever it was, and get on with her own job; she had no ambitions to move to the executive floor and spend her day worrying about stock issues, dividends and the price of paper. However, on rare occasions the corporate executives would venture into her domain with a timid suggestion or two, perhaps a report showing how many millions of dollars a year could be saved by cutting the magazine's huge, elegant margins a fraction of an inch, perhaps a suggestion that it might be cheaper not to rewrite every story after it had been set in type, possibly even the ultimate threat of an advertiser who wanted to be mentioned in a feature article as the price of a million-dollar campaign. Mrs. Lynch was equal to such challenges—she simply insisted that any emissary from the executive floor should come to *her* office—

after all it was no more than politeness, since she was a woman and a widow (two of her husbands had died).

Most of the senior executives found it difficult to cross the threshold of her office, and found themselves standing at the door with an uneasy and guilty sense of being out of place, like men who have taken the wrong elevator at a department store and find themselves by accident in the intimate lingerie department. It was one thing to promise they would be firm, even "hard-nosed," in the calm supportive atmosphere of the executive floor, where the walls were covered in sporting prints, the chairs were large, heavy and upholstered in tufted leather, the desks solid, masculine fortresses of mahogany and brass. Here, in the *fauverie* of Mrs. Lynch's lair, it was a different story. Determination ebbed as they tiptoed across the leopard-skin carpet looking for a chair to sit on that would bear their weight, trying not to brush any of the breakable *objets d'art* with their sleeves. Since there was no place to put their briefcases, they were obliged to leave them in their laps, like insurance salesmen. If they approached the subject at hand in a hearty, aggressive tone, Mrs. Lynch's secretaries would frown and cough. If they approached it delicately, Mrs. Lynch would reply with the vigor of a tugboat captain, throwing them off-balance.

She had, in any case, a gift for the vivid, dramatic turn of phrase. On one occasion she sent me to explore the possibility of using a woman skydiving champion as a model, the idea being to photograph her in midair wearing a variety of new sportswear. I returned from a disagreeable afternoon of hurtling through the sky above New Jersey, doubtful of the practicality of dropping the lady skydiver and a photographer out of an airplane simultaneously. What was more, I pointed out, the lady was not built for modeling clothes, either in the air or on the ground; she had the shoulders and muscles of a Marine judo instructor. Knowing that Mrs. Lynch did not like "pessimism," I lightened my report with the comment that the lady skydiver had informed me, during an evening spent touring the New Jersey roadhouses, that she always had an orgasm on the way down. "Why do you think it is?" asked Mrs. Lynch. I said that I thought it had something to do with the excitement of jumping, the fact that she was pushed out of the airplane by a handsome jumpmaster into the void, the speed of the fall. The whole thing, I reasoned, was a very Freudian experience. Mrs. Lynch thought about this a moment, then shook her head. "No," she said firmly, "It's the way the parachute straps rub on her crotch when she pulls the rip cord."

In the face of such frank logic and language, the senior executives of the corporation were helpless. Powerful men on their own floor, they were reduced to impotence on Mrs. Lynch's. From the moment they entered her office, their one thought was to get out as soon as possible, and return to the safety of their own offices, where they were respected as executives, men, husbands and fathers. "A spineless lot," Mrs. Lynch would say, as they retreated from her domain in defeat, and she was right. If they could have forced her to come to *their* floor, she would have been powerless.

Some women try to fight it out with men on a *mano a mano* basis; where men are tough, they are *tougher*. My friend Carla runs her department of a major television network with force and energy, swearing like a trooper, slamming down the telephone when she's finished one of her short, sharp conversations, lighting one Camel from another as she dictates the pungent and strongly worded memos that have made her famous in her industry. Carla ostentatiously refuses to accept any of the small courtesies usually extended to women. Long before women's liberation she would push men into the elevator before her, sometimes with considerable force, as if to show that *they* were the weaker sex. She refused to have any man pay for her meals, and was the first woman in her company to carry a brief case and use a dictating machine. As one executive said, "I'd always thought of dictating machines in a very traditional way, as if the separate units were of different sexes. You know, the male unit has a microphone, the female unit has a little plug that fits in the ear. When I saw Carla dictating into her machine, holding that microphone, it gave me a shock. I'd never seen a woman use one before, and it didn't seem to me *natural*. It was a very Freudian reaction, I guess." Since then, Carla has gone one better: she has a male secretary and dictates to *him*, and on occasions, when there are men in her office, sends him off to get coffee. Nothing stops her. When a senior executive broke off an argument by going into the men's room, Carla followed him in, and stood there talking while he answered the call of nature. "I wasn't embarrassed," she said, "and if he was, that's his problem. He couldn't show me anything I haven't seen before."

There's no doubt that Carla is a powerful woman, but the means by which she asserts and maintains her power are self-limiting. Nobody can take away from her what she's got, but at the same time, there's no way she can move up to something better. Like

most women, she plays power games *defensively*—
aggressive games interest her less. Her outspoken
combativeness more or less precludes her being promoted to a job that requires a tactful supervision of
several different departments, and her success at
her own job, since she's a woman, gives men an
excellent reason to keep her there. Carla has reached
the highest level to which her power games can carry
her. She is stuck.

Many of the games women play to secure power
are similarly limiting and defensive, which explains
why so few women, however talented and hard-work-
ing, get to the top. Perhaps the real reason is that
they have to fight too hard at the beginning of their
careers merely to be noticed; there is no easy path of
promotion for them, they start at a lower level than
men, spend longer in subordinate positions and have
to rise against far greater odds. Since they are seldom welcomed into the inner circles of power, they
have to fight their way in, which makes men resist
them all the more. Above all, they have no model of
power to follow. Most men learn early on to imitate
their elders in positions of power, but it is difficult
for women to imitate men, and in many respects, im-
practical. A woman wearing a skirt can hardly put
her feet up on someone else's desk, or share fishing
stories and football scores with the chairman of
the board in the elevator. In a world where men are
at the top, she remains an outsider.

Many women, of course, are content to accept a
limited amount of power and preserve it in their own
ways. A good friend of mine, for example, is an
executive in a motion picture corporation, a world of
ruthless and fiercely fought power games, in which
women have seldom played a part except as actresses.

Surrounded by people who curse, scream and spend their days and nights empire-building, she remains cool, calm and collected, firmly ladylike, implacably polite and soft-spoken. She never raises her voice and seldom argues. When opposed, she quietly repeats her point of view, always in a reasonable tone, making it perfectly plain that she will, if necessary, sit there explaining what she wants until she has got it. With her firm, determined mouth and her large, clear, slate-gray eyes, devoid of any guile, she is as immovable as a rock. She cannot be humored, shocked, threatened or won over by flattery. One look at those eyes tells you that—even if you're a man who has grown up in a business where wheedling, screaming, whining and Oriental flattery are the norms of behavior.

A part of her strength is that she is always perfectly dressed, in perfect control of herself, her hair and her pleats, one of those people whose clothes never seem to get wrinkled after a taxi ride in mid-August and who never seems to sweat, get smudged or even rained on. "It's as if she were always wearing a pair of little white gloves," complained one man, "no matter how angry I am at her, I see these white gloves, and it's like talking to a determined, obstinate child. She reminds me of my daughter, God help me, and I can't win an argument against either of them. They just look at me patiently, then go right on with what they want, in a nice, reasonable tone of voice as if I had to be humored. If she came on strong, I could throw her out of my office, but I know when I'm up against a brick wall, and that's what she is. And patient! Every time I say No to her over something, she comes back again and again, always very politely, and tells me that I'm wrong. The trouble is that I get to admiring her for her stubbornness, then I'm lost. You show me a man who can stare down a woman who's used to getting her own way! It's built into us. We give in. That's why the best agents are women now. Most men are simply programmed to give in where women are concerned."

Perhaps women do make good agents—certainly a great many of the major literary agents are women—but if they do it is hardly because men are "programmed to give in." When men do in fact "give in," it's usually a conscious trading-off of small concessions to protect their larger interests. Quite frequently men will seem to be in retreat when they are merely withdrawing to new positions. Pushed hard enough, they will give way on money, titles, large offices, expense accounts—anything but power. So long as a man can have the final word, he is reasonably content to give up anything else, though not of course without a struggle. Many women, anxious to rise and succeed, get bogged down in the struggle for the small things they want and know they deserve. Thus, a woman who has been made a vice president may find in succession that her new office is smaller than those of the other vice-presidents, that she needs someone else's authorization to have her name on the company's letterhead, that her secretary is making less money than the secretaries of her colleagues (a very neat way of humiliating a woman executive), that her name is still mysteriously omitted from all sorts of invitations and communications, that the announcement of her promotion in the trade press is unusually short and appears without a photograph . . . None of these things alone amounts to much, but the cumulative effect is to make her feel that her promotion is less valuable than a man's.

A woman who fights each of these small injustices

may soon find that her energies are being drained in meaningless and protracted quarrels over minor matters, while at the same time she's acquiring a reputation as a nag and a malcontent. At the same time a more subtle game is taking place in any exchange of this nature—all these small distinctions are being deliberately blown up into important matters. Few people, when you come to think of it, care much whether or not their name and title are embossed on their stationery, unless they've been told they don't have a right to this privilege, or find they need somebody else's authorization to order it. It then *becomes* important, of course, and a minor matter of prestige has been turned into a major issue. Men are adept at setting up these traps for women. A woman is promoted, an event which should, in principle, make her happy. She orders stationery with her name and her new title on it. Her secretary returns to say that the office manager can't put the order through without the authorization of a more senior executive— a man, of course. Furious, she now has to humiliate herself by getting the authorization from him. The beauty of the game lies in the fact that it is about a trivial issue. Men can make it as difficult as they please for her to get what she wants, then concede without having given up anything important. At the same time they can argue that it's typical of a woman to get so upset about such a trifling matter— "Haven't we got more problems than getting her name on her stationery, for Christ's sake?"

By turning small issues of prestige, comfort and tradition into major confrontations, men not only divert the attention of women from the larger issues of power and control, they build up an endless supply of small privileges they can offer, when the need arises, as if they were major concessions. You want an electric pencil sharpener? Fight for it, baby! Ten bucks a week for your secretary so she makes the same as the other girls on executive row? We'll talk overhead, six-month figures, restraint, until your mascara has run and your secretary has threatened to quit and take up free-lance weaving!

Of course, all these things, and many more, will eventually be conceded, but not before every one of them has been fought out—and how many concessions can you ask for? You want a raise? We gave you a new carpet, more money for your secretary, didn't we? You want to join the management board? We let you go to the convention after you'd nagged us to death on that one, didn't we? . . . And anyway, just between us boys, a woman who spends all her time making everyone's life a living hell over a bunch of chickenshit issues like these isn't exactly the kind of voice we need in a group that's supposed to discuss matters of policy, the big picture, in a reasonable, *cooperative* way, is it now? Isn't business the art of compromise?

All the same, there are women who have learned to use this game to their advantage, though it requires talent and perseverance to do so. They respond to these small digs by stubbornly arguing that they wouldn't have to waste other people's time with this kind of trivia if they had real power.

Cynthia Ransom, an executive in a medium-sized advertising agency, has carried this tactic to its extreme limits. She has talent, and works hard; without these attributes she couldn't operate at all, but how many women who work hard and have talent get power? Very few. Cynthia has it. She carries on a never-ending war of nerves against the management and all senior male executives, beginning every week, often every day, with a new demand, sometimes trivial, sometimes (but very rarely) major. She rightly anticipates that each demand will be met with anger, disbelief and rejection. She is careful to demand only what someone else, usually a man, already *has*—she never breaks new ground. If a man has a wall-to-wall cork bulletin board installed, she demands the same for her office; if the senior executives have telephone credit cards, she insists on one; if the top management take the first-class American Airlines flight to Washington instead of the shuttle, so must she. Each small demand for equality is accompanied by tears, rage, threats of resignation and interoffice *Angst*, and in almost every case the point is eventually conceded. Nobody wants to *lose* Cynthia, and few men have the stamina required to resist her for long. After all, she cares, and they don't, and what she's asking for, they usually have themselves already, which makes it hard for them to refuse it.

Her real cleverness is that she mixes major demands in among the minor ones as if they were on the same level of importance. The management has become so used to this guerrilla warfare that nobody now can distinguish between a meaningful demand from Cynthia and the usual piece of dramatic trivia. Thus, after several months of raising hell and tempers over the right to have an account with a limousine service or the right to have *engraved* business cards instead of the ordinary printed ones, Cynthia will slip in a request for a $5,000 raise, or ask to be made a member of the management committee, on which there has never been a woman executive. Such a demand, which would ordinarily cause horror and consternation, is treated as if it were merely another of her difficult whims, simply one more skirmish in the long-range battle of extortion that Cynthia carries on with her colleagues. They are so used to giving in to her on small things, that they give in on the large ones by reflex action, without even noticing that they have made a substantial concession that will materially increase Cynthia's power. What she has done is to conceal each demand for real power in a thicket of tiresome complaints. The fact that she has now managed to get onto every important committee, that she has a title, and that her autonomy is probably greater than that of any other executive in the company, has all but passed unnoticed. As Cynthia points out, when they *do* notice, it will be too late—she will have acquired enough power to protect her position in the agency, and a salary large enough to make it possible for her to "jump off," as the phrase goes, to a very lucrative job elsewhere, if she wants to.

"I'm careful," she says. "No parties to celebrate promotions, no public displays of power, nothing that could possibly frighten the men or make them think of me as a *rival*. I let them 'humor the little woman.' And I don't often ask for money, either. Money always scares them. The thing to do is to ask for the title, the respect, the power, without even *mentioning* money. That way they think you're an innocent, naïve, you're willing to be bought off with a title or a bigger office, you don't know what's really important. But once you have the title and the office, they can't very well turn you down on the money. Go for the vice presidency if you think you deserve one, but don't ask for more money. They'll eventually give you the title without a raise, and think they've gotten off cheap. But once you're a vice president, you can ask for the same salary as all the other vice presidents, and they can't very well say No to you. The money comes by itself, which is the way it ought to happen. Men are different. They always talk about money and power together, but I think that's a mistake. Get the power; then the money comes by itself."

In general, men suspect women of being more involved in trivia than they are, and are inclined to give in to minor demands after a brief and symbolic struggle. If a woman's *major* demands can be put in such way as to make them seem minor, she is likely to get what she wants.

Women have, in any case, certain advantages over men. In the first place, men are seldom inclined to see them as rivals, male chauvinist pride being what it is. In power struggles they consistently underrate women. Worse, men talk too much. Even those who have learned to keep their mouths shut in front of other men (and they are few) will talk openly in front of a woman, supposing that she is automatically "on their side," and of course anxious to impress her with their power and their plans. There is a natural tendency to *confide* in women, as if they were destined by nature to be approving listeners, and any intelligent woman can exploit this fairly easily, no more being necessary than a sympathetic air and a few words of encouragement. It is astonishing that men who won't tell their colleagues anything will tell a woman everything. "The smug bastards," Cynthia says, "they really think women don't count. They're so damned happy to tell you all the wonderful things they're doing, as if you were a high-school girl on a date, or a housewife washing dishes while her husband tells her what happened during the day . . . They just don't believe in their heart of hearts that a woman *counts*. When we were making a secret play for a big account—it was really a hush-hush thing and only top management were supposed to know about it, one of the executives told me the whole thing, I guess just to prove that he was important enough to be in on the secret and that I wasn't. Naturally, I found out I wasn't being included in the account group, so I went and complained. They wanted to know how I found out, and when I told them, they went to this guy and asked him why he'd opened his mouth. 'I didn't tell anyone,' he said, 'the only person I mentioned it to was Cynthia.' Naturally, I'm a no one! A woman who keeps her ears open hears everything. She knows far more about what's happening than any man does."

Since men don't as a rule consider women rivals for power, they have no way of mentally fitting them into the existing local power structure, which can be a great advantage to a woman. Men know exactly where another man should sit at a meeting, for example, but often find it impossible to know the right place for a woman, and are reluctant to tell her where they want her to sit. A man going into a meeting can look around and find his place in the power group instinctively; indeed, his major concern will be to place himself correctly, not too high and not too low, the former being dangerous, the latter weak. A woman, on the contrary, can usually sit anywhere she pleases, upsetting the power arrangement and often acquiring a power position that can have dramatic effects on her career. Men who would tell a presumptuous young male to move are reluctant to tell a woman the same thing—the old habit of respect and politeness dies hard, if at all. More than one woman, new to a meeting and to the ways of power, has sat down in a power spot and stayed there, and gone on to acquire the salary and title appropriate to the spot.

Imagine a meeting at which everyone sits in a rough circle, like this:

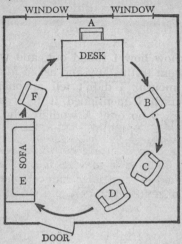

A (the desk) is obviously the position of control. The person whose office this is sits here. B, a straight chair without arms, is the second power position, since it is closest to the desk, and also isolates the person sitting in it, so that he or she will tend to dominate the room. It is also worth noting, in situations of this kind, that a straight chair is more powerful than a large armchair, like C and D. A person in a straight chair looks and feels more alert, and is raised higher than a person sitting in a low armchair. If one person is sitting in a straight chair and two people are slumped in armchairs (and most modern armchairs of the kind found in offices are designed for slumping), the person who is sitting high and straight will appear to be commanding and dominating the people in armchairs, and more important, they will *feel* that this is the case, however senior they are.

The sofa, E, is not a position of power, partly because it faces the wrong way, but also because people sitting on a sofa can never be sure how many more will have to sit down beside them. They may find themselves squeezed into an uncomfortable subgroup, and will, in that case, look powerless even if they're all senior vice presidents. In most meetings, the sofa is the last place to be taken, and will often remain empty until there's no place left for latecomers to sit. F, of course, is the position of least power, and a person sitting here may feel he ought to be taking notes and may in fact be asked to do so. Being asked to take notes reduces one, naturally, to the level of a stenographer, and eliminates one as a power factor in any group.

B, therefore, had always been the place where the second most powerful person sat, and it was that person's function to read off the items for discussion from a prepared agenda, and to present the various options and whatever information was available. It was the treasured place of one particular senior vice president, until the day when a woman, newly elected to the group, walked in and sat down there. No man would have done this, and in the unlikely event that one *had*, the senior vice president would simply have asked him to move. Since he was unable to ask a *woman* to move, partly because a woman did not seem to represent a serious threat to his power, but primarily because he was hindered by politeness (What is the etiquette of asking a woman to give up her seat?), he was obliged to squeeze himself in on the sofa, thus making himself part of the audience (for every meeting consists of players and audience).

284

Unfortunately for him, the chair itself, and the place it occupied, represented a power symbol. People were used to looking toward that chair, whoever occupied it, when they wanted facts and the next item for discussion. The young woman, surprised at being asked so many questions and treated with such unlikely respect, answered as best she could, and prepared herself better for the next meeting, at which she managed to take the same place by arriving early. By the third meeting, the place was hers, and with it all the responsibilities that had previously been those of the senior vice president. Before long, she was actually *made* a vice president, and the person whose seat she had taken was squeezed off the sofa, relegated to position F and reduced to keeping the minutes of the meeting. A successful career had been launched by sitting in the right chair.

No man could have gotten away with this, nor would any man have tried. As the woman herself remarked, "Women are just more free to break the rules and get away with it. They're not even expected to know what the rules *are*."

Not knowing what the rules are—and not *wanting* to know—can be very useful. One of the main fears that men have of women is precisely that they won't abide by the rules, whatever they are. The hierarchy of respect and power that men live in (and live *by*) differs from institution to institution, but is based on convention. A major executive's power is dependent on people's willingness to consider him powerful. He may of course be feared because he can fire people and because he can give or withhold raises, but ultimately his power depends on respect for his position and his person. By and large, men understand this convention, and are careful to give the proper respect to authority, if only because they can't enjoy their own places in the hierarchy unless they take the hierarchy itself seriously. This explains why men so often lose their tempers when women, even their wives, make fun of a man in their organization. No matter how much they may hate or despise a man in their own power group or hierarchy, they cannot allow an outsider to ridicule him—even though they may do it themselves all the time. No matter how ridiculous we may find our fellow members, we are obliged to respect them before strangers. If we don't, the group loses its meaning, and our membership in it then becomes meaningless. The chairman of a major conglomerate may be a short, unprepossessing and unpleasant neurotic, "a small, skinny hatchet-faced, vengeful child . . . a *lumpen* sadist, a mad god,"[2] but even though his executives may see him as such, they can hardly admit it to themselves, let alone allow others to say it. They must believe in each other and in him, whatever their innermost feelings and doubts. Above all, they must accept each other at face value. If they have to (and they often *do*), they will go to any lengths to overlook eccentricity, bad manners, physical gracelessness, lack of charm, bad breath or offensive personal mannerisms, since the very existence of the group depends on maintaining relationships among its members. When our own interests are at stake, the emperor's new clothes always look good to us.

What alarms men is the possibility that women may be more clear-sighted. They can be fairly sure of respect from their male colleagues in the hierarchy, who hardly even see them as human beings, after all, and can therefore accept or ignore their physical and emotional peculiarities. But might not a woman see them somewhat more plainly? They are all too aware that this is the case with their wives, their girl friends, if they have any, even their secretaries, and the notion of a woman as a colleague, *as a member of the group,* is therefore disquieting. One executive of a major financial institution told me that his chairman's behavior at meetings altered radically when he had to accommodate the first woman vice president. "Up until then," he said, "we hardly ever looked at Harry, I mean, who cared? He was chairman, and that was that. I guess I could have told you that he is fat, wears glasses and is going bald, but I never thought much about it, and neither did he. He had power in the hierarchy, and I had a place in it, and I thought of him as this—powerful *person.* When Sheila began to come to meetings, I suddenly noticed that Harry was nervous, and particularly that he had developed this special habit of stroking his head, as if he was trying to hide the fact that he was bald. Also, he began to take off his glasses a lot. It took me a while to work it out, but eventually I understood—Sheila made him unsure of himself. It wasn't anything sexual—she herself isn't exactly a beauty, and she's no spring-chicken either—but Harry was afraid she could see him in a way that the rest of us didn't. He wasn't sure that she respected him the way we did. In her presence his baldness mattered to *him,* whether it mattered to Sheila or not, and I'm sure it didn't. It threw him off-balance, which wouldn't have mattered, except that he became very sensitive to anything Sheila said at meetings, so that he took even the most harmless remarks as if they were personal criticisms. In the end, it taught me something: in a male hierarchy, a woman is always an outsider and a threat, no matter how talented she is. There's no way a woman can be one of the boys."

On the other hand, there are a good many ways in which she can outwit them. Men will do almost anything to avoid a face-to-face confrontation with women, and a woman is well advised to insist on them, rather than doing business by memoranda. Men have a tendency to dismiss anything in writing from a woman, but will usually give way rather than argue. As one woman says, "Men mostly want you to get out of their offices as fast as possible, so you can often get what you want by just going in and asking for it. The big thing is to sit down, put your handbag on the floor and look as if you might stay there forever. The handbag is important. Men have a horror of handbags, for some reason, and the sight of one in an office, particularly if you can put it right smack on the desk, tends to distract them." Cleavage is equally distracting, perhaps more so, not so much because men find it attractive (that depends on the man and the cleavage), but because in a world geared to power symbols, cleavage is a symbol of some other force, possibly more potent, but not easily assimilated in hierarchical terms. Men are so morbidly afraid that women may use their sexuality in negotiating for power and money that the slightest sexual signal is likely to frighten them: a woman doesn't have to do anything but *be* a woman.

With all due respect for the position taken by most women's liberationists, the imbalance between men and women in terms of power is so great that they would seem entitled to use any weapons they have. If you can move upward by exploiting men's fears and weaknesses, it seems foolish not to, especially since it's easy enough to do. After all, even so "successful" a woman as Katharine Graham, of the Washington *Post*, has commented that "Women aren't a minority, but they *are* in the business world

. . . There's still prejudice on the part of men everywhere, it's in our society, in ourselves—in women themselves." And Dorothy Chandler, described by one Los Angeles businessman as "the strongest individual who's been at the Times Mirror in the last twenty to twenty-five years," can still say: "I think I've proven *my* worth here, but even I have never been compensated the way a man would be . . . Here I am with a title that's a nonentity, and compensation below the men." If Mrs. Chandler, who raised $18,500,000 to help build the Los Angeles Music Center, is a major executive of the Times Mirror Corporation and a wealthy woman in her own right, can feel that way about her job, it is easy to imagine the feelings of ambitious women in most companies.[3] Under these circumstances, it makes sense to fight back, to play the power game twice as hard as a man would, to take advantage of being a woman in every possible way. Ample proof exists that dedicated hard work alone will get a woman nowhere, that money will be given to her grudgingly, that every effort will be made to prevent her from having real power. Until women have their proportionate share of power—which, to take an example, would imply something like fifty women United States Senators—they will more or less be obliged to fight their way into the world of power by clandestine methods, infiltrating what remains an obstinately masculine structure, with masculine symbols, traditions and laws.

I used to have a good friend named Dee, a handsome young woman with limitless energy and ambition. Her looks were, to put it mildly, striking (though she was not, as one says, "my type"), but what was most extraordinary about her was that she simply failed to recognize that being a woman could possibly be a disadvantage. I don't mean that she was *unaware* of being a woman—far from it, as we shall see—but she simply operated on the principle that no obstacles existed in her path, no discrimination was possible. It was as if she were deaf and blind to reality, which sometimes made her seem naïve and innocent, but as a tactic it worked.

It has to be said that Dee was smart and a hard worker, you couldn't fault her. She was eager to learn, so much so that she managed to frighten a number of the executives of the large financial firm that had hired her as an assistant to a security analyst in a half-hearted decision to comply with the demands of equal opportunity employment. She was, as it were, the token woman, though her job amounted to yet another Radcliffe summa cum laude doing clerical work that no Harvard graduate would have touched. Dee mastered with ease the comparatively simple tasks of her job, then pressured her boss— a fish-faced fellow, with damp, nervous hands and glasses so round and thick that they looked as if the lenses had been made out of the bottoms of Coke bottles—into allowing her to visit clients and attend meetings with him. Her mastery of facts, forceful manner and appearance soon put him in the shade, in addition to which he was widely assumed to have given way spinelessly to the demands of a woman, with the result that his reputation waned as hers waxed. Dee simply never accepted no for an answer. When she was refused an expense account on the ground that no young woman her age and rank had ever had one, she simply went out and opened house accounts at the restaurants she wanted to use and had the bills sent to her boss. No arguments, no pleas; she simply *acted*. And of course it worked. The accounts were in his name, all at restaurants he was in the habit of visiting, and he could hardly refuse to pay them without damaging his own reputation.

Dee spoke up where women were supposed to remain silent, treated men as equals and simply refused to behave like a woman or be treated like one. Within a year, she was ready to take over her boss's job, and he was ready to abandon it, even eager. At this point, she ran into the opposition of his superior, a male chauvinist in the old tradition, who had managed to avoid Dee as much as possible. They had, in fact, reached a working truce by each pretending that the other didn't exist, but it was now necessary for him to have a "heart-to-hearter" with Dee and explain why she couldn't have her boss's job—the main reason being, of course, that she was a woman, and a "pushy" one. Efforts to get through to Dee by means of an intermediary failed, and in the end Dee and the executive were obliged to have a confrontation in his office. Had she been a man, the whole thing would have been simple. A man would have respected the executive's power, argued perhaps, but with respect. A man would have sat at a distance, to show respect and recognition of his inferior position, and placed one hand on each knee, feet planted on the ground, the usual male posture of respectful submission, just one step above the humble position, in which the hands are clasped just in front of the stomach, while the whole torso inclines forward. (This is an important distinction: bending backward is a self-assertive, aggressive position, bending forward is an act of surrender, like offering one's neck to a conqueror, sitting upright is halfway between, and allows the sitter to adopt either of the two extreme positions quickly if he needs to.)

Dee did none of these things—she couldn't, it wasn't in her, and they wouldn't have seemed natural in a woman. She pulled up a chair so that she was next to the executive's desk (thus infringing on his space), put one arm on his desk, and leaned forward to expose a somewhat generous bosom, while looking him straight in the eye. Disconcerted, he proceeded to sum up the many spurious reasons why it was felt wiser not to give her the job she was entitled to. She listened gravely, in rapt and breathless attention. Then, when he had finished, she smiled like a little girl, mischievously and joyfully, and said in a clear, distinct voice, "I know you have to say that, and you know you have to say that, but now tell me why the fuck I can't have it, without any shit!"

There was an awful silence. It is one of the conventions of hierarchy that one always accepts a given reason for a decision from above, even when one knows it isn't true, *one operates within the rules*. The executive had no answer. He had prepared "the story," the explanation that a man would feel obliged to accept, but he couldn't bring himself to say, for example, "We recognize that you're qualified, but we're not about to give the job to a broad, so forget it." How can you reason with someone who won't accept your reasons? Possibly he could have fired her, but he hadn't prepared himself for that either, so he sat silent for a few moments, and his silence was a form of surrender. At last, he sighed. "We'll reconsider it," he said, and anxious to avoid a second interview he shortly afterward gave her the job.

She now has his.

PART THREE

Love of Power

CHAPTER NINE

Power Rules

A man can be a star of the first magnitude in gifts, will-power and endurance, but so well balanced that he turns with the system to which he belongs without any friction or waste of energy. Another may have the same great gifts, or even finer ones, but the axis does not pass precisely through the center and he squanders half his strength in eccentric movements which weaken him and disturb his surroundings.

—Hermann Hesse
THE GLASS BEAD GAME

He did not want R . . . as a successful rival, but he did not want him as an enemy either.

—Douglas Hurd
TRUTH GAME

You can't learn to acquire power by rules: it has to come from inside. But by following certain rules, you can develop an awareness of it. We all have a power potential, but few of us use it, or even know it's there.

In more "primitive" cultures, youths are initiated into the rites of power, sometimes in very complicated ways. The rules are absolute and clear-cut, and must be followed exactly, but they are intended to increase the initiate's awareness of himself—simply carrying out the rituals isn't enough. If in certain American Indian tribes young men bury themselves in pits up to the neck on lonely hills in the desert, it is to learn patience, concentration and the ability to stay motionless when necessary, however uncomfortable it may be. There's nothing mysterious about the process—a hunter who is fidgety or has to scratch himself when bitten by flies is unlikely to trap much in the way of game. Survival lies in the ability to control one's body and one's mind.

Our world is not so very different, noisy and complex as it seems, but we are less fortunate than the Indians. We are educated, at considerable expense and effort, but no wise teacher prepares us for the world we will face as adults. If we are lucky, we learn how to do a job, but for most people the price of survival is surrender. There is a place for almost everyone in our world, but usually on other people's terms rather than our own. Some of us learn how to *succeed* and may even become rich and famous; few learn how to use the world, instead of being used by it.

Those who grow up on the streets learn to rely on themselves, but pay a high price for the knowledge —the street teaches hard lessons. For most, the idea that we are personally responsible for our own lives comes late, if at all. Our system of education teaches us to put our faith in something else—a corporation, a marriage, a trade, a profession, a religion, politics, something, one might almost say *anything*, which offers us a set of rules we can obey and rewards us for obedience to them. It's safer to be a domestic animal than a wild one.

By the time we reach middle age the notion that we have an existence *apart* from what we do, the people we're married to, our children, our colleagues, our associates is hard to accept. The most we can do is to change our attachments with a new marriage, a new job or, more daringly, a new profession. We have been submerged in a community and spend most of our lives satisfying its demands.

Under the circumstances, it is not surprising that a good many therapists specialize in teaching successful, sophisticated modern men and women roughly what an Indian knows at the age of sixteen. One analyst has constructed an elaborate and ingenious layout of electric trains, with control boards at opposite ends of the room. Married couples "in difficulty" are given two trains, and asked to run them in opposite directions. Obviously, the trains will crash into each other if they meet head-on, but it requires skill and cooperation to shunt the trains onto sidings so that both can move freely without a collision. Needless to say, people with no sense of power find their train is always on a siding while their partner's is moving swiftly around the track. People with an overdeveloped sense of power try and force their partner's train *off* the track, and even invite collisions in a clearly self-destructive way. Those who understand power manage to work out a system that allows both trains to move freely at equal speeds. An Indian would probably have learned

297

that one can cooperate without sacrificing one's identity and without paying fifty dollars an hour.

One well-known existentialist analyst forces his patients to accept responsibility for their own actions by using a large blackboard, on which he outlines the foreseeable consequences of any given act. His specialty is middle-aged businessmen who feel their careers have bogged down. "That's not why they come to see me," he says, "they're usually here because of some sexual problem, mostly impotence or premature ejaculation, but when you get them to talk about themselves, it isn't sex they have on their minds at all. They're suffering from a feeling of inertia, helplessness, powerlessness. Their jobs and their offices are much more real to them than any of the women in their lives, and they're far more likely to talk with passion about their work than their wives or girl friends. Their sexual problems are secondary most of the time. They've simply lost all sense of identity. They see their lives as completed, finished, run by other people. Often they're strong, decisive men, but their ego is at the service of others, and when they need it for themselves, it isn't there."

The doctor, a thin, wiry and energetic man, questions everything they do and say, strips away the compromises and evasions of a lifetime, makes them aware they *exist*. He favors a hardbacked chair, not a couch, and sometimes lets his patients sit behind his desk while he takes the chair. "Let them take the position of power," he says, "they have to learn that I'm not a wizard or a magician who can solve all their problems. When they start fighting me, when they don't altogether *trust* me any more, they're on the way to being cured." At one end of the small, windowless room, brightly lit by overhead spotlights, is the blackboard. If a patient complains that he has been overlooked for some promotion he wanted (a common source of despair), the good doctor goes to the blackboard and brutally demonstrates the existing alternatives and their consequences. "A—you stay where you are and do nothing about it; B—you start looking for another job; C—you stay where you are and try to recoup your losses . . ." Swiftly he lists the consequences of each decision, probing for the facts: Could you afford a period of unemployment while you were hunting for a new job? How much money do you really need? Do you really want to be promoted? Have you really exploited the potential of the job you *have*? Is this an opportunity to do something else, to change your whole life? The patient is cross-examined, forced to ask himself what he wants to do, to accept the fact that he is both free and responsible for the consequences of his freedom. "Life," says the doctor, "presents choices and demands courage. We have to learn not to complain, or blame other people, or waste time fighting things that are inevitable. No self-pity! Skill, courage and power!"

Of course the trouble with this kind of therapeutic advice is that no analyst can share our experiences: he has to take our word for the nature of our work and the structure of our lives. In an Indian tribe, the teacher and the pupil share the same communal heritage; the wisdom of the old hunters is passed on to the young, the questions of the young have been asked in each generation. It's easier to be wise when life is simple and uniform, but very difficult when your pupil has to explain to you the workings of the international bond business before he can describe why he's unhappy with his life. Still, the rules of power are not very different from one culture to the next, when you strip them of their mythology. A good friend of mine is a student of "primitive" cultures (which are not, of course, primitive at all), and has spent most of his life living with obscure tribes, around the world. A tall, thin, ascetic man, a New Yorker by birth and education, he always looks as if he would be more at home in an Eskimo village or in the middle of an Indian ghost dance. He has the innocent look of a scholar, an impression strengthened by his green canvas bookbag and wire-rimmed spectacles, and one might easily suppose that there was something *unworldly* about him. Cynical city dwellers, steeped in the urban defenses, worry about him when he's here, as I did, until I noticed one evening the cautious way he walked down Amsterdam Avenue, not afraid, but keeping close to the edge of sidewalk, his eyes searching for danger, aware of every movement around him. He walked like a hunter, swiftly, purposefully, never letting anyone get too close to him, and did it without apparent thought or effort. In the streets of violence, he looked like, he *was*, a man of power.

But of course, he is. He understands power; when he gives a lecture (a rare and celebrated event), he enters the hall with the audience and sits down among them until it's filled, until everyone is beginning to ask where he is. Then, when they're staring expectantly at the empty stage, wondering if perhaps he's hiding behind the podium, or not coming at all, he rises from his seat and walks onto the stage. Powerful people have the ability to dramatize themselves and their actions so that even the most unimportant events acquire meaning. It's a talent, but it can be developed. My friend likes to arrive without warning, making his way past receptionists and secretaries so that he appears to have arrived by magic, and when he wants to go, he waits until I've left my office to take a telephone call or use the bathroom, so that when I come back, he's vanished. No good-byes: he has simply *gone*, and it's difficult to believe he was ever there. He has placed himself beyond other people's control, without giving up a success-ful and busy career, and as a result he's as much at ease in New York as in the jungles of New Guinea.

My friend and I are sitting at the Central Park Zoo, on the terrace of the cafeteria, one of those hot summer afternoons when the park is so crowded with people that the animals seem more human than one-self. To our right are the towers of commercial New York, a high, brutal cliff of great buildings, rising through the layers of haze like the dreaded tower of Barad-Dûr in Tolkien's *The Lord of the Rings*. I can understand how one can become a powerful man in simpler societies and cultures; it may be a long, hard initiation, but the distractions are fewer. The sheer size of the city distorts the ego. We are either reduced to the impotence of a meaningless daily routine—sleep, eat, work—made even more painful by the knowledge that we have no power over our lives; or worse, we destroy ourselves by trying to become bigger, more famous, more powerful than the city itself. Can one have power here, I want to know, in a life full of compromises, decisions, worries, pres-sures, in a place where even the mayor seldom seems able to control anything at all? I can understand the meaning of power in the desert, the significance of the rites of power, the sudden illuminations of self-awareness that come when one is alone with Nature —all that makes sense. But in an office on the thirty-eighth floor of a huge building in which thousands of people work? How does one seek power there?

My friend smiles. There are rules, they are the same for everybody, this terrace is not so very different from a jungle clearing. The rules of power do not change because one is on the subway, or in Central Park, or in an office without windows, where everything is made of plastic. "The first rule," he says, "is simple. Act impeccably! Perform every act as if it were the only thing in the world that mattered."

I can understand that all right. It's an old Zen principle—you put your whole soul and being and life into the act you're performing. In Zen archery your entire being wills the arrow into the bull's-eye with an invisible force. It's not a question of winning, or even caring, it's making the everyday acts we all perform important to ourselves. No matter how small the task, we have to teach ourselves that it *matters*. If we are going to intervene in a meeting, we must do so at the right moment, prepare for what we want to say, speak up at the crucial point when our intervention will be heard and listened to, make sure that attention is paid. Otherwise, it's best to remain silent. It is better to do nothing than to do something badly.

"Second rule: never reveal all of yourself to other people, hold something back in reserve so that people are never quite sure if they really know you."

I can see that too. It's not that anybody seeking power should be secretive—secrecy isn't the trick at all. It's more a question of remaining slightly mysterious, as if one were always capable of doing something surprising and unexpected. Most people are so predictable and reveal so much of themselves that a person who isn't and who doesn't automatically acquires a kind of power. For this reason, it is important to give up the self-indulgent habit of talking about oneself. The power person listens instead, and when he *does* talk about himself, it is in order to change the subject of conversation. Good players can always tell when someone is about to ask them to do something they don't want to do, and they effortlessly but firmly move the conversation onto a personal level. One of the best players I know can talk about himself for hours at the slightest sign of opposition or a demand about to be made on him. Even so, he reveals nothing. Sometimes he gives the impression that he has two children, sometimes three, occasionally none, and he has at various times given people to understand that he was graduated from Yale, Harvard, Stanford and Ol' Miss. Some confusion exists as to whether or not he is Jewish or Protestant, since he has claimed to be both, and also crosses himself when he passes St. Patrick's Cathedral. Nobody really knows the truth about him, and he is therefore respected. Once we know everything about a person, we have squeezed him dry like a juiced orange, he is no longer of any use or interest to us, we can throw him away.

"Third rule: learn to use time, think of it as a friend, not an enemy. Don't waste it in going after things you don't want."

Using time! Of course, but how seldom we do! Time uses us, we are merely its servants. We fight it as if it were the enemy, trying to force two hours' work into forty-five minutes if we're ambitious, or to stretch forty-five minutes' work into two hours if we're not. Powerful people devote exactly as much time to what they're doing as they need to or want to. They do not try to answer two telephones at once, or begin a meeting and then end it before a conclusion has been reached because "time has run out," or interrupt one conversation to begin another. They are willing to be late, to miss telephone calls and to postpone today's work to tomorrow if they have to. Events do not control them—they control events.

"Fourth rule: learn to accept your mistakes. Don't be a perfectionist about everything."

True enough. Half the people we know are rendered powerless by their need to be perfect, as if making one mistake would destroy them. Powerful people accept the necessity of taking risks and of being wrong. They don't waste time justifying their mistakes, either, or trying to transform them into correct decisions. Nothing makes one seem more foolish or impotent than the inability to admit a mistake.

"Last rule: don't make waves, move smoothly without disturbing things."

That makes sense too, even in our world. Half the art of power lies in arranging for things to happen the way we want them to, just as a good hunter stays in one place and draws the game toward him, instead of wearing himself out pursuing it. The skills of the hunter are not out of place in our world; they must merely be applied differently.

My friend smiles again. "What more can I say?" he asks, waving to the buildings south of the park. "It's your world. You picked it—telephones, Telex machines, credit cards and all. Myself, I wouldn't care to live in it all the time. I'm not interested in negotiating contracts, or buying a new car, or running a corporation—we don't have the same ambitions and desires. But I could live here as easily as I can anywhere else. You only need power. And since *you* live in it, you have to examine this world of yours coldly and clearly, as if your life depended on it. Because it *does*."

We live in a mass society, like members of a herd,

and conventional wisdom teaches us that safety lies in following the herd. But my friend is right: man is not a herding animal; his safety lies in his skill as a hunter, his ability to act, and be, alone. To *understand* the herd is part of the hunter's skill, to hide in the herd is a useful deception, but he cannot *join* it without sacrificing his essential nature.

The more mechanical and complicated our world is, the more we need the simplicity of power to guide us and protect us. It's the one gift that allows us to remain human in an inhuman world—for "the love of power is the love of ourselves." [1]

Acknowledgments

My special gratitude and affection to Lynn Nesbit, Erica Spellman, Nan Talese, Mildred Marmur, James Silberman and Selma Shapiro, for urging me to undertake this book after helping me through the experience of writing MALE CHAUVINISM! HOW IT WORKS. I am indebted to Phyllis Grann, Joni Evans and Joan Sanger for their suggestions, and to Paul Gitlin for his invaluable help, support and interest. For many conversations on the subject of power and encouragement, I am particularly indebted to: Barbara Bannon, Helen Gurley Brown, Ned Brown, Harvey Cox, Digby Diehl, Jonathan Dolger, Philip Evans, Robert Evans, Clay Felker, Elaine Geiger, Burt and Margaret Glinn, Tony Godwin, Dan Green, Henry A. Grunwald, Marc Jaffe, Phyllis S. Levy, Christopher Macleose, James Mills, Leona Nevler, Marie Reno, Morris Rittenberg, Deborah Rogers, Cornelius Ryan, Richard E. Snyder, Phyllis Starr, Irving Wallace, Jay Watnick, Patricia White, Ruth Whitney and Sir George Weidenfeld. Finally, I thank those I love for their patience and understanding.

Notes

CHAPTER ONE

1 Quoted in Frederick Meinecke, MACHIAVELLIAN-ISM, THE DOCTRINE OF RAISON D'ÉTAT AND ITS PLACE IN MODERN HISTORY, London, 1957 (originally published as DIE IDÉE DER STAATSRÄSON, Munich, 1924).

2 Frederick Nietzsche, THUS SPAKE ZARATHUSTRA.

3 Lord Acton, letter to Bishop Creighton, as quoted in Louis Kronenberger, ANIMAL, VEGETABLE, MINERAL, New York, 1972.

4 Edgar Z. Friedenberg, COMING OF AGE IN AMERICA, New York, 1965.

5 Silvano Arieti, THE WILL TO BE HUMAN, New York, 1972.

6 Alfred Adler, as quoted in THE INDIVIDUAL PSYCHOLOGY OF ALFRED ADLER (edited by Heinz L. Ansbacher, and R. Rowena), New York, 1956.

7 Rollo May, POWER AND INNOCENCE, New York, 1972.

8 Roberto Assagioli, THE ACT OF WILL, New York, 1973.

CHAPTER TWO

1 F. Scott Fitzgerald, THE LAST TYCOON, New York, 1925.

2 As quoted by Percy Sutton, NEW YORK TIMES.

3 NEW YORK TIMES.

4 NEW YORK TIMES.

5 FORBES, February 15, 1972.

6 NEW YORK Magazine.
7 Anthony Sampson, THE SOVEREIGN STATE OF ITT, New York, 1973.
8 Anthony Sampson, OP. CIT.
9 Erich Fromm, THE ANATOMY OF HUMAN DE-STRUCTIVENESS, New York, 1974.
10 Adolf Portmann, DAS TIER ALS SOZIALES WESEN, Zurich, 1953.
11 Bertrand Russell, POWER, New York, 1962.
12 FORTUNE, January, 1973.
13 FORTUNE, May, 1973.
14 FORTUNE.
15 FORTUNE.

CHAPTER THREE

1 NEW YORK TIMES MAGAZINE, October 28, 1973.
2 Harvey Cox.
3 Louis Spears, as quoted in Harold Nicolson, THE WAR YEARS, New York, 1967.
4 Erik H. Erikson, YOUNG MAN LUTHER, New York, 1958.
5 R. D. French Jr. and Robert D. Caplan, "Organizational Stress and Individual Strain," from THE FAILURE OF SUCCESS, edited by Alfred J. Marrow, New York, 1972.
6 Dale Tarnowski, THE CHANGING SUCCESS ETHIC, New York, 1973.
7 FORTUNE, June, 1974.
8 William Makepeace Thackeray.
9 Patrick Anderson, THE APPROACH TO KINGS, New York, 1970.
10 NEW YORK TIMES, June 2, 1974.
11 NEW YORK TIMES MAGAZINE, September 16, 1973.

12   James David Barber, NEW YORK TIMES, November 8, 1973.
13   As quoted in PSYCHOLOGY TODAY, November, 1973.
14   FORTUNE, November, 1973.
15   Erik H. Erikson, OP. CIT.
16   Rollo May, POWER AND INNOCENCE, New York, 1972.
17   Carlos Castaneda, JOURNEY TO IXTLAN, New York, 1972.

CHAPTER FOUR

1   FORTUNE, January, 1974.
2   FORTUNE, January, 1974.
3   PARIS HERALD TRIBUNE, August 10, 1973.
4   Thomas A. Leemon, THE RITES OF PASSAGE IN A STUDENT CULTURE, New York, 1972.
5   Niccolò Machiavelli, THE PRINCE AND THE DISCOURSES, New York, 1950.
6   "The Peter principle" itself is: "In a hierarchy every employee tends to rise to his level of incompetence." Laurence J. Peter, and Raymond Hull, THE PETER PRINCIPLE, New York, 1969.

CHAPTER FIVE

1   Marquis de Vauvenargues.
2   Lao-tse, as quoted in Rudolf Flesch, THE BOOK OF UNUSUAL QUOTATIONS, London, 1959.
3   Baltasar Gracian.
4   William Hazlitt.
5   Knute Rockne, as quoted in Robert H. Schuller, YOU CAN BECOME THE PERSON YOU WANT TO BE, New York, 1953.

6   Adolf Portman, DAS TIER ALS SOZIALES WESEN, Zurich, 1953.
7   Bartolomeo Vanzetti, as quoted in THE OXFORD DICTIONARY OF QUOTATIONS.
8   NEW YORK Magazine, March 25, 1974.
9   Edmund Burke, SPEECH ON CONCILIATION WITH AMERICA, March 22, 1775.

CHAPTER SIX

1   Robert Graves, THE GREEK MYTHS, New York, 1957.
2   Harold Nicolson, GOOD BEHAVIOR, Boston, 1955.
3   Colin M. Turnbull, THE MOUNTAIN PEOPLE, New York, 1972.
4   William Shakespeare, AS YOU LIKE IT, II, i, 56.
5   William Lamb, (Viscount Melbourne), as quoted in THE OXFORD DICTIONARY OF QUOTATIONS.
6   Logan Pearsall Smith.
7   Ladislas Farago, AFTERMATH, New York, 1974.
8   William Shakespeare, MACBETH, III, iv.
9   William Shakespeare, KING LEAR, V, ii, 9.
10 John Bradford, DICTIONARY OF NATIONAL BIOGRAPHY.

CHAPTER SEVEN

1   FORTUNE, October, 1972.
2   FORTUNE, November, 1972.
3   NEW YORK TIMES, August 26, 1973.
4   NEW YORK TIMES, July 17, 1973.
5   Bob Thomas, KING COHN, New York, 1967.
6   TIME, July 30, 1973.
7   Alan Harrington, PSYCHOPATHS, New York, 1972.

8   NEW YORK TIMES.

9   FORTUNE, September, 1973.

CHAPTER EIGHT

1   FORTUNE, April, 1973.

2   Alan Harrington, PSYCHOPATHS, New York, 1973.

3   FORTUNE, April, 1973.

CHAPTER NINE

1   William Hazlitt, POLITICAL ESSAYS.

About the Author

MICHAEL KORDA was born in London, England, in 1933, and educated at Le Rosey, in Switzerland, and Magdalen College, Oxford. He served two years in the Royal Air Force and moved to the United States in 1958. Mr. Korda has written for national magazines for several years. His first book was *Male Chauvinism! How It Works*. He is *Glamour's* monthly motion-picture reviewer, a member of the National Society of Film Critics, and vice-president of a major publishing house. Mr. Korda lives in Manhattan with his wife and child.